T0247562

WHITE ROBES
AND
BROKEN BADGES

WHITE ROBES
AND
BROKEN BADGES

INFILTRATING *THE* KKK
AND EXPOSING
THE EVIL
AMONG US

JOE MOORE

WITH JON LAND

HARPER

An Imprint of HarperCollins*Publishers*

HarperCollins books may be purchased for educational, business, or sales promotional use. For information, please email the Special Markets Department at SPsales@harpercollins.com.

FIRST EDITION

Designed by Leah Carlson-Stanisic

Library of Congress Cataloging-in-Publication Data has been applied for.

ISBN 978-0-06-337540-6

24 25 26 27 28 LBC 5 4 3 2 1

The only thing necessary for the triumph of evil is for good men to do nothing.

—ATTRIBUTED TO EDMUND BURKE

CONTENTS

PART III

FOREWORD

On January 6, 2021, the Joint Session of Congress met in the U.S. Capitol to receive Electoral College votes and complete the peaceful transfer of power. It did not go well. The proceedings were rocked by the explosive convergence of an attempted political coup from the inside and a violent insurrection from the outside. Donald Trump orchestrated the coup to overturn Joe Biden's victory and clear a path for him to immediately seize the presidency. He incited the insurrection to intimidate Congress and the vice president and force them into allowing the coup to proceed. In a constitutional sense, all of this chaos constituted an "insurrection," which nearly succeeded in toppling the 2020 presidential election and the American constitutional order.

Different component elements of danger came into play that day, including Trump's pathological refusal to accept his defeat in the 2020 election and the Trump network's effective manipulation of various social media channels to promote his Big Lie and supporting propaganda and disinformation.

But a key—and far less well known—part of the story was the mobilization of domestic violent extremist groups to act as the shock troops in the assault on the U.S. Capitol Police and the U.S. House and Senate. While Trump and his political lieutenants worked the phones on the inside and tens of thousands of rank-and-file followers filled the streets as violent extras, the organized violent extremist groups gave a fighting military-style structure and coherence to the front lines of the "Stop the Steal" protest. Domestic violent extremists, made up of well-organized racist and antigovernment forces, unleashed the brutal focused violence against police that helped turn the crowd into a vicious mob and the riot into a full-blown political insurrection.

Everything I learned as the lead manager of the House of Representatives prosecution team in Donald Trump's second trial, and as a member of the House Select Committee on the January 6 Attack, convinced me that we need to know a lot more about this dimension of the political assault on America.

In *White Robes and Broken Badges*, Joseph Moore tells the riveting back story of the Ku Klux Klan in America today and how its influence and recent history helped shape these shocking events and the street-fighting movement of white Christian nationalism.

America's "first organized terror movement" (in the words of Fergus Bordewich), the KKK is a white supremacist organization whose roots trace back to the end of the Civil War and whose operations have at various points of American history involved millions of members and supporters.

By recounting his remarkable involvement as a government informant in infiltrating and disrupting the Klan and its violent actions in the South today, Moore shows how the KKK remains a central entry point and organizing force for violent white nationalism in America. He also makes clear how brute criminal violence against African Americans and other political enemies remains the central instrument of power, control, and fear in Klan political culture throughout entire regions of America.

But Moore's fine-grained prose offers an even deeper analysis into the power dynamics that make the Klan a continuing threat to American democracy in the twenty-first century. Aware of the inevitable organizational security lapses that Moore describes, the Klan has begun to operate through slightly more sanitized groups that camouflage their violent white nationalism in the rhetoric of MAGA and right-wing extremism favored by Donald Trump and his movement. The "far right" of the Klan has begun to merge into the Proud Boys, the Oath Keepers, the Three Percenters, and countless other groups whose rhetoric and tactics continue to mutate and metastasize. But Moore treats all these moving organizational pieces as essentially interchangeable parts in the overall right-wing authoritarian threat to American democracy.

Although Moore's knowledge of the Klan is based on his personal bravery as an undercover informant and infiltrator, his book also reveals that it is the Klan's own systematic infiltration of law enforcement entities and government bureaucracy that is essential to its power. There are the sheriff's departments that allow racists to operate with impunity in many places; the police departments that can alert extremists to ongoing investigations and feed them vital logistical information; the motor vehicle departments that can procure followers driver's licenses and other forms of identification; and, at the national level, the armed services, which can provide fresh recruits trained to take orders and violent action. The Klan and its paramilitary affiliate groups thrive on the constant blending of racist vigilantism and terror with high-level official permission and bureaucratic support from within.

This should not be surprising. Violent white supremacy began as an official national ideology in pro-slavery America. The *Dred Scott* decision (1857) affirmed the Constitution as a white man's political compact under which African Americans had "no rights which the white man was bound to respect." After the Civil War and the Reconstruction amendments, it was the purpose of the Klan to recreate political and social white supremacy in southern states through a combination of terrorist violence and reorganization of the dominant white elites that had been defeated by Union forces.

Moore's riveting book tells an important part of the back story to how January 6 came to happen. It also depicts the character of the ongoing violent threat to American democracy today.

In the struggles ahead, all of us should show the courage and clear vision of Joseph Moore.

—*Congressman Jamie Raskin (D-MD)*

PREFACE

January 6, 2021, was only the beginning.

When I enlisted in the army in 1995, I swore an oath to protect the country and the Constitution against all enemies, both foreign and domestic. I served as a sniper and section leader for three years, during which I was deployed overseas defending the United States against foreign adversaries. I never imagined that years later I'd be deployed defending our country against enemies from within, in the form of domestic terrorists. Working as a confidential human source for the FBI and Joint Terrorism Task Force, I infiltrated the Ku Klux Klan twice within a ten-year period, between 2007 and 2017, and witnessed the seeds being planted for January 6, as well as what those seeds have sown: the nexus for right-wing extremists uniting toward a common goal, which is nothing less than a second civil war.

In my first tour inside the KKK—the nation's first domestic terrorist group, founded more than 150 years ago—I foiled a plot to assassinate then candidate Barack Obama, only to witness the Klan use his election as a rallying cry and recruiting tool that ignited a firestorm within the white nationalist right. In a subsequent stretch inside a second klavern, I watched a group that had long proclaimed itself the "Invisible Empire" gradually emerge from the shadows to unite the disparate forces that continue to roil this country today. It's estimated that somewhere between half and three quarters of all self-identifying Republicans either identify as white nationalists or hold white nationalist beliefs. That means as much as 30 percent of the United States population wants to see the country burn.

And now we are witnessing the smoke rising from the mass grave that powerful forces within our own country want to dig.

On March 29, 2023, a young man from Missouri rammed the U-Haul truck he was driving into the barriers protecting the White House. According to reports, he told Secret Service agents that he wanted to seize power and would kill anyone in his way, including the president. When he stumbled out of his wrecked vehicle, he pulled out a flag emblazoned with a swastika.

Just over a month later, a gunman opened fire with an assault rifle inside Allen Premium Outlets, a mall in suburban Dallas, and killed nine people, including a three-year-old boy. The shooter, thirty-three-year-old Mauricio Martinez Garcia, was wearing a tactical vest embroidered with the letters RWDS, which stood for "Right Wing Death Squad." What lay beneath the vest was even more telling: Garcia's body was tattooed with fascist symbols, SS lightning bolts, and a swastika.

A June 2023 report from the Inspector General of the Department of Justice states that "threats posed by domestic extremists have not only increased over the past few years, but are also becoming more complicated due to the emergence of new violent ideologies, the impact of social media, and the response to recent political and social events." According to the Southern Poverty Law Center, the hard-right movement's "fingerprints are everywhere: people's homes or schools, doctor's offices, libraries, bars, restaurants, churches, and other community spaces."

Earlier in 2023, Ohio education officials uncovered Nazi-approved homeschooling lesson plans that were created and shared online by white supremacists. More recently, swastikas were displayed in the hands of neo-Nazis who were storming a drag queen storytelling event in a park, also in Ohio. In June 2023, a man named Taylor Taranto, a known January 6 rioter, showed up at the Washington home of former president Barack Obama. When he was arrested, two guns and four hundred rounds of ammunition were found in his van. In 2022, Congressman Paul Gosar of Arizona (via video) and Congresswoman Marjorie Taylor Greene both attended a neo-Nazi convention, called the America First Political Action Committee conference, sponsored by avowed Nazi fanboy Nick Fuentes; Gosar also has two alleged white nationalist sympathizers on his staff. In regard to his apparent support for white nationalists like Fuentes, Senator Tommy Tuberville said in May 2023, "You call them white nationalists. I call them Americans."

Too many of those charged with protecting democracy, it would seem, instead appear fully committed to dissolving it.

In the state of Florida, vast numbers of books are being banned from schools and libraries. A librarian of the Kingsland Branch Library in Llano County, Texas, Suzette Baker, was fired for refusing to follow Florida's lead. On May 5, 2023, Georgia passed a law that allowed the legislature to remove (read: fire) any elected district attorney for any number of arbitrary offenses. North Carolina narrowly lost a case in the Supreme Court on June 27, 2023, requesting that justices place control of all elections in the hands of the state legislature, potentially allowing it to change the results of an election in which that legislature's preferred candidate did not emerge victorious. Alabama is currently refusing to follow an order by the Supreme Court of the United States to redraw its congressional districts, hoping to spur the justices to rehear the case because the state's elected representatives did not like the outcome the first time.

Everything we're witnessing today is a product of the sordid traditions and dogma of the Ku Klux Klan. But the Klan did not spawn the ideology roiling our country today; that ideology spawned the Klan and planted the roots for January 6. The January 6 insurrectionists may not have been card-carrying members of the Klan, but they demonstratively adhered to the same ideology that was the basis for the KKK's founding in 1865. As a whole, white nationalists and white supremacists today have increasingly focused their movements on that original Klan orthodoxy, to the point where their belief systems are nearly indistinguishable from one another, as if the KKK's offspring had collectively returned to the roots that had spawned it.

Now that same ideology has infested not just politicians but also the very forces that are supposed to protect us. A January 2021 analysis by NPR put the number of military veterans who participated in the January 6 insurrection at the Capitol at a staggering 20 percent. Also in January 2021, *Business Insider* reported that "31 police officers are under investigation over their suspected involvement in the Capitol riot, as departments face pressure to weed out white nationalists."

This came as no surprise to me, because I witnessed it firsthand during my two separate stints undercover inside the Ku Klux Klan. The virulent ideology that spawned that hate group has mushroomed across the country. Law enforcement officials who once shunned the Klan, whatever their respective feelings might have been, are now supporting, even embracing, the group openly in broad daylight instead of under cover of darkness.

The Klan's very existence is rooted in its self-identified status as the "Invisible Empire." The stated goal since the group's establishment in the wake of the Civil War has been to overthrow the government and replace it with one of its own making. At times, right-wing nationalist efforts toward that very goal have been as violent as January 6 or as subtle as the passage of bills in the dead of night. The Klan and the like-minded groups it has produced have learned to balance bullets with bluster and pistols with paper, both of which have the potential to do far more irrevocable damage on the state of our democracy than the former. The radical right cares nothing about process, only outcome. They're not interested in a civil discussion to work out differences, because they are so consumed by ideology that it has hijacked their civility. They have a clear vision of what they want the country to look like, and democracy itself is the only thing standing in their way.

In my years serving as an army sniper and section leader on numerous overseas deployments—which I'm not permitted to disclose—in hostile, authoritarian countries, nothing I witnessed in any of them scares me as much as what we're facing at home now.

Should we be afraid?

With the 2024 election looming, and democracy itself on the ballot, the answer is yes, we should be *very* afraid.

WHITE ROBES
AND
BROKEN BADGES

PROLOGUE

"This is our guy," the FBI SWAT team commander said, indicating me to the hundred officers dressed in camo fatigues before him. "He's one of us. Don't shoot him."

We were assembled at 4:00 a.m. in the Alachua Police Department parking lot, the early-morning darkness broken only by the pole-mounted floodlights shining down upon us. A large oak tree spread shadows over the scene that seemed to swallow pockets of the troops assembled, shifting with the whims of the wind. A natural earth berm blocked any view of the group by cars cruising past on State Road 441.

The SWAT commander turned my way. "Show us how you naturally hold your hands."

I let them dangle by my sides.

"Okay, cross your hands, left over right, just over your belt."

I put my hands in the low-compressed position, as instructed.

"That's the signal for the takedown. We'll move in once we see it and brace for the assault," the commander said.

When I'd arrived at 3:30 a.m., he'd told me they had almost deployed the FBI's elite HRT, the Hostage and Rescue Team, to take down Charles Newcomb, given his proven propensity toward violence.

Newcomb was a former patrol cop and prison guard currently working as a recovery agent, or repossession specialist, fancy terms for a repo man. He was stout and very muscular, with a wide build and piercing blue eyes. He claimed he had killed four people, supposedly in the line of duty, when he was a cop in Tennessee. Most recently, he had helped orchestrate the murder by the Ku Klux Klan of a former inmate who had run afoul of prison guards who were members of the klavern in which Newcomb served as Exalted Cyclops, effectively the chapter's mayor.

"What stopped you?" I asked the SWAT commander.

"We decided to use you instead," he told me, with a slight smile.

Five hours after the meeting's conclusion, at 9:00 am, I was sitting in my Kia Sportage almost directly across the street from the police station in a Home Depot parking lot. I was there to meet Charles Newcomb on the pretext that the national leadership of the KKK wanted me to build a bomb, and we needed to purchase the ingredients. As Grand Knighthawk for all Klan chapters throughout Florida and Georgia, and with my background as an army sniper, such a task was well within my purview, and Newcomb had no reason to suspect I was telling him anything but the truth.

"Subject is leaving his home," a voice from the surveillance plane flying twenty thousand feet over Newcomb's neighborhood announced though my earpiece. "Stand by."

That plane was outfitted with cameras that could read a license plate from four miles up in the sky. It would now be trailing Newcomb in his pickup truck the whole way to our planned meeting.

"Subject is turning onto Highway 20 West," the same voice reported.

At this point, FBI agents were already stationed inside the Home Depot, preparing to lock the site down for safety. Once Newcomb reached the parking lot, no one would be permitted to leave the store or enter the lot after him on the chance that Newcomb would resist arrest and it went to guns.

I had infiltrated this particular chapter of the Ku Klux Klan two years ago as a confidential human source for the FBI in an operation being run alongside the Joint Terrorism Task Force. This was the second time I had infiltrated a klavern, and the first time, which had ended six years before, had almost cost me my life.

The best I could hope for today was to walk away alive.

"Subject turning onto State Road 441," the voice in my earpiece crackled. "Stand by."

Charles Newcomb wasn't the only target of this operation. I had provided firm evidence on four Klan members, including the designated leader for both Florida and Georgia, Jamie Ward, and two members of the law enforcement community, Thomas Driver and David Moran. The charge lodged against Newcomb, Driver, and Moran was conspiracy to commit first-degree murder. For Ward, it was a federal firearms charge. The four-pronged plan was to arrest all of them simultaneously, so none of the four could provide advance warning to the others.

As I sat in my car waiting for Charles Newcomb to arrive, I knew a group of SWAT team members culled from both the FBI and numerous local police departments were closing in on the Florida State Prison commonly known as Raiford, located in Lake Butler, thirty minutes from my position, where two of the targets, Thomas Driver and David Moran, worked as guards. Their plan was to execute the arrests there during a shift change, when Driver would be coming out and Moran would be coming in, the perfect moment to snatch them up without gunplay. Another team would be converging in full force on Jamie Ward's house, while the largest detachment of all was already deployed unseen in the Home Depot parking lot, since Newcomb was considered to be the most dangerous of the bunch.

"Subject still proceeding north on State Road 441," the voice in my ear reported from the sky. "Approaching parking lot."

"Secure the building," the voice of the FBI SWAT team commander followed. "Secure the building."

I checked my watch. It was 9:25 a.m. Newcomb should be here any minute.

"Subject has turned onto surface road," the crackling voice reported. "Approaching target site."

I used those final moments to settle myself. I took a deep breath and then slipped into the 4-7-8 breathing ratio I had learned in my training to become an army sniper. It was the regimen I'd practiced before taking a shot in the field, an experience comparable to the one I was facing now. As I breathed, I focused on my wife and two children. Do everything by the numbers and I'd be home with them soon. Do anything that deviated from my norm and aroused suspicion in Newcomb and I might not be coming home at all.

"Subject is entering parking lot. Repeat, subject's truck is entering site parking lot. Begin lockdown now."

In that moment, the surface road accessing the Home Depot would be shut down in both directions to prevent any potential customers from entering the parking lot. With gunplay considered a very realistic, if not likely, possibility, the FBI needed to minimize risk to civilians at all costs.

I recognized Newcomb's truck pulling in, then making a long, lazy circle of the lot to make sure there were no surprises waiting—though in this case all the surprises were tucked out of sight, namely in staging vehicles and around the side of the building. A few moments later, Newcomb pulled his pickup truck alongside my Sportage. I climbed out in the same moment he did.

"KIGY, Brother," he greeted. "KIGY" is the acronym for *Klansman I greet you.*

"KIGY, Brother," I said back.

We shook hands and half hugged, with me ready to act in the event Newcomb felt the wire I was wearing. I noticed he had glued latex patches on the tips of his fingers to avoid leaving fingerprints on any of the bomb-making materials we were supposedly there to buy. After we separated, I watched Newcomb casually remove his firearm and tuck it under his driver's seat. I still had to assume he had a backup weapon on his person and act with that distinct possibility in mind. That wasn't just protocol, it was common sense.

We started toward the Home Depot entrance a hundred and fifty feet away. The FBI step van was parked half that distance away, at the juncture where the takedown of Newcomb would take place.

"This is a big assignment, Brother Joe," he said when we were almost there.

"I'm up for it, sir. I'm prepared to serve the brotherhood with the calling I was taught."

He smiled. "Just so long as it doesn't take you away from us."

Halfway to the entrance, just short of the step van, I put my hands in the low-compressed position I'd demonstrated at the staging session hours before, the signal we were a go. An instant later, a loud explosion rocked the air, coming from a spot well to our left, just beyond the outskirts of the parking lot, where a natural land depression utilized for drainage sat.

"What the hell was that, Charles?" I said, feigning shock.

The distraction achieved its desired effect of making Newcomb swing around in the direction I was already facing.

"There's a cloud of smoke coming up," he noted, pointing toward the heavy black smoke rising from the depression.

Our attention was still firmly rooted in that direction when we heard, "*LET ME SEE YOUR HANDS!*"

I raised my hands in the air, while Newcomb left his by his side. We turned together, and I found myself facing an M4 assault rifle six inches from my face, the finger of the FBI SWAT team member in full body armor starting to curl over the trigger.

PART I

Hell is empty, and all the devils are here.

—WILLIAM SHAKESPEARE, *THE TEMPEST*

CHAPTER 1

A CALL TO THE FBI

WORTHINGTON SPRINGS, FLORIDA
MARCH 2007

"I'm in trouble, Joe."

I got the call from my future brother-in-law, Ryan, midafternoon in March 2007. He'd been arrested after a cop pulled him over for a busted taillight and found a small waterproof hunter's box in his vehicle containing "marijuana residue." That's the drug possession charge he'd been booked on. But it was something else that caught my ear.

"I replaced that taillight," I told him.

"I know. And it was working, I'm sure it was. But the cop pulled me over anyway."

The cop also told my future brother-in-law the busted taillight gave him probable cause to search his vehicle. I majored in criminal law at Florida State and told Ryan that something was fishy. I asked where he was coming from when he was pulled over.

"I was at that truck stop in Worthington Springs. You know, Joe, the little convenience store inside. My cousin was there. So was the deputy who pulled me over."

In my mind, I could see how this had played out. Ryan and his cousin were not-so-friendly rivals. They'd been at odds for years, and I remembered the cousin had friends in the Union County Sheriff's

Office. I was guessing that the cousin knew about the busted taillight, so he told the deputy about it to settle a score between them, not realizing that I'd switched it out. He probably added a tip that Ryan was carrying drugs in the car. The cop must have followed Ryan out of the parking lot and then pulled him over down the road on a bogus charge.

Ryan's sister, Shannon, was the love of my life, which made him family to me. Shannon and I had only known each other for two months but were already living together, and I couldn't imagine spending the rest of my years with anyone else. The first time we met she shared her fried chicken lunch with me, so I guess fried chicken is the way to a man's heart.

At twenty-two years old to my thirty-six, Ryan was just a kid, and I wasn't about to let him get pushed around by a cop who was clearly in the wrong. A bad cop like that makes for the worst kind of bully.

"I'll be right there," I told him, and proceeded to pack up my gear at the power plant where I was working as a welder for an industrial contractor.

I went up to the jail in Lake Butler, a small agricultural community where people worked either as farmers or in some capacity at the state prison nearby that serviced thousands of inmates. Its sprawling structure was surrounded by a forest, which made escape virtually impossible. They let me take Ryan home, pending a preliminary hearing to set bail. He ended up being charged with drug possession, which could carry a stiff sentence, even though all they'd found in his car was that residue.

A few months after his arrest, the daylong trial got underway, with only two witnesses scheduled to testify: the deputy for the prosecution and me for the defense.

The prosecution went first and took the deputy step-by-step through the traffic stop and the arrest. It was a bench trial, and I could see the judge nodding through the deputy's testimony, likely figuring this was an open-and-shut case.

"Your witness," the judge said to Ryan's lawyer.

The lawyer rose. "Deputy, you say you pulled my client over for a broken taillight."

"That's correct."

"And you're certain the taillight was broken."

The deputy nodded. "I observed it in my capacity as a law enforcement officer."

Ryan's lawyer looked up at the judge. "No further questions, Your Honor."

When it came time to present his case, the lawyer called me to the stand.

"Mr. Moore, you are the defendant's future brother-in-law, correct?"

"Correct, yes."

"And you were aware of the defendant's broken taillight?"

"I was."

"And how did you become aware of it?"

"Ryan told me the taillight was broken, and I volunteered to replace it. I've got the receipt right here," I said, taking my wallet from my pocket.

Once I handed over the receipt for the replacement taillight, the trial was effectively over. The charges were dismissed on the spot, since the deputy had pulled Ryan over on false pretenses. The judge gave a stern admonition to both the deputy and the prosecutor, which should have ended things then and there, but not for me. I didn't like bullies and never had. So I called the local FBI branch in Gainesville and told them I wanted to swear out a complaint against the Union County Sheriff's Office.

"You'll need to come in here in person," whoever had answered the phone told me. "Just give your name at the front desk."

The FBI's satellite office in Gainesville was located on the third floor of a nondescript office building. There was nothing advertising that fact either outside the building or in the lobby, not even on the security door just beyond the elevator two flights up. I rang the buzzer, and a voice asked me through a nearby speaker to identify myself.

"Joe Moore," I said. "I was told to come in because I needed to file a complaint in person."

I heard a buzz. A young agent opened the door, inspected my ID, then asked me to wait in a small lobby sitting area. A few minutes later, an agent emerged through a secure door and approached me.

"Mr. Moore, I'm Special Agent Joe Armstrong. Let's go back and talk in my office."

Armstrong was middle-aged, looked to be of average height, balding on top with hair only on the sides of his scalp. We shook hands and he led me down a hallway into his office. I noticed a plastic cup maybe a third full of what looked like tobacco juice and a tin of Skoal atop his desk. I noticed his lower lip puffed out from the dark tobacco substance wedged between his bottom teeth and lip. He was dressed casually in a polo shirt and jeans, while the other agents I'd glimpsed were all wearing ties and dress shirts.

He closed the door behind him and took the chair behind his desk.

"Take a seat," he said, offering me the single chair before it, "Mr. . . ."

"Moore," I said.

"Mr. Moore," Armstrong said, readying a standard FBI FD-302 form to take my statement. "You have a complaint you'd like to file against the Union County Sheriff's Office, is that right?" He spoke rapidly, as if his voice were racing to keep up with his thoughts.

"It is, sir."

I proceeded to give him the blow-by-blow of the entire incident, including how I'd come to the conclusions I'd reached. Armstrong was definitely interested in what I had to say, though not necessarily for the merits of the complaint. He peppered me with questions, and I satisfied him with my answers to all of them.

"You have quite a memory for detail, Mr. Moore," Armstrong said once he'd finished questioning me.

"I picked that up in the army."

"You were in the army?"

"Yes, sir. I was a sniper. I was in charge of a section, which means I was taught intelligence-gathering methods. You can't always write stuff down when you're in a forward position, so you need to train your memory to recall everything you observe."

I figured Armstrong might have served as well. Either way, I could tell he was impressed. I had run track on scholarship at Florida State and enrolled in the ROTC program. If things had gone as planned, I would have graduated with a degree in criminal justice as a second lieutenant in the United States Army. But my mother came down with cancer, non-Hodgkin's lymphoma, so I resigned from the ROTC and dropped out of college in my senior year to assist my stepfather with caregiving duties. He was working incredibly long hours to keep up with the medical bills, which left no one to take my mother to her many appointments, which included chemotherapy sessions. I remember how weak and frail she became, unable to get in and out of the car without assistance. I had to support her when she walked down the hospital hallways. She'd tell the nurses and doctors we passed on the way to treatment that she was fine and really didn't need my help. She kept saying that, the weaker and weaker she got. I accompanied her on each and every visit to the hospital with no clear idea of her prognosis, but her attitude told me she was going to beat this thing. When she ultimately did, I enlisted as a private in the army, still holding on to a measure of my dreams.

Armstrong rose and extended his hand across the desk.

"We'll be in touch, Mr. Moore. And we'll let you know how our investigation proceeds."

Armstrong called me a couple of months later to tell me two FBI agents had paid a visit to the sheriff's department, where the sheriff himself assured them he would take care of the matter. But Armstrong wasn't really calling me about that.

"Would you mind coming back in, Joe? There's something else I'd like to discuss with you."

We set a time for the following week—this time not at the office in Gainesville but at a secret location I'm not permitted to disclose.

By the time I got there, Armstrong had a paper cup in front of him half filled with the dark grimy refuse of his smokeless tobacco.

"How are you with rednecks, Joe?" Armstrong asked me.

"I know rednecks," I told him, not sure where this was going. "But they're not my favorite people to hang around with. Why?"

"Sometimes, we need someone . . ." Armstrong let that thought dangle. "Tell me more about your background."

I provided additional details about being an army sniper and the head sniper for my section during my eight years of service. I told him about the training at Schofield Barracks in Hawaii and the various commendations I'd received. I was unable to disclose the specifics of the missions I'd undertaken because they were classified and under seal.

"Do you mind if we run a background check on you?"

"No, not at all. But there's something I'd like you to hear from me first before you read it in a report. . . ."

Near the end of my tour as an army section leader in August 1998, when I was twenty-seven, my platoon sergeant and battalion commander approached me about continuing on, only in a new capacity. He probed my interest in bringing my skill set to Special Operations. He said he'd been watching my progression all the way through the enlisted ranks to staff sergeant. I was the chief sniper and section leader of my detachment, and my accomplishments in extremely difficult, challenging missions had apparently captured the attention of an army Tier One unit.

I enthusiastically accepted the offer provided by this officer, but he was ultimately overruled and I was assigned to lead the army's recruiting efforts in Los Angeles instead. I was disappointed but hopeful I might get another chance at joining Special Operations if I performed my duties as a recruiter well enough to impress the brass.

Prior to moving on to my new assignment, while still stationed in Hawaii, I met a beautiful young woman at a nightclub, a schoolteacher from Nebraska who was vacationing there. We fell in love instantly. Over the course of the next six months, I visited her a couple of times in Nebraska and she returned to Hawaii twice to visit me. Then she uprooted her life in order to join me in Los Angeles and resume her career there. We quickly got engaged, and I counted my blessings that I'd ended up with this assignment instead of Special Ops, in which case I never would have met her.

The problem was that I'd developed a second love: gambling. I'd make up excuses why I couldn't be with her during a great portion of my off-duty time, so I could head to Las Vegas and play blackjack. I caught myself before things got out of hand, though, and enrolled in Gamblers Anonymous. I pronounced myself cured, was promoted to the next rank, and was making all the stated recruitment goals of the office.

When the recruiting battalion held a function at a casino in Palm Springs, California, I relapsed. I ended up bouncing some checks. When my commander found out, he pulled my stripes, a demotion that came with a dramatic cut in pay, down to less than six hundred dollars a month. My fiancée was understandably freaked out, and after we had been living together in LA for two years and starting to plan our wedding, she broke off our engagement and went back to Nebraska.

Meanwhile, I could no longer afford a place to live. Shelters weren't an option because they closed their doors to the homeless at five o'clock and I was still working at the recruiting office from 6:00 a.m. to 11:00 p.m. six days a week. I'd shower every morning at the LA Fitness health club because I had a prepaid membership, and did my best to look prim and proper, but it was hard while following a lousy diet and sleeping wherever I could find space. Several of my colleagues invited me to stay with them, but I declined because I didn't want their families to see this side of me. This was all my doing, and I needed to take responsibility for it.

Ultimately, my commander sent me to a psychiatrist at the local veterans hospital, and that doctor determined I was suffering from post-traumatic stress disorder. Drilling down deeper, he believed that the origins lay in the sexual assault I'd suffered as a young boy, memories I'd long repressed but that had come roaring back, triggered by the life-threatening missions I performed while deployed. I had been a warrior in the war against global terrorism, and now I'd become a casualty of it.

After serving three additional months under my reduced rank, my recruiting tour ended. I tried to reenlist to go back to fighting the global war on terror. After all that had transpired, though, my commanding officer barred me from reenlisting, and I was honorably discharged from the army. With no salary coming in, I had only four thousand dollars I'd received in back pay to get by. Fortunately, I was able to keep seeing the army psychiatrist, thanks to the VA, and got a job almost immediately at a drywall factory.

When I first got some time off after a few weeks of working at the factory, I decided to do some traveling on the cheap. I was in a restaurant near the airport when I began to get a heavy sensation in the left side of my chest and some pain in my left arm. I also felt lightheaded, almost dizzy, and got wobbly as soon as I stood up. My first thought was that somebody had spiked my drink, because I definitely didn't feel right. As a sniper, I had grown very attuned to my own body. I could feel the slightest deviation from the norm, and what I felt in that restaurant was anything but slight. I felt so off and strange that I decided to walk to a hospital only a couple of blocks away instead of driving, because I was afraid I might pass out behind the wheel. I also thought that walking in the fresh air might make me feel better. But I felt even worse when I got there.

The personnel in the emergency room believed I was suffering a panic attack. When they reeled off the symptoms, I checked every box, and was ultimately diagnosed as suffering from bipolar disorder, a condition that was bad enough on its own but was made much worse when combined with the PTSD, in large part because of the sexual abuse I'd suffered as a boy.

I spent enough time in the hospital for the doctors to settle on a drug regimen to treat my condition. In search of a fresh start, I left LA and moved to Florida, where my family lived, and found a job as a welder. It took me a while to get back on my feet, but in the years following I worked hard on my mental health. Even though I was fully recovered from that initial episode and had been prescribed the proper drugs to keep my condition under control, the stain of that experience was forever memorialized in my army file.

I was not ashamed to share this, or what a background check would reveal, with Armstrong. Like so many other veterans, my service came at an immense cost. After I left the army, I experienced some of the darkest times in my life. But I was proud of how I had rebuilt my life and climbed out of that darkness. I was confident in the man I was today—not in spite of what I had gone through but because of it.

I gave him my date of birth, social security number, address, phone numbers, and information about my family—all the boilerplate stuff.

Armstrong wrote everything down, and said, "Okay, give us some time to do this background check and we'll get back to you."

This was sometime around late June, early July. I'd figured my candidness about my background had disqualified me from working with the FBI, but then he called in August and asked me to meet him at the same undisclosed location. This time he was joined by Rich Vaughn, a local police officer and member of the Joint Terrorism Task Force as a Task Force Officer, or TFO.

"No issues on your background check," Armstrong told me. "Everything looks fine."

I waited for him to continue.

"This is about the Ku Klux Klan, Joe. We'd like you to infiltrate them. We'd like you to work for us as a confidential informant."

I was no fan of the KKK. Just like my mother's cancer was a bully, just like the cop who wrongly arrested Ryan was a bully, I saw Klansmen as bullies prone to terrorizing innocent people based on nothing more than the color of their skin or their religious persuasion. From my studies in law enforcement and criminal justice I knew what a confidential informant was: one of two categories of infiltrator, the other being a cooperating witness. The latter is generally someone who's committed a crime and is looking to make a deal to avoid or minimize jail time. A confidential informant, or CI, is someone who covertly joins a group, organization, gang, or anything else on the FBI's behalf, for the purpose of gathering intelligence to build an actionable court case against it.

In my case, I looked the part. I stood a hair over six feet, stayed fit, kept my hair trimmed high and tight, and maintained a polite and formal military-type bearing. But it was my active-duty background that caused Armstrong and Vaughn to feel I was the perfect choice.

"How do you feel about that?" Armstrong asked. "Are you willing to serve your country in that capacity?"

In the army, I'd sworn an oath to defend the Constitution against all enemies, although I'd always taken that to mean foreign enemies, as opposed to domestic ones. Not anymore, apparently.

"Yes, sir, I am."

Armstrong nodded, his gaze softening a bit. "That's what I was hoping to hear."

Confidential informants are not hired or trained employees of the FBI, although they can receive compensation in some instances for their information and expenses. According to the Attorney General's Guidelines Regarding the Use of Confidential Informants, "'a confidential informant' or 'CI' is any individual who provides useful and credible information to a Justice Law Enforcement Agency (JLEA) regarding felonious criminal activities and from whom the JLEA expects or intends to obtain additional useful and credible information regarding such activities in the future."

In this case, that JLEA was the Joint Terrorism Task Force, through the auspices of the FBI, working in conjunction with local law enforcement officials, like Vaughn. The Bureau doesn't use the term "informant" in official channels, preferring "confidential human source." Interestingly, the FBI doesn't actually place or insert such sources, as it would with actual undercover Bureau agents. Confidential human sources normally are people who are already in a position to know or gain information and willingly cooperate because they're concerned with something they've seen or heard. But Armstrong was asking me to infiltrate the KKK the way an FBI agent would, as opposed to recruiting a human asset who was already a part of the Klan or acting upon intelligence volunteered by someone inside. Right from the start, I sensed I was being asked to do something that stretched the boundaries of normal operations quite a bit. As I would later learn, though, the stakes called for it.

In October 2006, a then confidential FBI report titled *White Supremacist Infiltration of Law Enforcement* reported, "Although white supremacist groups have historically engaged in strategic efforts to infiltrate and recruit from law enforcement communities, current reporting on attempts reflects self-initiated efforts by individuals, particularly among those already within law enforcement ranks, to volunteer their professional resources to white supremacist causes with which they sympathize."

It seems that what attracted Armstrong to me was that my original reason for coming in was to report malfeasance by a Union County sheriff's deputy. That meant I was hardly averse to calling out rogue behavior by law enforcement personnel. Add to that my army background, and I checked all the boxes a senior field agent like Armstrong had been looking for.

"Because this is the KKK, you're actually going to be a counterterrorism operative," Armstrong told me.

What he didn't explain was that a counterterrorism operative acts entirely in secret. So all the paperwork, including the reports filed under my code name, listed me only as a confidential human source, the way I'm still listed to this day.

This was never a criminal investigation; it was a counterterrorism investigation. I wasn't charged with infiltrating the KKK to find evidence of a crime per se, the way the FBI does in mob cases. I was charged with gathering intelligence about the organization's inner workings and membership, while working to safeguard the lives of those the Klan might be targeting. In that respect, Armstrong wasn't holding back information to test me. The Klan was such an insular, compartmentalized organization that he genuinely didn't have any more information than the little he passed on. That's why it was so important to get someone on the inside.

When it came to matters involving terrorism, domestic or foreign, nothing was off the table. Around this time, the Klan was resurfacing as a very real threat, along with a bevy of other extremist organizations primarily comprised of white nationalists, having realized that they didn't need a majority of the country, just a willing minority, to achieve their goals.

The operation I would be part of was being conducted under the auspices of the Enforcement Act of 1871, aka the Ku Klux Klan Act, which had been passed in response to the political violence the Klan had perpetrated during Reconstruction in the post–Civil War era. That 1871 act seems even more relevant today.

Armstrong wasn't specific about what I was supposed to ascertain. All he told me was that a known KKK member named William Hawley (not his real name), who lived in Wayward, Florida, was selling a rifle, because that's all he knew. Purchasing that rifle was to be my way in, enabling me to establish the bonds necessary for me to ingratiate myself into an organization committed to the destruction of the United States as we know it.

"One thing," I said to Armstrong. "If I have to face these guys, I'm going to need to be armed."

Armstrong didn't have a problem with that. There was nothing in my background that argued against it, and plenty in my background to indicate I knew my way around firearms.

"As long as you follow the applicable Florida statutes," Armstrong said, "you can carry a gun in the company of Klan members. Let's just hope you never have to use it."

CHAPTER 2

WILLIAM HAWLEY

WAYWARD, FLORIDA
AUGUST 2007

My next meeting with Armstrong and Vaughn took place two months later, in a plain FBI-issue sedan. Vaughn was driving, with Armstrong riding shotgun. I sat in the back seat. They didn't tell me where we were going, and I didn't ask.

As we set out, Armstrong gave me my classified code name. It was what other FBI officials knew me as to safeguard my real identity from potential leaks, which was standard procedure.

This would be the first small step in the much bigger challenge I would face to maintain my own identity and stay true to the man I was while inside the Ku Klux Klan.

"This is who you are now, as far as the FBI is concerned. But with William Hawley, you're going to use your real identity, Joe Moore."

We were driving into Wayward. Armstrong wanted me to get the lay of the land and familiarize myself with how the town was laid out. I could see why the first question Armstrong had asked me was how I felt about rednecks, since Wayward was so typical of redneck life. The town was rural, set among smaller towns with populations between five and ten thousand that were common in this part of central Florida. The only employer of note was the local power plant. People worked either at the Walmart and Home Depot or at the smaller mom-and-pop shops and strip malls that were concentrated in the center of the town, which was only a small percentage of its total area. Wayward's infrastructure was defined by bass fishing, hog hunting, and gator hunting in the many lakes that dotted the land.

I'd never seen so many pickup trucks in my life. It seemed like ours was the only car on the road. *The Yearling*, the classic Pulitzer Prize–winning novel by Marjorie Kinnan Rawlings, was set in this very area of backwoods Florida, where her family settled in 1928 after purchasing a small orange grove in the town of Cross Creek.

"It is impossible to be among the woods animals on their own ground without a feeling of expanding one's own world, as when any foreign country is visited," Rawlings once wrote.

The Wayward, Florida, of 2007 may not have been a foreign country, but the area had an insular nature to it, a world unto itself, where outsiders were barely tolerated, and the phrase "Florida crackers" was accepted with down-home affection and pride.

On our drive, Armstrong never pointed out William Hawley's property to me, which I took to mean we never ventured close enough to avoid the risk of being spotted. He also never told me anything about Hawley, other than that he was a Klan member and was selling a rifle. The FBI was throwing me into a sink-or-swim situation.

Armstrong handed me a document with a standard list of rules for undercover operatives called admonishments. I reviewed it in detail, found everything to be acceptable, and then asked to borrow his pen to sign it. Then I handed the document back over the seat.

Armstrong looked at the signature pages and blew a gasket, showcasing a temper I would see flare several times during the course of our work together. "What the *fuck*! What the fuck did you do?"

I just looked at him as he jammed the now crinkled document back in my face.

"You signed your own fucking name! You were supposed to sign your classified code name. I told you!"

He hadn't, but I wasn't about to argue the point.

Armstrong called either the satellite office in Gainesville or the field office in Tampa to request fresh admonishment forms be faxed to a nearby police department. He was still livid when we pulled into the department's parking lot, and he bounced out of the car and slammed the door behind him, only to reemerge from the police station with the replacement forms in hand. He thrust them toward me after he got back into the car.

"I need your pen again, please," I said.

This time I signed the forms with my code name. Then we continued cruising about Wayward and the greater county, with Rich Vaughn doing most of the talking, acting as a tour guide. When they brought me back to where I'd left my car, Armstrong handed me a white envelope.

"William Hawley's phone number is inside. Give him your name, tell him you're interested in the rifle. He's selling it for seven hundred dollars. The money's inside too. You've got my number. Call me with an update after you've made contact. And when you call in, use your code name!"

Back in my car outside the field office, I called William Hawley's phone number on my cell and a man answered in a deep, scratchy voice with a slight Southern drawl.

"Yeah?"

"I'm calling about the rifle that's for sale."

"Who are you?"

"My name's Joe Moore."

"Can you come over first thing tomorrow?"

We set a time for the next morning, and I called Armstrong on the number he'd given me to report as much.

"Already?" he asked, surprise evident in his voice.

"Just doing my job," I told him.

The next morning, I drove into Wayward and followed the directions William Hawley had given me. His property wasn't hard to find. There wasn't a lot of tree cover, and I spotted the fence line from several hundred yards down the road accessing it. I could see that the fence was electrified and topped with barbed wire to discourage unwelcome visitors. The big, mangy dogs roaming about and the bevy of security cameras attached to the nearby Florida sugar maple trees furthered that impression. An eight-foot strip of grass had been cleared against the entire fence line, like the warning track of a baseball field, to reveal any footprints left by intruders.

I pulled up to a gated entrance and stretched my arm out the window to press a button on an intercom.

"That you, Mr. Moore?" the voice I recognized from the day before asked me.

"Yes, sir," I said, calling him that to show proper deference. I realized he was looking straight at me through a camera built into the intercom box.

"Drive on up."

The gate swung open electronically, and I slid through it along a flattened gravel road toward the one-level brick house. I could see a large figure already waiting for me there. William Hawley was a big, rawboned man in his early forties, with leathery hands from his career as a mechanic and steely eyes that looked black. He stood a bit taller than me at six two, was clean shaven, and was wearing a baseball cap over his bald head and logger boots laced up almost to his knees.

The air smelled of freshly chipped trees and dry dust. A freight train rode by along the tracks between the property line and the surface road, and diesel fuel joined those scents. I spotted three shooting ranges, which were backed up against earthen berms to catch stray bullets.

Hawley's property was a half mile or so from nearby Lochloosa Lake, long rumored to be a site where numerous people who "disappeared" have been dumped or fed to the alligators that call the lake home. Occasionally, human bones have washed up on shore, too degraded to be of use identifying who they might have belonged to. The property was a short drive from Rosewood, where an infamous massacre of African Americans took place in 1923.

As I drew closer, my first trained observation was that Hawley was dangerous, not so much because of how he looked or dressed as the way he carried himself. Broad shoulders canted to the side to make himself as small a target as possible. Right hand dangling low by his hip as if he had a pistol holstered there. Right away, I knew this situation could escalate from zero to violent in a heartbeat. And I hadn't come armed on this visit, because Joe Moore, the counterterrorism operative, needed to ingratiate himself and not appear threatening.

Hawley turned all the way around to face me as I stepped out of my car and approached him. I still couldn't ascertain whether he was armed. I was wearing jeans, work boots, and a hat, the clothes I'd normally wear to my work as a welder and mechanic myself.

"Nice to meet you, Mr. Moore," he greeted me, extending his hand. "William Hawley."

"Nice to meet you, too, Mr. Hawley," I said, taking it. "I can't wait to have a look at that weapon."

"She's a beauty, all right. In as good a shape as the day I bought her. Let's give you a look."

He led me through a front door made of heavy steel. The jamb and frame were steel, too, making the home impossible to penetrate that way without using explosives. The walls were made of reinforced concrete, and the windows were thick enough to withstand small-arms fire. With the perimeter fence surrounding it, William Hawley had constructed a virtual fortress.

I was also observing which doors opened in or out, left or right, according to the placement of the handle. Were there strike plates? How many steps had I climbed to enter the house? When you're trained as an army sniper, you're taught to pay attention to things nobody else ever would.

As Hawley led me through the house, I saw a .50-caliber anti-matériel rifle displayed on a wall across from a certificate emblazoned with what I recognized as the Klan symbol, consisting of a bold X adorned with four Ks. From my study of the KKK in the four months since Armstrong first raised the notion of my becoming a confidential human source in April, I recognized it as the Saltire Cross from Scottish religious tradition. It was an old Ku Klux Klan symbol that had been resurrected by KKK groups today. That X allowed for the symbolic placement of the four Ks that stood for "Knights of the Ku Klux Klan." That's why Klan members hold up four fingers at rallies. The Saltire Cross could also be found, appropriately enough, on the Confederate flag. It had been the mystic insignia of the KKK, also known as the Blood Drop Cross, from the group's founding in 1865 all the way through its first era until the start of its second era in 1915. That's when William Joseph Simmons changed the symbol to the Protestant Cross, an important change given that the Klan was a strongly Protestant organization.

"Is that what I think it is?" I asked Hawley, making sure to look appropriately excited.

"What do you think it is?"

"Are you a member of the Klan?" I asked, instead of answering.

"You interested in the Klan, Mr. Moore?" he asked me somewhat suspiciously, his head angled slightly to the side.

"Oh, for sure. I haven't found many people in these parts yet I like associating with."

"Okay, we can talk about that later. Right now, let's go get that gun."

He proceeded to lead me toward what looked like a closet that had been converted into some kind of vault. Hawley used a regular key to unlock it, and even a man of his size and strength strained a bit to open the door, because it was so heavy. A bright fluorescent light snapped on automatically, revealing a virtual armory.

The first thing I glimpsed was a second anti-matériel rifle, a fearsome weapon that fired .50-caliber shells powerful enough to penetrate armor up to twenty-five millimeters thick. That meant they could shoot through light-armored vehicles like troop carriers, enough to tell me that William Hawley was ready to fight a war.

I watched him lean in and lift a Browning BAR 30.06 hunting rifle from its upright perch on the floor.

"She's a beauty, all right," he said, handing me the rifle.

I went through a functions check, first making sure the safety was engaged and then confirming that there was no round in the chamber. I checked the heft and weight of the weapon. It would cost around two thousand dollars new, so seven hundred for a rifle in this condition was a steal.

I could tell Hawley was studying me, impressed by how I was handling the weapon.

"You've been around guns a little bit," he said.

"Yes, sir, in the army. I was stationed in Hawaii at Schofield Barracks."

I could tell that raised Hawley's interest. "You were in the army?"

"Yes, sir." I nodded. "I was a sniper and head of my sniper section."

I watched his eyes widen. "A sniper? Are you serious?"

I pulled out my phone and showed him my sniper certificate.

Hawley squinted slightly to regard it. "Not many like you around. Thank you for your service," he said, and handed me back my phone, his interest piqued. "Why are you interested in the Klan?"

"Well, I'm disgruntled with the way things in this country are going, and I'm kind of new here. I just want to be around people like me."

"Might you be of a mind to join us?" he asked me.

Something about the way he said that chilled me to the bone. "Yes, ab-so-lutely!" I said, feigning exuberance.

Hawley smiled for the first time since I met him. "Well, we'll see what we can do about that."

I forked over the seven hundred dollars Armstrong had given me and left William Hawley's house with the Browning rifle wrapped in a blanket. I had played my role well, it seemed, subjugating myself to Hawley in the hope he'd open up to me more. It was a master and student scenario, and I wanted Hawley to know I saw him as the master, the alpha. Men like him don't like to be challenged by someone they might then perceive as a threat, but they revel in loyal subservience.

Before I left, I gave William Hawley my phone number. He said he'd give me a call soon, that we'd have lunch or something to discuss the next steps of my joining the Klan.

"Just name the time," I told him.

CHAPTER 3

PASSING THE TEST

WAYWARD, FLORIDA
AUGUST 2007

I called Armstrong as soon as I left the property with the rifle lying across the back seat of my car. He directed me to a second location, where I was to turn it over and be debriefed.

His only reaction to the report I provided in response to his and Rich Vaughn's questions was: "Wow."

I had accomplished so much so fast that Special Agent Armstrong hadn't even finished obtaining all the necessary clearances for the operation to proceed. He thought I was just going to William Hawley's property to buy a gun. I'd left with not only the Browning, but also a straight path into the Klan.

We reviewed the chronology of my visit over and over again, Armstrong most interested in that certificate I'd spotted on the wall.

"Hawley didn't point it out?"

"No, sir, I observed it and recognized the X as the symbol of the KKK."

Armstrong was left shaking his head. I think he underestimated how army snipers are trained to notice *everything*, because anything can affect a shot or form a reason not to take one. Your focus is on your target, but you maintain a keen awareness of your entire surroundings. I had merely applied that training to my visit to Hawley's home, which was in fact, as I had explained to them, a fortified compound.

Armstrong listened intently as I described the interior of the house and the surrounding property. A siege on that property would clearly meet formidable and deadly resistance. It also suggested that William Hawley was high up in the KKK's ranks. All the task force had known until now was that he was a card-carrying member who had a rifle to sell. They had accumulated no additional intelligence until my debriefing. It was Confederate general Robert E. Lee who first proclaimed the Klan the "Invisible Empire" in May 1867. By all indications, its membership remained invisible in 2007.

"Good work, Joe," Armstrong complimented. "We're off to a great start."

"Thank you, sir. Now I need you to do something for me."

That night over dinner, I told Shannon that I had become a confidential human source for the FBI.

"Wow," she said, awestruck. "Are you going to be in danger, 'cause I'm worried."

"I'll be fine. Either way, I've got to do this."

I didn't want her to have to take me at my word, didn't want her getting anxious over all the time I'd now be away from the apartment we shared. So I asked Joe Armstrong to confirm the details face-to-face the next day. She squeezed my hand the whole time and smiled at me when he was finished.

"Go get 'em, Joe," she said.

The call from William Hawley came a couple of days later, still before the FBI had all their ducks in a row. But Armstrong wasn't going to let that stop the operation from proceeding. Any delay to the meeting Hawley called me to set up to discuss my potential membership risked raising suspicions and the ability to get a counterterrorism operative planted, at long last, inside. I was told to comply with Hawley's instructions.

"Can you meet tomorrow at my property?" Hawley asked me.

"Yes, sir, I can."

"See you at noon, then," he said, in what sounded more like an order, something I took as a good sign.

Before heading back to Hawley's the next day, I was fitted with a wire. During our meeting, an FBI agent would be parked down the road, a mile or so away, listening in and prepared to intervene if things went bad. Not that the Bureau expected they would—they didn't know what to expect because they hadn't been presented with such an opportunity before.

After being buzzed through Hawley's security gate again, I ended up spending much of the afternoon with him. The rapport I continued to build with him was the wild card in all this. He was starting to trust me, even confide in me, and that was something the task force had never managed to achieve before, never mind so quickly.

William Hawley and I didn't actually eat lunch at his home that day, the pretext on which our meeting had been set. Instead, he took me on a tour of his property. At one point, I noticed some tarps stretched over a big patch of land, clearly hiding something and preventing any disturbances in the ground from being spotted by aerial surveillance.

Hawley must have noted my lingering glance. "Something for another day, my friend."

We spent the bulk of my visit sampling his shooting ranges and testing out various guns. I had the sense Hawley was testing *me* as well—not only my skill with firearms but also my mindset, to see if I was a good fit for the Klan. Hawley had brought out a selection of his favorite weapons to show me in his living room, all of them Heckler & Koch and some of them having been illegally converted to fully automatic. I'd fired plenty of weapons like these, but never from this German brand. They were formidable weapons, easy to control.

The range was where we did the bulk of our talking, mostly about the KKK's philosophy and future. It wasn't an inquisition; Hawley never would have revealed himself to me this way if I hadn't already passed muster with him. He did a lot of explaining about the Klan's history, and how the current incarnation of the group differed from its past. It sounded like he was proselytizing, even preaching as he waxed poetic about the Klan being in the process of building an infrastructure that would support and enable their efforts to commit violence. Hate was the primary motivator for those actions and for their militancy.

But that wasn't all I took from that meeting. When a man like William Hawley shows you his guns, he's baring his soul. It's the ultimate show of welcome and indicates a kind of opening up of the circle to let you in. And Hawley was really going out on a limb promoting me for membership in the KKK, vouching for me even though he'd only known me a week. That told me he believed I could play an important role in the group, and the more important I was, the more intelligence I'd be able to gather. It was becoming increasingly clear to me by the way he presented himself, what trained operatives referred to as a "center of influence," that Hawley was very likely the leader of this particular klavern, a position known as the Grand Dragon. I also got the feeling he didn't trust a lot of people and saw me as a blank slate, someone he could mold and groom to his own liking.

Which suited me just fine.

That process continued over the course of the next two months. By October, I'd had six to eight meetings with William Hawley. Mostly, that meant meeting other Klan members from the area, as part of what I surmised was the process to vet me.

One of these members was a tall, lanky man Hawley introduced as Brother Brown. He owned a vehicle salvage lot and garage just south of Hawley's property. Hawley owned several Corvettes and other classic sports cars he kept garaged on his property, so I guessed this was the source of their friendship. When Hawley introduced him, he made a point of saying that Brother Brown had contacts at the Department of Motor Vehicles. I didn't grasp the significance of that at the time, but I would later.

Another time, we went to a local barbecue joint I'd later learn was a popular hangout for Klan members. Hawley steered me over to a table where a man sat alone, smoking a cigarette even though it was prohibited.

"Joe, I'd like you to meet Brother Bicky."

Like members of a biker gang, many Klan members boasted colorful nicknames. This was so they could keep their true identities on the down-low, and also an element of comradery that defined the Klan's parochial nature. I doubt very much the man seated at the table was called "Bicky" by anyone outside the organization. A cowboy hat sat on the table before him. He was an older man, mid-sixties maybe, and I quickly surmised that he was very experienced and knowledgeable about Klan activities going back several decades.

Bicky posed a number of questions to me.

Where you from?
Where's your family from?
What do you do for work now?

As I answered each question, I could tell he was observing my expressions and body language. I got the sense Hawley used him as a kind of human lie detector, and this meeting at the barbecue joint was an opportunity to get Bicky's seal of approval.

Or not.

That would explain why he was seated by himself, even though he was a celebrity among the group. The questioning was interrupted at one point by a waitress refilling my iced tea. I noticed her hand was shaking so bad she could barely manage the task. I'd later learn she was terrified because Hawley had told her I was a hit man.

When we left the barbecue joint, Hawley pointed out a liquor store.

"Blacks used to hang out there," he said, slowing his truck. "We drove by in a van one night and opened up with an assault rifle on full auto over their heads. Took out the whole damn window." He grinned. "The Blacks don't hang out there anymore."

There was pride in his voice as he said that, even though he was admitting to several felonies that could have put him away for twenty years. I took that as a sign he'd received positive feedback about me inside the restaurant, most prominently, I thought, from Bicky.

"I think we're ready to take the next step, Joe," he said as we climbed out of his truck back at his house. "There's just one more hoop you've got to jump through, that being you need to be interviewed by the Klan's national leader, Charles Denton. He'll be in town next week. That's when we'll make it happen."

I could only imagine what Armstrong and Vaughn would make of the fact I was about to meet the Imperial Wizard of the United Northern and Southern Knights, one of five separate families that made up the national organization and for which the klavern Hawley led was considered a flagship, based in the heart of Klan country. Denton directly oversaw all the individual chapters under his domain. He was infamous in Klan circles and had been since his youth. In the 1960s, he'd been affiliated with a Klan sect known as the Mississippi White Knights and closely acquainted with Edgar Ray Killen, who murdered the civil rights workers James Chaney, Andrew Goodman, and Michael Schwerner in 1964, during what was known as Freedom Summer, on behalf of that group.

That groundbreaking investigation became known as "Mississippi Burning" and was the basis for the great 1988 film of that name starring Gene Hackman. Denton had attended the Killen trial from beginning to end, posing as Cole Thornton, the name of the character played by John Wayne in the movie *El Dorado*. The Mississippi White Knights, while following the same doctrine the Klan did nationally, had a propensity to resort to violent extremes to achieve their ends, essentially staying true to the original ideals of the Klan set forth upon the group's founding. While other chapters preached those same ideals, they didn't necessarily enforce them to the same degree.

"And if things go well," Hawley told me, "he'll likely participate in your naturalization ceremony himself."

At my debriefing the following day, Armstrong and Vaughn were blown away by the rapid progress I'd made in ingratiating myself to a man they hadn't even known was the leader, the Grand Dragon, of this particular klavern. When I told them I was going to be interviewed by Charles Denton himself the following week, they were astonished. I wondered if just for a moment they thought I was making this up.

But it was all on the recordings that came courtesy of the wire I wore to all my meetings. From a procedural standpoint, it was much easier to get authorization to make covert recordings because this was a counterterrorist, as opposed to a criminal, investigation. All we needed was a local assistant U.S. attorney to sign off instead of a federal judge, mostly to avoid putting that judge in danger. When and if my intelligence-gathering efforts and assessment led to proof of criminal behavior, then we'd need to go before a judge to proceed further in the investigation. It would still be classified under the counterterrorism moniker; only the process would change. And the purpose of that assessment would be to determine the threat to the general public posed by the particular chapter of the KKK. In other words, mine was a proactive investigation, meant to prevent crimes from occurring, instead of a reactive investigation, designed to bring to justice those responsible for crimes that have already occurred. In that respect, my initial efforts were about putting myself in a position close enough to William Hawley to assess the danger posed by the klavern he led.

The following week, Hawley told me we needed to find a location where the meeting with Charles Denton would take place. My first thought was a restaurant or club friendly to the Klan and supportive of its interests. But the search for the ideal spot took us deep into a state forest that rimmed Lochloosa Lake, the rumored dumping spot of numerous Klan murder victims over the years. Denton had learned to always conduct such meetings outside, as far away from civilization as possible. For this reconnaissance drive I had no FBI backup, but I was wearing a wire to properly authenticate the meeting. By this point, there were already fifty personnel from the Joint Terrorism Task Force involved in the operation, which stretched all the way to Washington and involved both the FBI and Homeland Security.

Hawley had some work to do that day, so we took two vehicles, with me leading Hawley in his truck along a narrow dirt road that cut through the woods pocked by exposed tree roots and depressions left by puddling after the major storms common this time of year. I had told him I was already familiar with the area, which I was, but I'd also scoped it out for myself in advance of this trip. We drove slowly, approaching the spot Hawley ultimately selected for the meeting, when we came upon a man out looking for his lost hunting dogs. He started cursing at me because my tires had kicked up dust into his face. Then he just kept screaming, cursing, and threatening me as I drove on.

I didn't think anything of it, but William Hawley must have heard the whole thing through his open window, because he jammed on his brakes, reversed slightly, hopped out of his truck, and approached the man. Hawley wasn't carrying a gun at the time, but the man had a hunting rifle. This didn't stop Hawley from punching him so hard in the face that the man banged hard against the truck and slumped down the fender. In my rearview mirror, I watched Hawley beating the man to a pulp, and by the time I got out of my car and approached, he had dropped his rifle and was begging for his life. Hawley saw me and cast a slight smile my way. I thought in that moment he was going to kill the man, and that I'd have no choice but to go along with it, even help Hawley dump the body in the lake if it came to that.

The man continued pleading, and Hawley looked over again and flashed me another smile. That smile said a lot of things, but mostly that he was enjoying himself, that he took pleasure in bringing pain to others. He didn't even seem to be breathing hard. Just as I became certain the guy on the ground was about to take his last breath, Hawley stepped back from his limp body, retrieved his rifle, handed it back to him, and told him to "drive the fuck out of here" as he pointed to the truck the man had left parked nearby. Hawley didn't seem remotely concerned that the guy might turn the rifle on him; maybe he wanted him to try.

Until then, everything had been about proving myself to Hawley to end up in his good graces. But I had the sense from this incident that he wanted to prove himself to me, to show that he had my back. It was almost like he was saying, *Now that I trust you, I want to give you reason to trust me.* I was truly being welcomed into the family, and the head of that family wanted my approval.

I got back inside my SUV and suddenly felt lightheaded. An oddly familiar stench of stale sweat mixed with unwashed clothes seemed to fill my car's interior—the violent encounter I had just witnessed had triggered an intense flood of memories, from my first experience with true evil as a young boy. I felt like I'd been transported decades back in time, to the three-month stretch when I'd been sexually assaulted by a pair of men. They lived in the neighborhood and had good reputations in the community. I closed my eyes, unable to stop flashbacks to the pain and anguish I had suffered at their hands, how weak and helpless I felt. They were bigger, they were stronger than I was. There was no way I could fight back. During the assaults, I would conjure up visions of Superman in my head, imagining him flying to my rescue. But he never came.

The abuse went on for months but I was too ashamed to tell anyone. No matter how hard I tried to stay away from them, they'd lie in wait after school or watch for me on the bus back home so they could drag me out into the woods and have their way with me. The abuse I suffered at their hands extended from fall into winter, and I remember the frigid feeling of the snow against my skin when they pressed my head down. Finally, one day I managed to pull free and ran up a nearby hill. I could hear their boots smashing through the snow, closing on me, when I spotted my uncle, whose family we were living with in Indiana at the time, chopping wood with a double-edged axe up ahead. He was a Vietnam veteran and as tough as they came. I don't know if he saw the men, but they must have seen him, because they swung around and hightailed it away. That was the last time I ever saw my two abusers, and I didn't share the experience even with my mother until I was in my thirties. We'd moved back to Florida from Indiana soon after, driving the whole way in my mother's Chevy Vega with a busted heater, so she could reunite with my father for the second time. The experience left me with no tolerance for people who had power using it against those who have none.

I have hated bullies with an indescribable passion ever since those men bullied me in the worst possible way. In retrospect, I think that's why I joined the army: to fight for the oppressed, those who couldn't stand up and fight for themselves. And I saw the same thing in William Hawley's expression that I had seen in the faces of those men who had assaulted me. He was no different from them, and that redoubled my resolve to see this through as far as I needed to.

I met Denton a week later, a mile or so down the dirt road from where William Hawley had performed that beatdown on the stranger who happened to be in the wrong place at the wrong time. Hawley and I arrived and parked next to a black pickup truck with dark windows that kept me from seeing who was inside. I watched Charles Denton, Imperial Wizard for the United Northern and Southern Knights, climb out of one side of the truck, and his wife, who Hawley informed me would be present, climb out of the other.

We had gathered in a small clearing just off the road, not far from the turnaround vehicles used to reverse direction down the one-lane dirt road. Thick, towering pine trees climbed for the sky, creating an umbrella of shade from the hot sun. Besides some ground brush, they were the only vegetation in the area.

Another potential Klan inductee met us in the woods as well, arriving just after Hawley and I did. I barely paid any attention to him, because my focus was rooted on Denton. He was not physically impressive at all, a few inches shorter than me and slight of build, looking more the part of a CEO in a suit and dress shirt sans the tie. I suppose that was appropriate because in the Klan hierarchy he was a kind of CEO. I knew how dangerous a situation this was, and the presence of Denton's wife didn't ease my concerns very much at all. Her subservient demeanor was typical of what a Klan leader would have expected from his wife. She never said a word and we were never introduced. She was playing the role of a refined Southern lady, her dress and heels utterly wrong for the landscape, but she knew her place, which was to be deferential to her husband. She never took her gaze off me while her husband spoke, and there was something cold and calculating in her eyes.

In his suit, for the moment Denton was doing his best to play the part of an old Southern gentleman, to match his wife and make this appear to be the business meeting he was treating it as. We shook hands, Denton's soft and feathery in contrast to Hawley's leathery ones. His fingernails were clean and trimmed, like he'd just had a manicure.

Denton asked me what I used to do and what I was doing now. He probed my interest in, and potential dedication to, the Klan.

"Why do you feel you belong with us?" he asked me, getting to the point.

"I don't like the way the government and the world are going. I don't like the fact that I can't find steady work. I'm new to the area, trying to start up and make friends with people who think like me. I'm starting fresh and I think this is the life for me," I said, referring to the Klan.

He talked to me a lot more than the other man, because I'm sure William Hawley had briefed Denton on the resources I could bring to the organization. While he was feeling me out, he was also ingratiating himself to me. Establishing a bond and a rapport, trying to impress me with his own background. The attention he paid me made me believe that Hawley had provided a worthy assessment of my background and bona fides, of all the boxes I checked. I knew he'd have a lot of questions and, although I hadn't rehearsed or memorized any potential answers, I had put myself into the proper mindset by listening to the Guns N' Roses song "Ain't It Fun" over and over again on the drive to Hawley's.

"Oh, ain't it fun when you feel like you just gotta get a gun," I sang along, every time that line rolled back around.

It helped me leave the man I really was behind, because it wasn't a song I'd normally listen to, and its dark message and bluesy beat helped me get into the sinister role I had been entrusted to play by the FBI. The song continued to play in my head as I answered the questions posed by Charles Denton:

Where are you from?
Tell me about your family.
Do you have any Black friends?
What's it like being a sniper in the army?
Where are some of the places you served?

I told him about my deployments overseas and otherwise more than satisfied him with my answers. Denton had risen through the ranks of the Klan in large part because he was an "original" member, meaning he must have come from Klan stock. Denton sounded like he was preaching from the pulpit about the infrastructure the organization was building to commit violence, just as Hawley had on the shooting range. I had the sense something big was brewing.

Our exchange seemed to go on forever, but only thirty minutes had passed. I knew I had won over Charles Denton from the way he was looking at me and nodding.

"You ready to become a Knight of the Ku Klux Klan, son?" he finally asked.

"I am, sir."

Denton looked pleased. "In that case, let's get you naturalized into the brotherhood. No time like the present, I always say."

LIGHT AND DARKNESS

WAYWARD, FLORIDA
OCTOBER 2007

From our meeting in the forest clearing, we went straight back to William Hawley's property. I think it was around noon, maybe closer to one. Either way, the sun was burning high in an utterly cloudless sky.

The first thing I noticed were a dozen or so vehicles parked close to Hawley's house. Their drivers weren't outside, meaning they must have been inside, likely preparing for the initiation ceremony the Klan refers to as naturalization. The group is like the mafia when it comes to such things, in that very few accounts of the actual process have ever been written. What I was about to witness—and be a part of— was something that no other undercover informant had ever seen. If I made it through the ceremony, the information I would be able to give Armstrong and Vaughn would be the first of its kind.

William Hawley led me and the other guy about to be initiated up to the front door. Charles Denton was on my other side. This time, his wife did not accompany us. I could feel Denton studying me the whole time, trying to get a read on my facial expression to see if I was scared, apprehensive, excited. I did my best to look like I was taking things in stride, not wanting to do anything that would attract undue attention, even though my heart was racing and I could feel sweat beading up on my forehead. He knew me as an army sniper, so doing my best to remain stoic and calm seemed the best way to approach this. Not quite just another day at the office, but nothing I couldn't handle either.

"Stay here," Hawley said, indicating a bench on the front porch, to the right of the heavy door.

Hawley left me and the other guy there, while he and Denton entered the house, closing the door behind them. A few minutes later, a pair of Klansmen came outside. One grabbed hold of the other guy and took him inside, while the second remained with me, hovering nearby.

At that point, I remember thinking, *Breathe, focus, don't break a sweat* . . . I focused on observing anything I could, including listening to whatever sounds emanated from the house. I heard a creaky metal door slam closed. I heard something banging. I detected sounds of a struggle, maybe someone being thrown against a wall, and then that metal door slamming again. Partly I was trying to distract myself from the man looming six feet away, partly I was trying to get some notion of what I'd be facing when it was my turn inside. But I was distracted by the news Shannon had shared with me just a few days earlier. Though we had yet to tie the knot, she told me she was pregnant with our first child. I was overjoyed—starting a family with Shannon was all I ever wanted. But it also changed the way I thought about the inherent risks of my work undercover. Suddenly the stakes were even higher. As I anxiously waited to be brought into the house for the initiation, I struggled to stay focused and calm. But succumbing to fear wasn't an option. I now had a family to protect.

Fifteen minutes after they brought my fellow initiate into the house, the two men who'd originally come outside led me through the front door together. They immediately fitted a black pillowcase over my head and pulled it down tight. The world went dark, that bright sunlight now a memory. I kept telling myself to *focus and observe, focus and observe, focus and observe.* Of course, I couldn't see anything through that pillowcase, but I could still hear and feel, and I wanted to remember every detail I could to properly complete my report. I breathed steadily, willing myself to remain calm.

I took twelve small steps forward and then twenty more to the right, which I assumed meant we'd turned down a hallway. They pushed me through what felt like a heavy curtain or drape that smelled musty. Then one of the men threw me against the wall and patted me down. That same person pushed me back and forth, a test to see if I'd get rattled. I couldn't help but wonder what happened to would-be Klan members who didn't pass, figuring their bodies might have been among the many lying at the bottom of Lochloosa Lake or inside the stomachs of gators.

That's when the other man yanked the pillowcase off my head. It was still pitch black, except for a sliver of light pushing through a small hole in the curtain that was now behind me. One of the men rapped his knuckles against what must have been that metal door I'd heard clanging a few times from outside the house.

"Enter," I heard from beyond the door.

I heard the creaking sound again and knew the door was opening. I felt one of my escorts put a hand against my back and push me inside, into a thin spray of flickering light cast by fourteen candles inlaid into a white wooden cross: seven going up and down and seven more going across Then the metal door slammed behind me. My eyes adjusted to the light, and I saw four robed, hooded figures standing before me. The nearest wore purple, the others white, green, and black respectively. The figure in black stood to the left of the cross and candles, making him the klavern's Grand Knighthawk, who was responsible for security and defense, the so-called Keeper of the Flame. The man in the purple robe was about Charles Denton's height. Set between me and the figure garbed in purple was a wooden table covered in a white cloth with a Bible resting atop it next to a broadsword more than a yard long. Behind me, I heard the distinctive sound of a shell being racked into a 12-gauge shotgun, the noise as loud as a gunshot itself.

"Kneel," the figure robed in purple ordered, and I recognized the voice as Charles Denton's.

I did and looked up at him.

"Do you swear to protect the Klan with your life?"

"I do," I replied.

"Do you swear to give your life for your brothers?"

"I do."

"Do you swear to protect the white race, uphold the purity of the white race, and to die for your white brothers?"

"I do."

Another of the robed figures lifted the broadsword from the table and lowered the blade until it touched my collarbone, scraping across my neck in the process. I could feel the weight of it—this was no prop. It must have been an authentic battle sword that had likely drawn blood at some point. I realized then that there were only two ways this naturalization ceremony could end: with me being accepted into the Klan or never being seen again.

"State your full name," Charles Denton instructed.

"Joseph Moore."

I focused on my breathing again, trying to get my heart rate back under control. I didn't want to start perspiring, nothing that would show any weakness or fear.

"Do you swear your allegiance to the Knights of the Ku Klux Klan?"

"Yes."

"Are you willing to die for the Knights of the Ku Klux Klan?"

"Yes."

"Do you swear by the Almighty God to uphold the values of the brotherhood, to keep its teaching close to your heart, and to value the brotherhood above your own life?"

"I do."

There was a pause, and I heard the hiss of the sword cutting the air before me. Then the blade landed on my collarbone again, feeling even heavier.

"Rise."

I stood up, fighting the stiffness in my legs from kneeling.

"You are now a Knight of the Ku Klux Klan," said the robed, hooded Charles Denton, the tension gone from his voice. "Welcome, Brother Joe."

CHAPTER 5

FIREWORKS

WAYWARD, FLORIDA
JULY 4, 2008

"Can I fix you a plate, Brother Joe?" asked a woman I recognized from the bar where I'd initially passed muster from the most senior members of the klavern, including Bicky, prior to being naturalized.

She spoke from behind a serving station packed with hamburgers, hot dogs, sliced pig fresh off the spit, and all the fixings. William Hawley's Fourth of July Summer Bash was in full swing, heading toward the evening's annual fireworks celebration. As far as I knew, Hawley didn't have a permit to shoot them off, but that clearly was of little concern to him, based on how he greeted the half dozen law enforcement officers from nearby communities, including Wayward. They weren't in uniform, but I recognized them from earlier encounters over the course of the past nine months since I had become a member of the Klan. Those months had been dominated by a lull in activity for this particular klavern, with little to report on to my FBI handlers, but things were about to ramp up in a big way, as I would soon learn.

"Do you need me to bring anything to the barbecue?" I'd asked Hawley when he invited me.

He flashed a big grin. "Anything Black."

This was the Klan in all its glory, on the surface as American as apple pie, as the saying goes. The members had brought their families, and the women mostly stood off to the side, chatting among themselves and showing deference to their husbands.

The previous month, my future wife, Shannon, had given birth to a son we named Jordy. It was the happiest day of my life and also changed my outlook about the importance of my work inside the Klan for the FBI. Whereas before I was doing it out of duty to the country and the oath I'd sworn to the Constitution, now my paternal instincts had kicked in. It wasn't just the country I was doing this for anymore, it was my own son, who I didn't want to see grow up in a world dominated by division and hatred. I could either put the responsibility for that future on myself or risk leaving it to someone else.

My choice was obvious.

When I arrived back home in Jacksonville from Los Angeles in 2002 to live with my mother and stepfather, I was able to continue working as a welder for the same industrial company that employed me in LA. They specialized in maintaining power plants, and there was no shortage of them in Florida. Five years later, I joined a crew rebuilding the lone elevator inside a building housing the local power company. As luck would have it, my future wife worked for the power company. Shannon had been assigned to play the role of a glorified elevator operator, controlling the cab's movements in the intervals it was online, a truly thankless job. In the first two days on the job, we smiled at each other a few times, and then, on the third day, her gaze lingered on me outside at a picnic table where we were eating lunch—well, at least everybody else was; I hadn't brought anything.

"You look hungry," Shannon said, tilting her paper plate toward me. "Want some fried chicken?"

I accepted her offer, and it was the best fried chicken I ever had, probably because of my feelings for the young woman who'd handed it to me.

"I think you're fun," she said to me. "I like you."

"Then I think we should go out on a date."

We never looked back after that. We started dating in February 2007 and moved in together the following month, right around the time I helped her brother, Ryan, out of his scrape. If it hadn't been for that incident, I almost surely would never have become a confidential human source for the FBI. I'd never been happier in my life and accepted her family as my own, though my first impressions of her mother, Sharon, and especially her stepfather, Rusty, were bad, to say the least. Rusty was all of five foot four and a scrawny 120 pounds, and fit the very definition of a punk. Almost immediately I judged him as the type prone to compensate for his slight stature by dominating those closest to him. This was confirmed by how Shannon reacted in his presence. She turned skittish and subservient, acquiescing to all his opinions without voicing any of her own. That was enough for me to form my opinions about Rusty and Sharon, but I stopped short of voicing them to Shannon, because I was so much in love, I didn't want anything to come between us.

That included the display of Confederate flags along with other paraphernalia and literature all around Rusty and Sharon's home, suggesting their embrace of both white supremacist and anti-government movements. Rusty expressed clear disdain for my military service when the subject came up, shaking his head and scowling at my level of commitment and embrace of my duty. He made his contempt for the government plain and was clearly miffed that my beliefs represented the polar opposite of his. He positioned himself closer to Shannon, as if to draw her away from me, and looked at her any number of times, as if studying her reaction in the forlorn hope it would mirror his. When it didn't, he became even more irked at me and my attitude, but I resisted responding in kind because I didn't want to add to the discomfort I sensed Shannon was feeling. But it was clear that Rusty resented not only me but also the fact that I was taking her away from him.

Even though Shannon had moved both physically and emotionally away from her mother and stepfather, they continued doing their utmost to win her back and get her to come back to their home and to their beliefs. I had to tread a fine line between mitigating that and letting Shannon preserve some form of relationship with them for her own mental well-being, because of her attachment to her mother.

I didn't propose to Shannon until spring 2008, just before she gave birth to Jordy, and a few months before William Hawley's Summer Bash. We took a trip to one of our favorite places, Little River Spring in O'Brien, Florida. It was where we could be with nature and each other at the same time. On this beautiful, sunny day blessed with low humidity, it turned out we were the only people in the area, and when she wasn't watching, I placed her engagement ring in the crystal-clear, still water next to a rock. I didn't even consider the possibility of it floating away, because I was so committed to making this moment special.

"How about that," I said, after leading her to the water's edge. "Looks like somebody lost a ring."

With that I plucked it out of the water and dropped down to one knee.

"Will you marry me?"

I had come alone to the Summer Bash, because the Klan did not know I had a fiancée and son. I didn't want William Hawley, or anyone else associated with the Klavern, to ask to meet them and ingratiate themselves with my family. Not only was this for my family's own safety, it was also crucial to my desire to keep my two worlds separate.

The Klan certainly didn't need to know that the only way to get my infant son to fall asleep was for me to sing Elvis's "Can't Help Falling in Love" to him. Having a child brought everything home to me in a hurry. The safety of Shannon and my son was all on me, but so was my work as a confidential human source inside a historically dangerous organization. To say the least, it was a difficult mix to sustain. As much as possible, I needed to separate the man I was when inside the Klan from the man I was outside it, especially at home.

I got the sense that there was ample precedent for that in the form of members committed to the Klan and the klavern who saw their activities as taking place removed from their families. For these men, the Klan was like a social club, albeit one chartered in hatred and bigotry. While plenty of men leave their families behind when they go golfing or boating or to a de facto men's club, these men left their families behind when they went shooting, were training or planning, or potentially executing operations.

I noticed Beth, Hawley's wife, mingling about, and their nineteen-year-old son, Joey, was mixing with young men around his age. Although they both lived on the premises, I hardly ever saw them because they were never around on the numerous occasions Hawley summoned me to his property. When there was business to attend to, they made themselves scarce, which was easy for Joey since he worked for his father.

Young kids maybe half Joey's age rushed about Hawley's property wielding toy guns that made soft popping sounds when fired, an eerie emulation not only of their Klan parents, but also of those who founded and built the group in the wake of the Civil War.

Unable to accept defeat, veterans of the Confederacy gathered at a social club in Pulaski, Tennessee, on Christmas Eve 1865 to establish a group that would continue fighting for the values that had spawned the war in the first place, namely pertaining to slavery. They assembled in the common purpose of not wanting to see the old South die, as reflected in the name of their new organization. "Ku Klux" stemmed from the Greek word *kyklos*, meaning circle. According to some historians, Robert E. Lee was approached about becoming the group's first leader. When he declined, the job went to the Confederate general Nathan Bedford Forrest.

Forrest had no formal military training, but nonetheless had rapidly risen through the ranks from private all the way to lieutenant general. His motto when leading troops into battle was, "Get there first with the most men." Known best for guerrilla-style tactics focused on upending Northern supply and communication lines, Forrest is infamously remembered for perpetrating a massacre of Black troops at Fort Pillow in April 1864, even though they had already surrendered. At the time, the reputation that incident earned him made Forrest the perfect candidate to run what was clearly envisioned as an anti-government organization, especially once Congress passed the Reconstruction Act to ensure enforcement of the Fourteenth Amendment, which granted equal protection to former slaves.

From its passage in 1867 onward, men who'd been no more than property ascended in public and political life, with men like Forrest and his minions bearing witness to something they would never accept and were committed to stop at all costs. Toward that end, by 1870, the KKK had established a foothold in every Southern state. Though decentralized, these groups shared a common ideology that persists to this day. In essence, they never stopped fighting the Civil War, and in response to that, Congress passed the Ku Klux Klan Act in 1871, giving the government the right to crush the Klan and its activities, especially under President Ulysses S. Grant. As Reconstruction efforts faded, though, the Klan's white supremacist doctrine caught renewed fire, spawning the cross burnings the group became infamous for. By 1876, their grip on the South was tighter than ever.

When he turned down the role of Grand Wizard eleven years before, Robert E. Lee is reputed to have requested that his support for the Klan remain "invisible," spawning the group's moniker that also encapsulated its mission statement: the Invisible Empire.

As I stood amid all the revelry on William Hawley's property, my gaze lingered on the children, who represented the future. I noticed the eldest of the group, ten or eleven years old, had a pellet gun that looked very much like the real thing. A pecking order had been naturally established—the younger kids played out their shooting games in a ring closest to their parents, while the older ones strayed out farther, closer to those tarps I'd gotten my first glimpse inside of months before. A tear welled up in the corner of my eye from the sorrow I felt over the thought that my newborn son, or any child, could follow the same path these kids were on.

For the past nine months, since the naturalization ceremony, I'd been sticking as close to Hawley as I could, gathering intelligence and passing it on to Armstrong and Vaughn. Since I was a mechanic, much of our visits were spent working on the collection of cars he kept in the old barn on his property he'd converted into a garage.

Among that collection were a vintage 1979 Corvette and a monster truck—a yellow school bus rigged with tires taller than both of us that he drove in local parades to loud cheers from those assembled along the route.

The best way to continue winning someone's confidence is to bond with them over what they perceived to be a mutual avocation, in this case cars. I made my living as an industrial mechanic, a welder mostly, so I knew my way around machines and machine parts, and that included a close familiarity with motor vehicles. Although being schooled in those skills had nothing to do with going operational for the FBI, they proved vital in generating the trust of William Hawley. Most of what we talked about was engines, drive shafts, and the like. But Hawley also sprinkled in plenty about the operational priorities and structure of the Klan in small talk. The more cars we worked on, the more he took me into his confidence, and the more intelligence I was able to pass on about the inner workings of the organization. Most of the information pertained to the individuals Hawley made it a point to introduce me to, enabling the FBI to establish an elaborate dossier on the members of this klavern, identities previously unknown to them, which shed light on the size and scope of the group.

On that Fourth of July, I took advantage of all the activity to get an extended look at the inside of Hawley's house, alone for the first time. He hadn't brought in any Porta Potties for the occasion, so everyone was using a bathroom just off the home's foyer. It was the perfect excuse to get inside the house. I made a stop in the bathroom first—I was wearing a wire at the time and smiled at the thought of how this portion of the tape might be transcribed. Then I made the most of the few minutes I had to scope out the house before my absence might draw attention, in search of anything that might have changed from my last time inside. The first thing I noticed was that the second of Hawley's two .50-caliber, armor-piercing rifles still hung over the mantel in the same room in which his KKK regalia was on full display. Nothing had been moved, and I didn't have the time to riffle through any drawers or cupboards, which likely wouldn't have yielded much anyway; whatever William Hawley had that might be actionable would, no doubt, have been kept under lock and key. And although my army intelligence training had included a primer on lock picking, I didn't have time for the full reconnaissance of the place that would have required my skill.

Almost everything I provided was information the FBI was hearing for the first time. In 2008, domestic terrorist groups weren't nearly the priority they are today. The country was only seven years removed from 9/11, and most of the task force's attention nationally was focused on foreign extremists. For their part, Armstrong and Vaughn seemed most interested in digging deeper into the confidential 2006 FBI report titled *White Supremacist Infiltration of Law Enforcement*, while I was also providing a treasure trove of additional information.

Many of my conversations with William Hawley included discussion of Senator Barack Obama's nascent presidential campaign.

"I can't see him getting the nomination and can't see him coming anywhere near to winning if he does," Hawley said once. "If it appears otherwise, we'll have to step in."

The veiled threats never went much beyond that until the Obama campaign gathered steam and started to build a formidable lead over Hillary Clinton. Initially, Obama's run invoked caustic conversations about a *Black* man in the *White* House. As Obama's delegate tally continued to mount, though, shoulders stiffened, voices lowered, and the talk turned more ominous. Given the Klan's sordid history, the possibility of such an ascension was impossible to accept. While members expressed their open disdain for Hillary Clinton, Barack Obama was like a bogeyman to them, antithetical to everything they represented, and a reality they never expected they'd have to face.

Much of what I learned from the naturalization ceremony forward was more about the inner workings of the Klan than any actionable specific crimes or operations they were planning. The information I was providing was still invaluable to the FBI, since those inner workings had never been documented to the degree I was providing. Indeed, law enforcement in general had seldom, if ever, enjoyed the benefit of a confidential human source planted this deep as a full, card-carrying member. To that point, I was consistently included in high-level meetings and made privy to things like what William Hawley had recently shown me, something he shared with extraordinarily few of his Klan brethren.

A few months before the Summer Bash, he led me across his sprawling property, swinging a big key hanging from a thick ring. We reached those big camouflaged tarps, and he pulled them back to reveal the entrance to what were clearly underground bunkers. Hawley fit the key into a padlock in the first heavy steel double doors and yanked them open. A single dome light snapped on, flickering briefly until it finally held, and we used a small ladder to descend into the bunker. Before me, I saw a dozen Russian-made Kalashnikov AK-47 rifles hanging across brackets on the wall and several cases that must have contained more stacked up across the floor. I also noted the presence of open boxes of converter kits that turned the semiautomatic rifles to full automatic. Off to the side, stacked against the wall, I noticed more cases, made of hardwood that might have been maple.

Hawley squeezed between the containers of AK-47s and raised the heavy lid on one of wooden containers, extracting a weapon I recognized immediately.

"What do you think, Brother Joe?" Hawley asked me with a grin, back in klavern leader mode.

He handed me a Heckler & Koch 91 .308-caliber battle rifle. The HK91 carried that name for good reason. It featured an eighteen-inch heavy target barrel and fixed plastic stock. It was a fearsome weapon, generally considered to be among the finest in the world. And as near as I could tell, this was the latest model.

"That's some weapon, isn't it?" Hawley asked me.

I tested the heft and balance, raising it to my shoulder while keeping my finger well clear of the trigger. My next thought, on top of the array of ordnance amassed down here, was about the resources in terms of funding it had taken to acquire such a weapons cache. The Klan was clearly far better financed than the FBI and JTTF had ever conceived.

"For sure," I said, handing it back to him.

The worst thing an undercover like me could do in such a situation would be to ask too many questions, like *How many of these have you got?* Questions like that were certain to raise eyebrows and suspicions in a man like William Hawley. I resolved to stay in character, playing the dutiful subordinate at once enamored with and fully loyal to the Klan.

The second bunker contained a collection of 9-millimeter pistols, boxes and boxes of ammunition, canned food and MREs (Meals Ready to Eat), stacks of flak jackets stretching all the way to the low ceiling, ammo vests, tactical gear, and even some night-vision goggles. Such a massive display of ordnance suggested one thing and one thing only:

The Klan was getting ready to go to war, returning to the roots established at the outset of the group's second era in 1915 with the release of D. W. Griffith's movie *The Birth of a Nation*, called "the most reprehensibly racist film in American history" by the *Washington Post*. The Klan had faded by then, not quite into obscurity but to a point where its efficacy, influence, and membership had severely declined.

That all changed on the movie's opening night in early December 1915, when a local preacher named William Joseph Simmons led committed Klansmen wearing Confederate uniforms atop hooded horses down Atlanta's Peachtree Street, firing rifles into the air. Simmons, himself an otherwise unremarkable man, used an early screening he had seen of *Birth of a Nation* as inspiration to rebuild the Klan. Accompanied by a group comprised of a combination of Klan veterans and new recruits, he climbed to the top of Stone Mountain just outside Atlanta and lit a cross for all to see. In a ceremony that night, he proclaimed himself Imperial Wizard of the Invisible Empire of the Knights of the Ku Klux Klan.

The revived Klan was given a further boost the first week of January 1923, when members spearheaded a riot in the town of Rosewood, Florida, in the wake of a white woman allegedly being assaulted by a Black man in the neighboring town of Summer. A mob of several hundred white men led by Klansmen killed every Black person they could find and burned almost every structure in Rosewood. For several days, survivors from the town hid in nearby swamps until they were evacuated to larger towns by train and car. The town was abandoned and, basically, ceased to exist.

No arrests were made for the Rosewood massacre, not a single one, convincing the Klan that it could practice its wanton violence with impunity. Virtually overnight, the group became reinvigorated and restored to its place of prominence in Southern culture, culminating in what some estimates indicated was a sixty-thousand-strong march through Washington, D.C., on September 13, 1926, with all participants donning white robes and the KKK's trademark hoods. They marched in daylight straight toward the building they fully intended to someday occupy: the White House.

At this point, the Klan's national membership was estimated to be between three and five million. Figuring that for each of those there may have been as many as ten sympathizers or downright supporters, that number swells, potentially, to as high as between thirty and fifty million. Since the population in the United States at the time was only 117 million, that represents a huge percentage of the population.

Simmons knew he needed to win over hearts and minds to keep the Klan growing at its unprecedented pace. So he hired a pair of public relations specialists out of New York, Mary Elizabeth Tyler and Edward Young Clark, to improve the Klan's image. The pair published positive articles about the Klan in local newspapers nationwide and helped build a national campaign to have statues of Confederate Civil War heroes erected in community parks, further boosting the group's profile and efficacy.

The mentality espoused by the Klan reached somewhat of a peak in 1940, when Catholic priest Father Charles Coughlin used his wildly popular radio program, broadcast out of Michigan, to stir up an armed rebellion. Coughlin's audience numbered in the tens of millions, and any number of them were either avowed Nazis or those who shared such beliefs, which to a great extent even then included the Klan. The priest himself reprinted a speech from Nazi propaganda minister Joseph Goebbels. He blamed pretty much every problem on the Jews, further uniting him with not only the far right but also Klansmen, under something called the Christian Front.

Under that name, a formidable cache of weapons and explosives was acquired, men recruited to the cause, and plans laid by early 1940 to overthrow the United States government. The plan included systematic bombings, assassinations, and creating the chaos needed to usurp the country's leadership and replace it with something the Klan knew all too well: an Invisible Empire.

By then, the Klan had been decimated by federal tax evasion charges instigated by the Roosevelt administration over fear of the group's increasing power and influence. Its members, for a time, may no longer have called themselves Klansmen, but they took the ideology the Klan spawned with them to other groups that primarily included the Christian Front, where many became foot soldiers in Father Charles Coughlin's war on America. The plot may have failed, but it was as impactful as how close the rioters of January 6, 2021, came to preventing a peaceful transfer of power. The fact that neither worked pales in comparison to the resources brought to bear and the commitment of the perpetrators to do anything necessary to make sure they succeeded the next time. And that proclivity was front and center here in Wayward on the nation's birthday in 2008.

"I'd like you to meet someone, Brother Joe," William Hawley said, calling me over to a sinewy man with hairy arms and pockmarked face beneath his scraggly beard. "This here's Brother Deke."

"Heard a lot about you," a grinning Deke said, shaking my hand. "Always nice for a Klan lifer like me to meet the new blood. I come from stock that perpetrated the Rosewood massacre. A lot more were killed than you ever heard told. I know this because I'm descended from the man in charge of burying the bodies in a mass grave big as the Grand Canyon."

I later reported that to my handlers, but the FBI lacked the resources to dig up or dredge the area where Brother Deke suggested the mass grave was located.

Part of my mission that Fourth of July was to make sure I took pictures of the license plates of all those in attendance, around ninety vehicles in all, virtually all of them trucks. That would provide a bounty of intelligence riches for my FBI handlers, unprecedented really, since it would allow them to assemble a roster of the klavern's membership and sympathizers.

Charles Denton, the Klan's Imperial Wizard, reveled in telling me that Fourth of July about his days with the Mississippi White Knights and his support for Edgar Ray Killen.

Initially, Mississippi government authorities and law enforcement officials turned a virtual blind eye to the murders of James Chaney, Andrew Goodman, and Michael Schwerner, performing only a cursory investigation. Incensed by the lack of action, Attorney General Robert F. Kennedy took matters into his own hands. Kennedy dispatched the FBI in force in one of the most concerted investigations in Bureau history.

Symbolically and otherwise, Mississippi formed the heart and soul of the Klan in these years. Back in 1964, one of the reasons Edgar Ray Killen believed he could kill three civil rights workers with impunity was that local and even state law enforcement either looked the other way when it came to the Klan's actions or were outright members in secret. That was the tradition Denton (aka Cole Thornton) intended not only to uphold but also to expand across the entire Klan.

Denton didn't mention anything about the November 1979 Greensboro [North Carolina] Massacre, but he might as well have. "The Greensboro massacre, as it became known," *Politico* reported in an article titled "The Massacre That Spawned the Alt-Right," "was a coming-out bloodbath for the white nationalist movement that is upending our politics today. . . . The seeds for this iteration of white supremacy were planted 40 years ago in Greensboro, when the white wedding of Klansmen and Nazis launched a new, pan-right extremism—a toxic brew of virulent racism, anti-government rhetoric, apocalyptic fearmongering and paramilitary tactics. And this extremism has proven more durable than anyone then could imagine."

At the Summer Bash, Denton admitted to me without prompting that his goal was to turn the entire Klan of today into a nationwide version of the Mississippi White Knights. And I took the fact that he had risen to become one of five KKK Imperial Wizards as a strong indication that he was succeeding in his attempt to transpose those radical, militant views and actions onto the contemporary Klan as a whole. He expressed to me how proud he was that the Mississippi White Knights had put a hundred-thousand-dollar bounty on the life of Martin Luther King.

"This man running for president is a gift from God," Denton told me as the barbecue was winding down, referring to the final weeks of Barack Obama's campaign. "Going to be a huge boost to the kind of members we need to give this country what it needs."

He grinned at me as he said that, and I was thinking of Charles Denton as I continued to observe the presence of those six police officers, at minimum, from nearby communities, mixing among the klavern's membership. There were a lot of people there, families mostly, a portion of whom I didn't recognize, making me wonder how many more law enforcement officers might be on the grounds.

Night had fallen, and I was sticking as close to William Hawley as possible to discern anything I could about who he was talking to and about what, when my cell phone rang with SHANNON lighting up in the caller ID. She had no idea where I was or what I was doing at the time.

"Hey, babe," I said, walking discreetly away, while not wanting to do anything that might make Hawley or any of those he was entertaining suspicious.

"Jordy misses his daddy," Shannon told me.

I could hear him crying in the background. "I miss him too."

"I can't get him down. Do you think you could . . ."

She let her question trail off, but I knew what she wanted.

"Sure," I said and, after waiting for her to lower the phone to our son's ear, I began to sing. *"Wise men say only fools rush in . . ."*

Here I was, standing forty feet away from Klan members I was trying to put in jail, trying very hard not to draw any attention to myself. A few of them glanced over and I wondered if they heard me doing my best impersonation of Elvis singing. But Jordy wasn't sobbing anymore, so I kept going.

At that point, Shannon got back on the phone.

"Mission accomplished," she whispered. "He's sound asleep. See you when you get home."

"Love you, babe," I said, ending the call and feeling my heart settle in my chest.

I took a deep breath to steady myself, an instant before explosions rocked the night. I held my breath, my whole body locking up, until I looked up and saw the majestic colors and shapes bursting in the night sky above, while in the company of men who fully intended to topple the government of the United States.

The fireworks show had begun.

CHAPTER 6

CAMPAIGN VISIT

WAYWARD, FLORIDA
SEPTEMBER 2008

The black pickup truck sped down the surface road, dragging a curtain of dust kicked up from the dry gravel that ran parallel to the highway. I watched it ride along the fence line enclosing William Hawley's ten acres.

It was my virtual one-year anniversary (eleven months) of being naturalized into the Klan, and I was sticking closer to Hawley than ever. It wasn't hard, because he liked having me around. As I was a former army sniper with a background in intelligence, he had even proclaimed me the klavern's "hit man." If something needed to be handled, I'd be the guy who'd handle it. I had stopped by, as I often did, to follow my orders.

In the last twelve months, my life had changed dramatically. Working undercover gave me a newfound sense of purpose, and I was proud to be serving my country once again. But in the past few months, especially since my son had been born, the toll of living two lives had started to wear on me. I was constantly toggling between two versions of myself. The real me: a new husband, a new dad, a normal guy; and the undercover me: a hateful racist capable of unthinkable violence. My only solace was knowing that I was succeeding in my undercover role. Hawley viewed me as not only a trustworthy resource but a confidant.

When the pickup turned onto Hawley's property and headed down the drive, I noticed police lights built into the grille. I didn't recognize the stocky man with well-groomed, close-cropped hair who climbed out, but the dogs seemed to, and his boots clacked against the pebble-strewn gravel as he approached us. A second man, the truck's passenger, walked slightly behind him. Neither of them acknowledged me at all, just a quick glance before turning their attention to Hawley.

Hawley closed his stance—body language for whatever these two men had come to discuss with him didn't include me.

"Let's take a walk," he said to them in a Southern twang more common in Georgia than Florida.

They moved off, stopping just out of earshot. I returned my gaze to the pickup, splotches of shiny paint showing through the coating of dust it had picked up on the surface road that accessed Hawley's property. It was illegal in the state of Florida for anyone outside of law enforcement to have police lights on their vehicle. Such lights were easy to spot and could lead to the owner being arrested and his vehicle confiscated. Florida, enough of a Wild West state already, took such offenses seriously. That was enough to tell me this guy was likely, almost surely, a cop.

We weren't formally introduced, but I'd later learn his name was Donny Edwards, and he was a police officer from a nearby community out on medical leave. I suspected the man who'd accompanied him to Hawley's property was a fellow police officer, but didn't confirm that until later. I'd heard that cops and other law enforcement personnel were joining the Klan in increasing numbers, though this was the first time I'd witnessed such an association up close in the wake of the Summer Bash.

William Hawley loved participating in community functions, like parades, where local Klan leaders were treated with respect and even worship. About five weeks before his Fourth of July celebration, I was on his property while he was getting ready to participate in a Memorial Day parade. I witnessed a county deputy arrive to personally escort Hawley and his monster truck school bus to and from his property, as if the deputy were the Klan leader's own personal bodyguard.

I was too far away to hear what Edwards was telling William Hawley, but I could tell Hawley was interested, excited even. He seemed to be peppering Edwards with questions, and for his part, Edwards didn't lack a response to each that left Hawley nodding in satisfaction.

A few minutes into their conversation, Hawley opened up his stance and looked my way, a signal he was ready for me to approach.

"Brother Joe, this is Brother Donny," he said, indicating the man I had pegged for a cop. "He's brought us some interesting news today. It seems a certain Democratic presidential candidate is going to be visiting nearby Kissimmee in two months' time, a couple days before Halloween. That presents us with an opportunity we'd like your advice on." Hawley aimed his next words straight for Edwards. "Under no circumstances while we're around will he ever become president."

"Amen, Brother," Edwards followed. "Amen."

I collected myself in my car once the meeting broke up. I had actionable intelligence that an attempt was going to be made on the life of Democratic presidential candidate Barack Obama, who was leading in the polls at that point and was generally considered the favorite in the upcoming election. I already had a meeting scheduled with my handlers for later that day, so there was no need to schedule something on the fly.

We met at our usual location, and I think Armstrong and Vaughn could tell there was something making me anxious.

"What's up?" Armstrong asked me.

"There was a meeting at William Hawley's property this morning," I said, keeping my voice level. "The subject was assassinating Barack Obama."

Armstrong and Vaughn exchanged a glance, then both leaned forward in their chairs. "Where and when?"

"Kissimmee, on October twenty-ninth, which is six days before the election on November fourth."

They traded another glance.

"That's not all," I resumed. "There was a police officer from Fruitland Park."

"Fruitland Park," Armstrong repeated in a tone that told me it meant something to him.

"What is it?" I asked.

"You remember all those photos you took of license plates at William Hawley's Fourth of July barbecue?" Armstrong asked. "Well, it turns out two of the license plates you shot pictures of belong to two high-ranking members of the Fruitland Park P.D."

Hawley's Summer Bash hadn't been for mere hangers-on; only naturalized members and highly committed supporters had been invited. Donny Edwards, for example, hadn't been there, but apparently his two immediate superiors were. I didn't know what either looked like, and I hadn't been introduced to them. But the implications of this were clear: the Klan would be provided with intelligence about Obama's schedule and motorcade only known to insiders. At this point, he was still only a candidate and thus lacked the rings of Secret Service protection afforded a president. And now William Hawley would be privy to the times he was most vulnerable.

As for me, I couldn't get the thought of that .50-caliber armor-piercing rifle hanging on his wall out of my head. It made for an excellent sniper system, deadly accurate up to a very long distance. From five hundred yards, for example, I could put five bullets inside the same water glass with that rifle.

"Are we going to report this to the Secret Service?" I asked Armstrong.

"We're not there yet. You need to go get us more intelligence."

More came a month later.

WAYWARD, FLORIDA

OCTOBER 2008

"We need to go see somebody, Brother Joe," William Hawley said when I arrived at his property one afternoon.

That was always the way it was with Hawley. I seldom had any fore-warning of when we'd be working on something operationally, and he'd remained characteristically tight-lipped about the Obama assas-sination over the course of the past few weeks. Other than picking my brain a few times about things like muzzle velocity and the penetra-tion power of a .50-caliber shell, it was like the meeting with Edwards in his front yard had never happened.

"Will passing through armor or bulletproof glass change the tra-jectory of a shell like that?"

"No, sir," I told him. "It's a high-powered shell moving at a velocity that cuts through armor like paper without any redirection, some-thing called barrier blind, meaning that passing through the object doesn't alter the trajectory."

"What would be an ideal distance to shoot from?"

"There's no such thing. It depends on the shooter, the wind, the weather, the sight lines. Too many factors for there to be one easy answer."

"How about, say, from a hundred yards?"

"With a rifle like that, a hundred yards would be child's play."

I started to figure that Hawley had already worked up at least a tentative plan he hadn't run past me. I had the distinct feeling in that moment that I was going to be the one to take the shot; it made per-fect sense, given my background. At that point, though, Hawley had not made an indication either way, though he was about to.

"Let's take a drive, Brother Joe. There's somebody I want you to meet."

We climbed into his truck and drove to an auto repair shop owned and operated by Mr. Brown—that's all I ever knew him as. Hawley never mentioned his first name or used it around me.

"KIGY, Brother Brown," Hawley greeted the grease-splattered man with an untrimmed beard and squirrelly, evasive eyes that didn't stay fixed long on anything when we entered the garage.

"KIGY, Brother William," Mr. Brown said.

"This here's Brother Joe."

He shook my hand and it came away sticky with oil. Brother Brown seemed to acknowledge that and finally ran his hands through a rag that was already covered in grime.

"Take a look at this," Brother Brown said, grinning through a missing tooth in the front. "Came in this morning," he added, leading us to a car that was bashed to hell. "Old lady driving got stuck on the train tracks and couldn't make it out before the train did its business."

I peered inside the wreck of a car I recognized as a Toyota Corolla. There was blood everywhere, and I spotted a locket amid it on the driver's-side floor, where the mat must have been. I reached inside, picked it up, and handed it to Brother Brown.

"You may want to get this back to the victim's family," I said to him, realizing I had blood from the locket on my hand.

"Why?" he said with a grin, opening the locket to reveal a picture with a blood drop on it.

Then he slid the gold locket into his pocket.

"What do you think about the candidate, Brother Joe?" he asked me.

"I'm with Brother William on this," I said.

I had skirted giving an opinion because that was an important part of the duality that had come to define my personality. All this time, for a full year now, I had been two people: the family man whose first child had recently been born, and the Klansman who was participating in the planning of the assassination of Senator Barack Obama. I was afraid that if I stated my own opinions, even fabricated opinions, I'd risk dropping into a rabbit hole where I could sink deeper and deeper. That's the thing about a deep-cover human confidential source: getting in is hard enough, but getting out can prove even harder, and I wasn't going to let that happen to me. It also explains why I never uttered the N-word, even for show or to enhance my credibility with the klavern. These boundaries were crucial in preserving my sense of self.

"Can you meet me back at my house?" William Hawley asked Brother Brown, loath to talk anywhere he wasn't absolutely certain was secure.

"Straightaway, Brother William. Just let me close up shop."

Even though this was 2008, the Klan did not trust electronic communication. That's why Hawley hadn't just picked up the phone to summon Brown over. Instead, he drove to Brown's garage just down the street to have the same conversation with him.

Brother Brown joined us in William Hawley's kitchen a few minutes after we got there.

"What do you need from me, Brother?"

"Two trucks, open with no camper on top, because that's where each of the shooters will be stationed. We also need clean paper on the vehicles from the DMV and a way to dispose of the vehicles once the deed is done."

Brother Brown was grinning again, showcasing that missing tooth. I smelled a combination of grease and body odor wafting from him. He took off his ball cap to reveal short, knotted hair framing a bald spot he hid with that ball cap I'd learn he always wore, stained with oil and grime along the bill.

"Well, I got a contact in the DMV who can handle the paper no problem," Brown told us. "And I got a friend owns a junkyard who can smash those two trucks into yesterday. What about guns? You looking to acquire a couple of those too?"

Now it was Hawley who smiled. "Nope. We got that covered."

Hawley and I proceeded to watch footage he'd recorded of candidate Obama's other motorcades to see how the vehicles were lined up. The Secret Service didn't have the personnel to shut down entire areas, including roads, and were left with a basic alignment of vehicles in pretty much a straight line outside the venue in which he was speaking. In Kissimmee, Obama would be speaking at Osceola Heritage Park, which featured both outdoor and indoor venues. The setting would be irrelevant to the plot, since the formation of the Secret Service motorcade would be the same either way. And it would conform perfectly to the alignment and spacing they used in all the recordings we studied. I mean, were they trying to get him killed?

"You know your way around an L-shaped ambush, Brother Joe?" Hawley asked me, after pausing the footage with Obama's motorcade frozen in place.

"I sure do."

I proceeded to sketch out the basic plan of staging an L-shaped ambush with two shooters, in this case one in each truck. The shooter on one side of the L would be on the far side of the motorcade, assigned to prevent extraction and use his .50-caliber rifle to make sure the vehicles stayed where they were. The shooter on the perpendicular top side of the L would be in a truck positioned a hundred yards from Obama's vehicle, placed in the center. He wouldn't shoot until the candidate was inside and stationary, since neither reinforced steel nor bulletproof glass would change the bullet's trajectory. The rifles were semiauto and came equipped with eight-round magazines to house the eight-inch-long shells. Their power had the added advantage of being able to swiftly bring down any close air support in the form of helicopters.

I still hadn't asked William Hawley about who was going to take the money shot and who he was thinking about for the second shooter. Asking that kind of question made targets suspicious and got informants found out. I had thought initially that the shooter positioned at the top of the L was going to be me. But now I figured I had grown too important to William Hawley's and even Charles Denton's future plans to sacrifice—not my life necessarily, but whoever manned those weapons was going to be in the wind fast and would never be able to return. Hawley's plan was to have the shooters retreat to a cabin he owned on Cypress Key. Getting away would pose an easily surmountable challenge, because the shooter at the bottom of the L would have rendered the motorcade effectively blocked in, and by the time the locals got in the game it would be too late. This all sounds like tough stuff, but for someone like me, a former sniper who's been trained to engage as many as two hundred enemy troops at once, it was pretty routine.

Meanwhile, I kept coming back to the fact that this was all happening thanks to information provided by police officers. I even wondered how many of those officers assigned to Obama's detail would rather help the shooters than catch them.

The day in question was less than a month away, and now I had gathered intelligence about the scope of the entire plan. If the assassination succeeded just a few days from the election, we'd be looking at a full-fledged civil war. And without the concentric rings the Secret Service uses to establish a perimeter and keep the president safe, I had to believe the outcome stood a very good chance of being successful.

I alerted Joe Armstrong about the enormity of what was happening, and he told me to come in to provide a full report.

CHAPTER 7

TRICK OR TREAT

WAYWARD, FLORIDA
OCTOBER 2008

The day after that phone call to Joe Armstrong, I met him at our usual meeting place. Rich Vaughn was not there, having other business to attend to for Homeland Security. That meant I was about to provide very sensitive information to the men who served as my handlers for a vital operation, and only one of them was present. This was not just some guys yapping away in a garage. These guys had the goods. The assassination was going to happen, unless we prevented it.

I laid it all out for Armstrong, who listened with an expression that wavered between dumbstruck and pained. Atypically, he never cut me off to ask a question and let me tell the entire story unbroken.

"You think Hawley's still in contact with these cops out of Fruitland Park?" Armstrong asked me after I'd finished my report.

"I have no doubt," I told him. "I haven't found evidence of other law enforcement involvement, but I'm sure it's there."

Armstrong nodded, more to himself than me. "Okay, let's stay on it. Catch as many people in this sweep as we can."

I was under the impression that we'd be handling this according to FBI guidelines and that the Bureau had jurisdiction, as opposed to the Secret Service; since we had uncovered the threat, it was up to us to deal with it, which meant it was up to me.

"We've got faith in you, Joe," Armstrong continued. "We know you can get the job done."

My first thought was, *What am I going to do? Did the FBI expect me to take everyone out on my own?* I assumed Armstrong was playing this by the book, following his orders, which meant I had to follow mine and do whatever it took to prevent the assassination of Barack Obama.

Because I was the only one who could.

William Hawley had hinted at the fact that he'd wanted me to work with his shooters on the ranges set up on his property in the days leading up to the assassination. I could take them out then and there, and knew I just might have to do that, which would fall directly into the marching orders Armstrong had given me.

Whatever it takes . . .

Since that would blow my cover, and potentially lead to a gunfight with Hawley himself and others, like Brother Brown, I sought alternate means to preempt the plot. If I was going to continue in my role, the decision to abort had to come from Hawley. He could be acting on information I provided him, but the call had to be his.

A potential way out of this dawned on me one day while I was standing outside staring at a plane soaring high in the sky, a mere speck on the horizon, flying at maybe thirty-five thousand feet. Knowing that William Hawley detested all forms of electronic communication, I showed up at his property unannounced two days before Obama's planned visit to Kissimmee, and four days before Halloween, with a well-rehearsed warning about what I'd concluded awaited us just six days before Election Day.

He ushered me into the kitchen, where Brother Brown was seated at the table drinking a beer, even though it was morning. Brown was wearing the same grease-stained overalls I always saw him in, as if he didn't have another pair. Fortunately, Hawley's wife, Beth, and son, Joey, were nowhere about.

"Brother William," I said, addressing Hawley, "we've got a problem."

Hawley cast a sidelong glance toward Brown. "Speak freely, Brother Joe."

"I was reconnoitering the objective and noticed black specks up in the sky, twenty thousand feet maybe, flying in a circular pattern," I continued, using that kind of professional terminology to establish subject-matter authority.

"Go on," Hawley instructed after I'd paused for effect.

"They were Predator drones, Brother William," I continued, trying to instill restrained panic in my voice. "The Secret Service must have been test-flying them for Obama's appearance on the twenty-ninth."

"You sure they couldn't have just been airplanes?"

"Yes, sir. The circular flying pattern gave them away."

Hawley swallowed hard. I could see his mind working, coming to grips with what that meant. I waited for him to respond, not wanting to continue unprompted.

"What kind of problem does that pose for us?" he asked finally.

"Predator drones carry four Hellfire missiles each. The operators can read a man's watch from twenty thousand feet. If they spot our men in those trucks . . ."

"Twenty thousand feet is a long way up, Brother Joe."

"I've seen what those Predators can do up close and personal while I was serving, Brother William. They are precise enough to be fired through your kitchen window over there," I said, indicating it.

I was pushing the absolute limits of my cover, hoping Hawley would either default to my expertise or figure I was an informant. Either was possible, and I could only hope both would lead to him aborting the mission, although the latter could end up getting me killed. I was straddling a line between giving up too much information and not enough.

I could see Hawley looking toward Brother Brown, who was twisting the beer can between his hands, looking deferential while remaining silent. My mind was spinning. If Hawley decided to stick with the plan, my only choice would be to take out his chosen shooters once they were deployed in the trucks on the day in question.

I had my own .50-caliber rifle to make the shots.

Those nerve-racking final forty-eight hours passed in agonizing fashion. I began to fear the worst and plan for it, knowing I was going to have to kill two men to save the life of a Black man who was the odds-on favorite to become the next president of the United States.

Finally, the day before Obama's visit to Kissimmee, Hawley summoned me to his property. We were alone this time, which comforted me a bit, but I was alert to any motions he made for the pistol he routinely wore holstered on his hip.

"Brother Joe," he started, "we've decided to postpone the operation."

I felt relieved, but still on edge because I didn't know what was coming next. All I knew was that the original plan had been shelved and no attempt on Barack Obama's life would be made by the Klan during his campaign stop in Kissimmee the following day.

"The decision's been made," Hawley continued, "that the event will achieve much more of an effect if we wait for him to win, and we've begun gathering information about what his Secret Service detail will be like with regard to positioning after he becomes president-elect. We'd love to hear any thoughts you have on that subject."

CHAPTER 8

GONE FISHING

WAYWARD, FLORIDA
JANUARY 2009

Shannon and I set the date of our wedding for December, six weeks after the election of Barack Obama. Jordy, now six months old, got to watch the ceremony, and I was careful to choose a church far away enough from Wayward to ensure no Klan members who might recognize me happened to meander by.

That's the thing about working undercover. It never stops, even when you're technically not working. Shannon had come to grudgingly accept that. She was nervous, but her anxiety was mitigated by the stabilizing influence I'd been in her life, a kind of rock. So while she certainly feared losing me, she had confidence that I was a rock outside of our relationship as well, someone she knew could hold his own in any situation—to the point where she should have been more worried about the fate of anyone who tried to do me, or our family, harm. Since I had saved her, she was convinced, I could certainly save myself.

We didn't go on a honeymoon. The closest I came to going on any trip at all was when I got a call from William Hawley.

"I'm heading out to do some deep-sea fishing this week," he said to me. "I thought you might like to join us."

Of course, I had no idea who "us" was. It was early January 2009, two months since I'd managed to foil the Klan's attempt to assassinate Barack Obama, and I still wasn't sure about my status in the organization. Had William Hawley settled on the fact that I was an informant? Was he intending to kill and dump me in the Gulf of Mexico?

I settled on two things going forward. First, that I had to go on the fishing trip or I'd risk losing whatever trust and credibility I still maintained in the klavern. And second, that, if necessary, I would kill anyone on that boat if the plan was for me to never return.

Preventing the attempted assassination of Barack Obama, meanwhile, had strengthened my bond with my handler Joe Armstrong even more.

"You're a rock star," he said, smiling from ear to ear when I issued my report on William Hawley's last-minute decision to abort the mission, after hearing my fabricated story about the Secret Service flying Predator drones capable of taking out both of his shooters in a heartbeat. "I never doubted for a second that you could handle this, and I was right, wasn't I? You're a rock star," he repeated.

Vaughn also began treating me with a level of deference and respect he hadn't before and made it a point to tell me how impressed he was with my work. Apparently, his previous attempt to infiltrate the Florida chapter of the Outlaws biker gang had been an abject failure, so he knew how hard it was to achieve success inside such an insular criminal world.

In our meeting to discuss the fishing trip, Vaughn and even Armstrong were adamant that I shouldn't go. They stressed again and again how they wouldn't be able to cover me miles out to sea. They didn't dare use a follow boat, which could be spotted easily. And though a surveillance aircraft or drone could follow the action on Hawley's thirty-two-foot cabin cruiser, there was no way for anyone to get to me in the event things went south. I didn't know if the fishing trip represented a test William Hawley was giving me or not. But I knew I had to go to make sure he knew I trusted him and had no reason to fear anything on his part. And if push came to shove, I'd have a pistol holstered appendix-style in my jeans. Appendix carry is typically concealed inside the waistband in the one or two o'clock position, or right in front of your hip. The positioning facilitates quick drawing, an added bonus to keeping it hidden.

Fortunately, on the day of the fishing trip, it was a chilly day for Florida, around sixty-five degrees, making it easier for me to hide the pistol inside jeans instead of the less bulky clothing hot weather may have called for. I arrived at Hawley's house dressed in jeans, a T-shirt, and work boots and was relieved to see him dressed in virtually identical fashion, as was his nineteen-year-old son, Joey, who'd be the only one accompanying us. The presence of Hawley's son didn't ease my trepidation about what was to come, because if Hawley did intend to kill me and dump me at sea, who better to keep quiet about the effort? Joey was just as tall as his father, but even broader, with short, coarse hair. The two of them would be formidable opponents in a fight, which was why I was glad I was carrying a Sig Sauer P229 9-millimeter pistol concealed in my jeans.

Wearing jeans, or pants in general, was important for another reason. In the army, I had trained extensively in water survival. One of those survival techniques was how to take the ends of your pants, tie them in a knot, put them over your head, and then clap air into the waistband of the pants. That forces the pant legs to fill up with air, creating a makeshift, donut-shaped flotation device every bit as effective as a life preserver. All you have to do is hold the waistband with your hands and you can float like that for days, or for however long you can hold on, and come away with only a bad sunburn on your face. An added trick is to hook your thumbs into the belt loops of the pants, so you don't risk getting tired from using your grip strength. So although I could just as easily have concealed my gun in a pair of shorts, I wore jeans specifically for the potential survival tool they represented.

Before we left, I went inside the kitchen to pick up a cooler Beth had packed with soft drinks, beer, water, and sandwiches. We exchanged smiles and pleasantries and left it there. She was a petite, demure woman with curly brown hair and an easy way about her. By that time, Hawley had confided to me that he also had a girlfriend who resided in the house, too, a living situation I had trouble grasping, but wasn't really surprised about given the penchant for Klan leaders to traditionally believe that they existed above the need to conform to the norms and mores of a society they were determined to bring down. In this case, that belief system served as a rationale to pursue not only an illicit affair but also to do so under the same roof as his wife.

Although there are women who were naturalized as card-carrying members of the Klan, most acted as support personnel, knowing when to make themselves scarce and what their role was. The Klan remained a male-dominated organization; even naturalized women who attended meetings remained subservient in Klan life and totally subordinate to the male members at every turn.

Going all the way back to the Klan's founding, a parallel or adjacent organization was formed, called the Women of the Ku Klux Klan, aka the Ladies of the Invisible Empire. Their goals to pursue traditional morality and practice religious intolerance and racism pretty much mirrored the views of the men, the primary difference being that WKKK went about their business through nonviolent means. Not surprisingly, spikes in membership of males coincided with spikes for females, primarily in the 1920s, 1940s, and during the Civil Rights movement of the 1960s. At their most effective, the WKKK would organize boycotts of anti-Klan businesses, while the male-dominated wing would be more likely to firebomb the buildings.

As the three of us climbed into William Hawley's truck, with a boat trailer holding his cabin cruiser attached, I remained painfully cognizant of the fact that some of that violence might soon be visited upon me. I was confident I could handle whatever came up, not so much playing the role of an informant but in my actual identity as a former sniper. If William and Joey Hawley were determined to murder me at sea, I had to make sure they were the ones who would not make it back to port alive.

When we arrived at the dock of Cedar Key Marina around ninety minutes later, my first priority was getting Joey alone. I wanted to endear myself to him in a way that would lead him to question his father's intentions, assuming those intentions were truly nefarious. I didn't expect to turn the young man totally against his father, but at the very least I could create doubt, which would be more than enough to tilt the advantage my way if this came down to me against them. In combat, or any deadly physical altercation, a moment of hesitation was all I would need to turn the tables on my potential attackers.

As luck would have it, once Hawley backed the trailer onto the boat ramp that dropped into the sea, it fell on Joey and me to guide the boat into the water, while Hawley parked his truck amid the nest of trucks in the parking lot with similarly empty trailers that had followed the same process we'd just completed. Cedar Key was the primary marina serving the west coast of Florida for a hundred-mile radius, and it was busy even in the so-called slower winter months when the weather wasn't always ideal for boating.

I used that opportunity provided by Hawley parking his truck to praise Joey for the job he was doing.

"Man, you're strong," I said, smiling. "Bet you don't even need my help to steer this thing into the water."

Then, a few moments later, when it came time to tie the boat down to the ramp, "No problem for those strong hands of yours to untie that knot."

I wanted the young man to feel comfortable in my presence, to question why his father might be planning my execution in spite of the demeanor I was displaying. Again, all I needed was to create that flicker of uncertainty if and when the fateful moment came.

It was even cooler on the water, and all of us needed every bit of the clothes we were wearing to ward off the chill of the wind whipping against us. William piloted the boat several miles out to sea, between three and five, though it was hard to tell exactly because no land was visible in any direction. He cut the engines and let the boat slow to a drift. Since the water was several hundred feet deep at this point, the anchor would do us no good, and we would be at the whim of the tides. There wasn't a cloud in the sky, and I wished I'd brought a windbreaker along, not only to ward off the chill but also to even better conceal the pistol I was packing.

We tucked our fishing rods into the buckets built into the boat's stern. We were using smaller bait to attract groupers, mahi-mahi, and spotted trout as opposed to the whole-fish bait we would have employed if we were after big-game fish like marlin. The body language of both William Hawley and Joey suggested nothing deadly was in the offing. There were no sidelong glances, unspoken signals, or furtive gestures, and there was nothing about their positioning on the deck relevant to a coming attack. Still, I didn't relax.

Army snipers aren't just shooters; we also serve, perhaps even primarily, as intelligence gatherers and battlefield-assessment experts. Reading enemies and potential enemies through a scope isn't all that much different from viewing them up close and personal, as I was doing today. And everything I was observing about William and Joey suggested I need not fear any foul play, especially given the direction my conversation with Hawley turned after we'd caught a couple of big groupers right off the bat, later joined in our fish cooler by spotted trout and mahi-mahi. Before the day was over, we'd exceeded the legal limit for grouper. Wouldn't it be ironic for William Hawley, who'd existed under the radar of law enforcement for so long, to end up getting nabbed by Florida's Fish and Game Commission?

"The Klan owes you a great debt, Brother Joe," he said, in a moment when both of us had lifted our fishing rods from the buckets to reel in a fish.

"I appreciate that, Brother William. But what for?"

"Being on the ball about the Obama action. You know what two weeks from today is?"

"Inauguration Day," I said, without pause.

"That's right, Brother Joe. We're already seeing a spike in membership nationwide. But once Obama takes office, the numbers are sure to skyrocket even more. The Klan was born out of the injustices of the Civil War. Now we're positioned to gain new power, thanks to the injustice of a man like that becoming president."

We both continued to reel in our catches, a combination of all three species we were after, Hawley's line appearing to be a little ahead of mine.

"Obama's going to be the gift that keeps on giving," Hawley went on. "We take him out while he's in office and the government'll bring the wrath of God down upon us. I should tell you that's the talk among the national leadership, Charles Denton included. He thinks this is the Civil Rights era all over again, the perfect time to spend stocking up for the days to come. You see what I'm getting at here?"

Our fishing lines broke the water at the same time, twenty-pound-plus groupers dangling. We raised the fish into the boat, where Joey was waiting to put them on ice in the big cooler with the rest of the bunch we'd already caught.

"Yes, sir, I do: we've got a golden opportunity to boost our ranks, while a successful assassination would risk decimating them."

Hawley cast me a long look while our fish flopped atop the moist deck. "If I'd asked you to take the shot a few months back, would you have done it, Brother Joe?"

I flashed an unforced smile born out of the fact I no longer feared an attempt was going to be made on my life. "Not if there were Predator drones in the sky, Brother William."

Within another hour, our cooler was packed full with fish, including those groupers that went way beyond the allowed limit.

"Keep an eye out for the Fish and Game patrol boat," Hawley advised me and Joey. "And keep the cooler out of sight, just in case. Don't want to get boarded by the game warden and have our catch confiscated, do we now?"

We certainly didn't, but I was after bigger fish than we could pack in a cooler. The small talk we engaged in made for another crucial step in the level of my infiltration. The day kept me within the Klan's comfort zone, while also reassuring me that my cover had not been blown.

After three hours, we headed in. Back at the dock, it took Joey and me to lift the cooler into the rear of Hawley's pickup truck. We drove back to his property and repeated the process, only this time we brought the cooler into the house and loaded all those fish into a freezer.

"Quite a haul we pulled in today, Brother Joe," he said before I climbed back into my car to drive home, stinking of fish. I couldn't wait to jump in the shower before my wife had a chance to sniff the air.

Then he flashed a smile that was different from any I'd ever seen him display before. It lingered a bit, along with his gaze, in a way that told me the fishing trip had endeared me to a Grand Dragon of the KKK in just the manner I had hoped it would.

"But we got lots bigger hauls ahead of us," Hawley said.

CHAPTER 9

MAKE THE GUY PAY

WAYWARD, FLORIDA
MARCH 2009

It turned out that these "hauls" William Hawley referred to had nothing to do with fishing. In the months following our deep-sea expedition, Hawley and other Klan leaders witnessed a massive membership spike—not just in naturalized Knights of the Invisible Empire but also supporters, sympathizers, and most dramatically, nonmembers who cited Klan ideology and orthodoxy in committing crimes based in the racial hatred that was the foundation of the organization's very existence. This was accompanied by a significant rise in hate crimes across the country, coinciding with a Black president moving into the White House. That served up a galvanizing issue for the Klan to boost its numbers, a trend line that continued to rise through the Obama presidency.

But that's not all.

In the very klavern I infiltrated, I watched in horror as more and more members of the law-enforcement community came into the fold. And if it was happening in Florida, it was happening nationwide. Prior to Obama being elected, law enforcement had kept their distance, but now their membership in the Klan was an open secret they no longer saw a reason to hide. Pre–November 2008, such law-enforcement officials had nonetheless been vital to the organization's efforts in providing intelligence and looking the other way at the most opportune times. Now they had moved from the fringes into the center of the movement, resulting in a culture of white supremacy sprouting in police departments all across the country, predominantly in Florida, Alabama, and Louisiana. But scandals were everywhere, at least a hundred of them in forty states "in which individual police officers have sent overtly racist emails, texts, or made racist comments via social media." Many of those who stopped short of joining nonetheless became the Klan's foot soldiers, embracing its rhetoric and working to further its aims, while the Invisible Empire to a great extent remained invisible.

I could always tell the relative nature of any Klan meeting I was asked to attend, not only by William Hawley's tone but also by how he characterized it. A "prayer meeting," for example, meant we were going to have discussions that centered around illegal activity, in contrast to a more routine membership meeting or something more ceremonial, like a cross burning or naturalization.

In March 2009, two months after the boat trip, I received a phone call from Hawley. I was struggling to maintain my two separate lives. My son, Jordy, was about nine months old, and I wanted to be there for him as his father and not a Klansman.

"Brother Joe, this is Brother William," he began. "We're having a prayer meeting over at the compound Saturday morning and need your participation."

Though we spoke every week, often several times, something about his tone was different. It was more businesslike, instead of celebratory or matter-of-fact. That told me something big was up, potentially suggesting illegal activity.

"I'll be there, Brother William," I replied.

The fact that he said "we're" implied there would be more than just the two of us. That told me this was likely a more official meeting that could involve a larger-than-usual gathering of the klavern's cadres. Given the potential significance, I resolved to wear two recording devices to make sure I had a backup.

The dogs were out roaming Hawley's property when I arrived on Saturday morning. I was always prompt, and he was waiting for me outside to call the dogs off so I could safely exit my car. Hawley put the dogs at heel and escorted me around his home to a screen door in the back. My defenses were alert because we'd never entered his home this way before. In that moment, I began to suspect my cover had been blown somehow and that Hawley had figured out I was an informant. Just over eighteen months had passed since I'd first made contact on the FBI's behalf about that rifle he was selling, and that was an eternity for a confidential human source to be inside an organization as dangerous as the KKK.

Sure enough, as soon as we walked through the back door of his home, I noticed plastic had been laid across the floors and layered over the walls. The kind of plastic you use if you want to kill someone and wrap up the body to avoid leaving any evidence behind. The next thing I noticed were the dozen men standing in a room just off to the side in a semicircle, all wearing identical Klan T-shirts, including Brother Brown, who was wearing his draped over his overalls.

I was still making sense of what was happening here when Hawley handed me a matching T-shirt.

"Put this on, Brother Joe," he said. "Then we've got some business to discuss."

Hawley expected me to switch the shirt I was wearing for that one then and there, and all I could think of were the wires that would be exposed as soon as I took mine off.

As I was taking off my T-shirt, I managed to unclip the wire that was connected to the recording device hidden in my groin area. The backup, taped to the small of my back, was hidden by my pants, so all I had to do was face front to ensure no one would notice the slight bulge.

I managed to ball the wire up inside my T-shirt, and fortunately the tape holding it in place held. I handed it to Hawley and watched him fold it up, holding my breath against the possibility that he or another member of the gathered group would notice the wire as I slipped on the T-shirt he had given me.

At that point I was already contemplating my next move, should my fears be realized. I had come armed. I knew the first thing the grouping of Klansmen would do was back up to draw their weapons before they started shooting. That would give me time to burst out through the screen door. I was carrying a Sig Sauer P229, the same one I'd taken on the fishing trip, with a fifteen-shot magazine, and I had a spare magazine in my pocket. It might have been twelve against one, but being closest to the door gave me a tactical advantage. Once I was through it, the men following me would emerge in single file, so I'd still have the advantage when I got outside. If flight proved my best option, I'd shoot the dogs and do that. If I felt taking the men out gave me my best chance, I'd opt for that. Otherwise, I'd rush to safety across the road to a drainage culvert, where I'd have cover.

But Hawley simply handed my shirt back to me and I moved in to join the others. My attention remained on their hands, not their faces, still wary of a move being made against me. Of the twelve, I recognized only three, including Brother Brown, from whom I'd recently bought a 1989 Jeep Cherokee in mint condition for only eight hundred dollars. It was one of several he had lovingly restored but made available only to "family," as he called it.

That meant there were nine of them I'd never seen before, even at Hawley's Summer Bash. It could have been a matter of availability, but it could also be these were klavern members who doubled as civic leaders, even elected officials, and would have wanted their association with the Klan to remain private. Living in Worthington Springs, I wasn't as familiar with public figures here in Wayward. And I remained more cognizant of their hands than their faces.

"Brothers, we have a situation," Hawley addressed us. "In September of 2008, a thirteen-year-old girl named Frances Margay Schee was killed in a school bus accident on US 301, not far from North Marion Middle School, that she attended as a seventh grader. A Hispanic man named Reinaldo Gonzalez was driving the semi that rammed the bus from behind while it was stopped with flashers going and killed Frances. Nine other children were hospitalized."

I heard someone behind me mutter, "Spic."

"It was a horrific scene," Hawley continued. "But what's even more horrific is that all this time has passed and Reinaldo Gonzalez is still a free man. He was never arrested, even though the investigation revealed he wasn't looking at the road at the time because he was talking or texting on his phone. He claimed he never saw the school bus."

I heard several of the men utter what could best be described as a low growl.

"Brothers, the killer of Frances Margay Schee must be punished outside the law by god-fearing people like ourselves. So the matter before us today is to take a vote on whether we should make this guy pay—you know, a life for a life. Anyone have anything to say on the matter?"

Heads shook stridently. Nobody raised their hands.

"In that case," Hawley resumed, "all in favor of serving justice on Reinaldo Gonzalez, raise your hands."

Thirteen hands rose into the air, including mine.

Hawley nodded, remaining impassive. "Then the next order of business is to figure out how we're gonna get this done."

"I'll take care of it," I chimed in, leaving it there.

All the eyes in the room turned toward me, the gazes flashing satisfaction and gratitude at my volunteering to spearhead the action. The fact that I knew hardly any of these men didn't mean they didn't know me, at least by reputation as the klavern's so-called hit man.

Brother Brown was the first one to come up to me to offer his support. "Whatever you need, Brother Joe, I'm here. You'll need a vehicle with clean paper and we can get that worked out."

The others followed, approaching me one at a time with offers of assistance or just to say they had my back. A few squeezed my shoulders. Their eyes showed admiration for my efforts. I could see William Hawley nodding, as if he'd been hoping I'd step forward just as

I had done. I had acted on impulse, determining on the spot that the best way to save this man's life was to volunteer to take it.

Even though my relationship with Armstrong in the wake of how I had handled the planned assassination of Barack Obama was stronger than ever, I had no idea really of how he'd react to my volunteering to "take care" of Reinaldo Gonzalez. Had I overstepped my bounds? Had I acted out of turn and put the FBI in an impossible spot?

Because of the potential importance of this meeting, Armstrong was waiting for me in a parking lot a mile away from Hawley's compound. I climbed into the front seat of his Ford 500 and briefed him on what had gone down, and he started grinning from ear to ear.

"You're a rock star again!" he said, beaming.

And why not? If I could pull this off and ended up nailing the leadership of one of Florida's largest and most notorious klaverns, including its Grand Dragon, it would be a career maker for Armstrong. This was a case supervisory agents stuck running a backwoods Bureau office dream of. We knew the situation would remain fluid, and the more we let William Hawley run things, the better off we'd be in terms of implicating him and the other twelve men wearing matching T-shirts while standing atop the plastic I thought might be meant for me. This was a classic case of conspiracy to commit murder, and if I played my cards right, every one of them would be going down.

My next meeting with Hawley only upped the ante more. I had spent a few days the way I would have if I was actually planning to kill Gonzalez: by watching his house and his movements to find the best spot to take the shot. When I met with Hawley, I brought along pictures of his home and truck, along with a detailed dossier of his regular comings and goings, and the time he normally left the house to head out on a long-haul route, which was his specialty.

Hawley nodded, clearly impressed by the planning I'd already done and the progress I'd made. He went over to his gun cabinet and came back with a Walther P38, the infamous Nazi sidearm.

"No one knows I've got this," he said, handing it to me. "It's not registered. Call it a collector's item I'm willing to part with for a cause this just."

I took the pistol in hand and checked its heft and balance, after making sure it wasn't loaded. "We're going to need to get it fitted for a silencer," I said, again on impulse. "I know a machinist who can handle that."

"Just keep the Klan out of it, Brother Joe."

"He's a sympathizer, Brother William. Even if he has an inkling of the truth, he'll be glad to help. And he owes me a favor."

Of course, no such machinist existed. At my next meeting with Armstrong and Vaughn, I turned the Walther over so the FBI could handle the task of fitting it for a silencer. And by the time my next meeting with Hawley came along, I was ready.

"What do you think?" I asked him, handing over the remodeled pistol.

He inspected the threading a gunsmith retained by the FBI had done to the barrel so it could be fitted for a silencer.

"Very impressive," Hawley noted, complimenting the work.

"I thought so too," I told him. "The silencer's being made as we speak. My buddy has to do it on off-work hours."

Prior to returning the Walther to me, the FBI had cleaned it thoroughly so no prints remained. So now the only prints that could possibly be on the gun were mine and William Hawley's. I watched him handling and examining it and knew we now had his fingerprints on a gun he had provided from his own collection to murder a man.

"What's next?" he asked, handing the Walther back to me.

"I'm gonna take some more pictures. Find us the ideal spot to get the deed done."

Tailing Gonzalez revealed he was a creature of routine, as most of us are. On Monday mornings, when he set off on his route, his first stop was always ninety minutes down the road at a particular truck station on Interstate 75. He would fuel up at the pumps, then park his rig alongside the multitude of others that used this stop as a way station, while he went inside to grab some food. I determined that the best opportunity to take him out would be while he was exiting his truck in a parking lot cluttered with other vehicles that would cover the car, supplied by Brother Brown, we'd be using for the hit.

"I'll take the shot from the passenger seat," I reported to Hawley four weeks later at a meeting also attended by three other klavern leaders who'd been standing atop the plastic the day of the vote. "Because of the silencer, no one will hear a thing, and we'll be long gone by the time somebody comes upon the trucker's body."

I had taken detailed photos to share with the group on the pretext of them being able to visualize the logistics. The real reason was to capture their fingerprints as well. Those prints, along with the recordings, would be all the FBI needed to swoop in and make the arrests for conspiracy to commit murder. I even announced we'd decided upon an upcoming Monday for the hit, because that's when Gonzalez's schedule was most predictable. I explained how we'd utilize a lookout, so the car in which I was riding wouldn't need to be there until the last possible moment.

The scant security cameras in the lot posed no problem, since I'd be wearing a mask and the license plates would be fake. Once I took the shot, we had arranged a drop point for the vehicle where Brother Brown would pick it up and get it disposed of in the same manner we would have followed had the assassination attempt on Barack Obama gone forward.

Two weeks prior to the day the hit was planned for, the FBI informed the Florida Highway Patrol that Gonzalez was going to be killed. He was arrested on April 8, 2009, and charged with vehicular manslaughter and reckless driving with serious bodily injury. I can't explain why the arrest hadn't been made earlier, since the accident had taken place in September, seven months before. Because he was in custody, though, the planned hit was called off.

Meanwhile, we still had more than enough to charge William Hawley and a handful of upper-echelon klavern members with conspiracy to commit murder. Even though the attempt on Gonzalez's life was never made, the conspiracy remained a serious crime that could send Hawley and the others away for up to twenty-five years, decimating the Klan in Florida and sending shock waves through the organization nationally.

I realized then that all the hours I'd put in and all the stress I'd endured infiltrating the Klan and spending every day for nearly two years as a trusted member seemed well worth it. We had built a strong case against Hawley and his minions. All that remained was to move in and make the arrests.

Until something else intervened.

CHAPTER 10

THE CASE THAT WASN'T

WORTHINGTON SPRINGS, FLORIDA
APRIL 2009

The deeper I became entrenched in the Klan, the more of a challenge it became to leave all that at the door when I went home to my wife and son. It seemed like whenever I was home, all I could think of were Klan activities, and all I could visualize were members kicking in the door to come get me after learning my true purpose. And when I was at Klan meetings and social events, all I could think of was getting home to Shannon and Jordy. That left me on high alert 24/7, with no respite on Sundays or holidays. I had been undercover for nearly two years, and it was becoming increasingly difficult to compartmentalize the overwhelming anxiety and fear—not just for my own safety but the safety of my family. The whole time I was undercover, I wasn't working another job, making us reliant on a monthly disability payment I had been receiving from the VA because of the PTSD and depression with which I'd been diagnosed back in Los Angeles and that had been deemed service connected. I was also receiving a modest stipend from the FBI.

A week after Gonzalez was arrested, and just days before the FBI planned to arrest Hawley, I noticed some odd behavior from my son

Jordy. My in-laws regularly watched him while Shannon was at work and I was busy with Klan business.

When Jordy began acting strangely, my suspicions naturally turned to Rusty and my mother-in-law, Sharon. They were rednecks in the worst sense of the word, and I'd seen nothing over time to change the negative first impression I'd formed of them. I continued to keep my thoughts to myself to keep the peace in my own home, and because I knew how important it was for Shannon to maintain a relationship with her mother. But I did take the provocative step of surreptitiously recording my mother-in-law in Jordy's company, as much to assuage my own concerns as anything else. I did this with the full knowledge that such taping may have been an illegal act, unless it was illegal activity that ended up being recorded. That was the case according to Florida State Statute 934.03, which also stipulated that all that was required to take such an action—taping—was a *belief* on the part of the parent or guardian that such activity may have been taking place. The statute specifically referenced suspected sexual abuse of a minor.

And that's exactly what happened. That night, after picking Jordy up around nine o'clock, I listened to the tape, disturbed by some of what I heard suggesting that my mother-in-law might have been abusing my ten-month-old son. As a survivor of childhood sexual abuse and trauma, this was obviously something I was extremely sensitive about. I could not let it go without responding. Shannon couldn't believe what she was hearing either and came to the same conclusion I had, that we couldn't take any chances.

I called the local sheriff's office to make a report. My wife wanted to confront her mother herself, but I insisted that we needed to get the authorities involved. We were told deputies were being sent out immediately to interview my in-laws, which was standard operating procedure in the case of suspected sexual abuse of a child.

Then, around 1:30 in the morning, we heard hard banging on the door of our home in Worthington Springs, which we rented from my in-laws, who were now being investigated for sexually abusing our son. It was Sharon and Rusty. They barged in as soon as I opened the door. My wife's stepfather was screaming and swearing. He wanted to start a fight with me, maybe hoping I'd beat him up so he could file a countercharge of assault and battery against me, but I left my hands by my side and refused to be goaded into knocking him into tomorrow, which was what I wanted to do.

My mother-in-law, meanwhile, just kept screaming and shouting, with spittle flying in all directions.

"I didn't do nothing to that boy and you know it!" she ranted.

"I don't know that you did nothing," I shot back at her. "And the recording says you certainly may have."

"I was just playing with him! It was just a game!"

"It didn't sound like a game to me."

"You don't get to talk to me that way, you ungrateful son of a bitch!"

"And you don't get to talk the way you did to my son. You can call it a game, you can call it anything you want—it was still wrong, and maybe criminal."

"Fuck you!" my father-in-law added.

"Get out!" my mother-in-law ranted to my wife. "This is our house and I want you out of here now!"

"Mom—"

"Don't 'mom' me," my mother-in-law said, cutting off her daughter, "not after the sheriff's deputies showed up at my door tonight. I want you gone! Pack up and leave! Get out of my house, girl!"

Shannon swallowed hard. I knew she was convinced the recording was real, but she was in a state of denial about what to do about it, thanks to the subservience she still felt to her mother and stepfather. I remained calm, managed to defuse the situation, and by 2:00 a.m., my in-laws were gone. But we now faced the daunting prospect of moving immediately. I'd already been homeless once in my life and would never let my family experience that ignominy. And before I could even think about packing, I faced the equally daunting prospect of reporting this to Joe Armstrong.

By the time I climbed into the front seat of his car at our usual meeting spot the next morning, my in-laws had already called the local FBI office and spoke to him as the supervisory agent. They didn't know I'd infiltrated the KKK, thankfully, but they knew I was doing something for the FBI because Shannon had told them. They had been working hard to drive a wedge between us by trying to convince her I was unfaithful, given how I would disappear for long periods of time. And Shannon felt she had no choice but to counter such a claim with a measure of the truth.

"What the fuck is going on?" Armstrong shouted, and I saw brown drops of juice from the tobacco he was chewing spray the dashboard and windshield. "Your in-laws called and were screaming that you're crazy, that you've gone nuts!"

"Joe—"

"What the fuck did you do?"

"I had strong reason to believe that my mother-in-law was—"

"I know what you accused these people of. I'm asking how the fuck you could jeopardize the whole operation by doing it."

"We're talking about my son here," I said, raising my voice an octave.

"And I'm talking about two years of work we've got invested in you. It's done, it's over. The operation's fucking toast."

My stomach sank. I had just accused my mother-in-law of molesting my son, and now the operation I had given two years of my life to had blown up in my face. On top of all that, we had to move. My whole world was crumbling. I felt like an enormous failure. All I could think of in that moment was how things had ended for me in the army as well, before I relocated here. And now I'd be moving again. I just wanted to put every bit of this behind me and start over wherever we ended up.

"I'm sorry. My family comes first," I said, defeated.

"Fuck your family!" Spittle continued to fly everywhere, and Armstrong was hammering the steering wheel so hard I could feel it vibrating from the passenger seat. "Thanks to all this shit, we have to pull you out and you can't even testify. That means everything you did was for nothing. Without your testimony, we haven't got shit on William Hawley and the others."

I didn't bother reminding him that I had very likely saved the life of Barack Obama, so all this had hardly been for nothing. I'd be lying, though, if I said the inability to prosecute Hawley and the others we had on conspiracy to commit murder charges didn't sting.

"You should have goddamn fucking handled this differently!"

Armstrong enunciated his remark by pounding his fist into the dashboard. I thought it might be about to crack, but remained silent. There was nothing I could say or explain that would satisfy Armstrong, and truth be told, I didn't blame him. The fact that my in-laws knew I was working with the FBI on something meant operational security had been compromised. As overt Klan sympathizers and supporters, who's to say they wouldn't approach William Hawley or someone else inside the klavern to exact revenge on me? My cover was blown and the only way I'd ever see William Hawley again was if he showed up to take action against me, wherever we ended up settling.

"You know what happens now?" Armstrong continued, without giving me a chance to respond. "Social Services is going to investigate. What do you think happens when you have to tell them you're working undercover for the FBI? What happens if their investigation determines your home to be an unsafe environment?"

I hadn't thought of that, or something else he said next either.

"It means your status as an informant becomes public record."

I'd said all I could. There was no reason to respond.

"Get the fuck out of my car!" Armstrong raged.

"I'm sorry," I said to him, as calmly as I could manage.

"GET THE FUCK OUT OF MY CAR!"

And I did, wiping off the tobacco juice he'd spit all over my clothes.

Three days later, we moved into an apartment in the beach town of St. Augustine, on the northeast coast of Florida, about a hundred miles away. It had long been a dream of my wife to live there, so close to the ocean, near where her grandmother had taught her and her eight cousins how to swim in a motel pool. Strangely, her grandmother hadn't even known how to swim herself, but she was committed to making sure her grandchildren didn't suffer the same fate, so her swim lessons always took place in the shallow end.

In St. Augustine, we were free of my in-laws, and my wife and I decided not to press charges. The whole case would go away, ensuring things didn't get any worse than they already were, and we could keep what little remained of the peace. I could only imagine what Armstrong might have made of that, since in his mind I'm sure the reckless actions he'd deemed I'd committed had resulted in nothing at all.

I had plenty of regrets but harbored no guilt. If I couldn't protect my own child from monsters, how could I protect the country from them? Now, at long last, my wife would be free from the reach of her mother and stepfather and close enough to the ocean to smell the salt air in our new home. The stress that accumulated between the incident involving my in-laws and the way my infiltration of the KKK had ended, though, caused both my depression and PTSD to spike. It got to the point that it was affecting my reliability once I tried returning to my job as a welder, which is a dangerous job to begin with.

Then I caught a break. Not long after we got settled in St. Augustine, the Veterans Administration stepped in out of nowhere and awarded me an additional two thousand dollars a month in veterans disability payments after finally fessing up to the fact that my army experience was part and parcel of both the depression and PTSD I'd been treated for back in Los Angeles. Meanwhile, Shannon returned to her chosen profession and passion as a home health care worker for the elderly, while I stayed home with Jordy as a true Mr. Mom. Spending those hours with Jordy turned out to be the best therapy imaginable. It gave me a sense of purpose and filled me with a desire to find the strength inside myself to be the best father I could possibly be. And that meant overcoming the effects of the mental illness I was experiencing.

Meanwhile, the Klan might have been out of sight, but they were far from out of mind. Even though we had moved away from my double life, I didn't think we were by any means free from danger, but

I had no way of knowing for sure how the klavern had greeted my sudden disappearance. Did they suspect I was an informant, and if they did, what steps would they take? I had seen firsthand the extreme lengths the Klan would go to, to satisfy their perverse sense of "justice." Because of the inauspicious manner in which the investigation had ended, I wasn't in witness protection or protective custody with someone watching my back. I was totally on my own, facing the very real possibility that William Hawley would try to kill me or, more likely, arrange for me to be killed. I had to assume that my absence could only lead him to conclude I'd been an informant the whole time, and Hawley wasn't the kind of man to just let that go. I couldn't keep tabs on the goings-on in the klavern I'd infiltrated or in Wayward in general. And with all my FBI contact broken off, I had no idea how Hawley and the rest of the group had greeted my leaving without explanation.

The stress and anxiety I endured over worrying about whether the Klan would find me were monumental. At night sometimes, I'd sit in sight of the front door with a gun, waiting for the inevitable moment when heavy boots would kick it in and men who came to kill me stormed inside. All I could do was try to move forward in spite of that. We lived spitting distance from the beach, I enjoyed the time playing house dad for Jordy, and I was starting to look forward to whatever form the next phase of my life would take. The spring and summer months passed without any indication the Klan knew our whereabouts or the reason why I had vanished in the first place, leaving me to settle into a routine and compartmentalize my fear.

While I was keeping my mental health in check, though, my physical health started to rapidly decline. I felt very weak and got exhausted doing the simplest things, despite having been so obsessive about staying in shape. I was easily distracted and couldn't focus on anything for very long at all. My mind would wander, fixating on all the lowest points in my life, from being homeless in Los Angeles to not being able to finish what I started after infiltrating the KKK.

It continued to get worse until one day, feeling weak and feverish, I drove myself to the local hospital. Upon being checked in at the ER,

I was found to be spiking a fever of 105 degrees and was immediately admitted to the Intensive Care Unit. They took extreme measures to bring my fever down, including draping bags of ice over my body, and pumping all kinds of fluids into me to get my body to cool. Doctors quickly determined that my system had become septic, and at one-thirty in the morning in October 2011, my heart stopped and I stopped breathing.

The hospital called my wife and, without telling her how dire the situation was, told her she needed to get to the hospital as fast as she could. By the time she got there, with Jordy in tow, I had been revived but remained in critical condition. Mumbling, I asked her to bring me a pad and a pen so I could write out my will, because the doctors weren't at all sure I was going to make it through the night. My odds were fifty-fifty at best.

But I lived to see the morning and spent the next seven days in the ICU, suffering from an acute form of diverticulitis, an intestinal infection. It was further determined to be far more likely than not that the condition had been severely exacerbated, if not outright caused, by the residual buildup of stress I was experiencing, first from those nearly two years I was leading a double life undercover and then from the strain of constantly looking over my shoulder the past two and a half years.

A psychiatrist I had been seeing likened this to living in a perpetual state of fight or flight. When the body is in this state, it shuts down peripheral components, like much of the immune system, in order to focus almost solely on survival. From a psychological standpoint, it was essentially the equivalent of spending four straight years on the battlefield. Trauma piled upon trauma, given that I had been treated back in Los Angeles for serious complications resulting from PTSD coupled with childhood sexual trauma.

I was discharged after a week, determined to set my life back on course. I had lost some weight and strength, but not enough to curtail my efforts. In three months, I was bench-pressing four hundred pounds and running five miles a day. I got into the best shape of my life since college and later the army. Then, just as I began to treat my body differently, the psychiatrist I was seeing sent me to a mental health therapist who specialized in PTSD, specifically in how to manage the kind of daily activities everyone else takes for granted. That therapist taught me how to discard all the stresses before they got bottled up and spilled out in what could resemble a panic attack. Treatment educated me on how to manage my past, so I could focus on looking forward instead of back. I still kept an occasional gaze cocked over my shoulder just in case someone from the KKK came gunning for me, but I taught myself how to be cognizant of my surroundings without being paranoid about everything and everybody. When I was operational, my life was on loan. And when it came time to pay up, I almost paid with my life.

Not anymore.

Though my monthly stipend from the VA had relieved me of the need to make a regular paycheck, I had taken a job at a local shooting range teaching precision rifle to current law-enforcement and active military personnel, as well as veterans. It was mostly volunteer work, but I did receive some modest compensation from those who could afford it, while never taking money from those who couldn't. I enjoyed being on the range and shooting, as well as teaching the skill to others, which proved therapeutic in its own right. Meanwhile, we were still living close enough to the beach to hear the waves at night through windows I was no longer afraid to leave open.

Then one day in April 2013, the phone rang.

"Hello," I answered.

"Hey, Joe," a voice I immediately recognized as my former handler Rich Vaughn said, "it's Rich."

"Been a long time, Rich," I answered.

"How you been?"

"Good, real good. Thanks for asking."

"Joe, I'm not going to mince words here," Vaughn said, dispensing with the small talk. "We need you back."

PART II

Not all those who wander are lost.

—J. R. R. TOLKIEN, *THE FELLOWSHIP OF THE RING*

CHAPTER 11

THE CALL

ST. AUGUSTINE, FLORIDA
APRIL 2013

It turned out that Vaughn and his colleagues were qualifying one day on the same range where I served as a part-time instructor when he spotted someone teaching what was clearly advanced stuff.

"What's going on over there?" he asked the rangemaster.

"Army sniper leading a class in precision rifle shooting."

On second glance, Vaughn realized the instructor was me. That, he explained to me over the phone, was the impetus for him to reach out to me.

As it turned out, though, there was something else.

"What do you know about Klan activity in the area, Joe?" he continued.

"Not much, Rich, nothing at all really. I haven't been following any of that stuff."

"But you could dig around, tell us what your thoughts are, right?"

"I suppose."

"A week enough time for you?"

"It is."

"Then I'll talk with you then."

I guess I knew where this was leading, but I wasn't resistant. Truth be told, a big part of me was glad Vaughn had called out of the blue. Digging into local Klan chapters based in this part of Florida wasn't hard. There were three, and it would take someone familiar with how such klaverns operated in order to distinguish between them. They all freely announced themselves with websites and 800 numbers, though one clearly stood out from the rest in terms of its organizational capacity and messaging that left just enough unsaid—a chapter of the Traditionalist American Knights of the Ku Klux Klan, or TAK.

A week later, I climbed into the front seat of Vaughn's car in a parking lot where he'd told me to meet him. There was a young woman in the back seat. I judged her to be in her midthirties, maybe ten years younger than what I had Vaughn pegged as.

"How's the family, Joe?" he asked me, after we shook hands.

"Good."

"Your son . . . He must be, what, six now?"

"Still five."

"And your wife?"

"Back working in the career she loves."

I could see Vaughn stiffen slightly. "What about your in-laws?"

"I'm keeping the peace, what's best for everyone."

Vaughn nodded, ready to move on from the small talk. "Joe, this is Lindsay Campbell. She works out of the Jacksonville FBI office and is currently assigned as that office's liaison to the Joint Terrorism Task Force."

I exchanged nods, smiles, and pleasantries with Campbell, who impressed me right from the start with her focus and professionalism.

"I've got a question," I said to Vaughn.

"Shoot."

"Am I going to have to work with Joe Armstrong again?" I asked him, smiling tightly.

Vaughn forced a smile. "No Joe Armstrong this time."

"That's good," I said, smiling more broadly.

That was enough to tell me that if this went much deeper, Vaughn would take the handler role previously filled by Joe Armstrong, while Campbell stepped into his shoes as backup. Even though she was seated in the back seat, I could guess she was around five seven, and noted she was wearing athletic-style flat shoes so she could sprint or run after a suspect if called for. That, and the tattoos that stretched over both shoulders, exposed by a sleeveless top above her slacks, told me she was a former cop. Her accent suggested somewhere up north—all facts I was later able to confirm. It turned out that she'd started her career in Philadelphia.

"So what can you tell us, Joe?" Vaughn prodded.

"There's one group you need to worry about," I informed him from all the research I had done. "By all accounts, they're a traditionalist group, operating the way the Klan did all the way back in the nineteenth century, believe it or not. What caught my attention on their website was all these First Amendment disclaimers to create plausible deniability. There's a group of First Amendment lawyers who go around the country to teach these so-called nonviolent organizations what to say publicly."

"I wasn't aware of that."

"The nonviolent language is designed to put a buffer between the leadership and the foot soldiers."

"But this particular group piqued your interest?"

"Yes, sir, it did. They call themselves the Traditionalist American Knights, one chapter of many scattered across the country."

"So that's the one." Vaughn exchanged a quick glance with Campbell in the back seat. "And if we wanted to get an agent inside, what would be the best way to do it? Could you do an assessment for us?"

"I could, yes."

I knew Vaughn was testing me, gauging the level of my interest and commitment to what I'd been forced to walk away from four years before.

"Can we meet again as soon as you've got something for us, Joe?"

Meaning that's when he wanted my assessment.

"Sure."

That night over dinner I told Shannon what I'd felt in my gut from the moment I recognized Vaughn's voice on the other end of the phone line.

"I think the FBI wants me to go operational again."

She just looked at me and went right on eating.

"You don't have anything to say, babe?"

"I know if you want to do it, you're going to, no matter what I say. Jordy and I will be there for you, no matter what you decide to do. Just don't get killed."

She left things there, her response short and sweet, because I think Shannon knew me better than I knew myself, knew that I couldn't be the husband and father I needed to be unless I could be the man I knew I was. A few days later, when Jordy was in school, we decided on a whim to go fishing. We headed out to one of our favorite spots, Vilano Beach Pier in St. Augustine, and cast our lines off the pier. There was only one solitary figure there already. I guess those who normally crowded the pier had checked the weather; before we knew it, a typical Florida rainstorm blew in.

"Wanna quit, babe?" I asked Shannon.

"Hell, no. We came to catch some fish. Let's catch some fish."

So I plucked our rain jackets from the storage box that held our fishing gear and we zippered them up to fight the storm off as best we could. And, as fast as the storm had washed in, my line got a bite. I hauled a twenty-six-inch red drum out of the water, which was just short of the legal limit. That one guy standing on the pier getting soaked couldn't believe it.

"I been here all morning and haven't even felt a tug," he said, shaking his head.

We took that fish home and made dinner out of it for several nights, moments of normalcy that were like the calm before a figurative storm. In the end, I knew I had to go back undercover, despite the fact that I'd nearly lost myself the first time around. I had to face the dragon again, and this time I had to kill it. The fact that I'd left that initial go-round with the KKK unfinished had a lot to do with me saying yes to Rich Vaughn. More important, though, it was about loyalty and duty. I knew better than anyone what the Klan was capable of; imagine if their attempt to assassinate Barack Obama on the eve of the 2008 election had been successful? I knew the havoc they could wreak and their utter disregard for the Constitution I had sworn to uphold. I knew President Obama's reelection in 2012 had only galvanized their convictions and reinforced their stated desire to foment a second civil war. If I turned Vaughn down, I'd never be able to live with myself.

But I resolved to do it differently this time, so I would not lose myself again in the darkness of despair. I had already experienced what psychotherapist Thomas Moore had covered in his book *Dark Nights of the Soul* when he wrote that "life is never as bright and successful and meaningful as you might imagine." This time I would achieve the success that had eluded me the first time, and I would find the meaning I'd been denied then. And maybe that was the only way I could finally brush the darkness, which had long riddled my soul, aside with light once and for all.

The next day I placed a phone call to the 800 number for the Traditionalist American Knights and left a message on their voicemail just saying I was former army interested in more information about their organization. Two or three days later, I got a call back. I knew they were likely getting lots of phone calls these days and took it as a good sign that the return call had come so quickly.

"I'm looking for Joe Moore," I heard a stranger's voice say when I answered the phone.

"Speaking."

"Joe, this is Jamie Ward. I'm the chief recruiter for the Traditionalist American Knights."

"KIGY, Brother," I said, using the tried and true greeting among Klan members.

"AYAK?" he said back, his voice laced with surprise. *Are you a Klansman?*

"I was, yes, sir. But it was an organization that was disbanded because of prayer activity that went sideways."

I was referring to the klavern William Hawley ran back in Wayward. I had no idea whether it was still functional or not, but I was relying on the Klan's reputation for decentralization among chapters to keep Jamie Ward from learning anything further. Ever since its founding, the Klan has been obsessive about secrecy, to the point of keeping communication between chapters virtually nonexistent. That way, if one chapter was decimated by the authorities, the arrested members wouldn't be able to give up any of the members, especially the leaders, of neighboring klaverns. Given that a lot of these chapters now had websites and 800 numbers, they may have known of another's existence, but would rarely have contact with it, even if separated by only a hundred miles. Almost exclusively, contact would occur at mass rallies.

"You sound like a man we'd like to have aboard, Brother Joe. I look forward to meeting you."

He told me he'd call me back to set a time and place. I imagined that would provide the opportunity to probe a bit deeper into my story about my previous chapter having disbanded. Worst-case scenario would be that he somehow made direct contact with William Hawley, in which case I'd never hear from Ward again.

My next meeting with Vaughn and Campbell took place two weeks after that call, at the Jacksonville field office, in Campbell's office, where I reported on the progress I'd made so far. Vaughn and I sat in chairs across from Campbell, who was behind her desk.

"You expect him to call you back?" Vaughn asked me.

"I believe he will, depending on whether he happens to make contact with the Wayward chapter. You hear anything in that regard?"

Vaughn shook his head. "The task force's interest and involvement ended with you, Joe. We haven't been keeping tabs." He leaned closer to me. "We're going to have to run another background check on you before you can become operational again. That should be a formality. Any surprises we should expect?"

"Well, I almost died . . ."

I proceeded to give Vaughn and Campbell the blow-by-blow of my near-death experience in October 2011, eighteen months earlier. He listened expressionless throughout, nodding a few times.

"Okay," he said when I was finished. "How do you plan on avoiding the same fate? You might not be as lucky the next time."

"I've been doing a lot of thinking about that and have come up with a process I called C-I-G-S, pronounced 'sigs.'"

Picture the letters C-I-G-S laid out vertically from top to bottom, like this:

C

I

G

S

I'd drawn that acronym, to a great extent, from the lessons of the therapy I'd been undergoing for several years now. I explained to Vaughn and Campbell how it encapsulated the protocol I was going to follow, starting with the lowermost *S* and then working my way up. The *S* stood for Shadows, since initially that's where I'd be. I'd be probing and nothing else, lying low to win their trust without any risk of compromising myself. In the next stage I'd be a Gray Man, *G*, only answering questions or offering information when asked or requested, never volunteering information in a way that made me stand out. Next would come *I*, Interrogative, in which I would not appear as a subject-matter authority, and in that guise would just be asking questions. Then, finally, I'd get to Character, *C*, at which point I could answer questions and display a level of expertise since I would already have won their trust. You only go from the bottom to the top, not the top to the bottom, because that's how you could risk compromising yourself.

I told Vaughn and Campbell that essentially I'd be creating a doppelgänger, a fictional character I could leave at the door when I got home and not take inside to live with the way I had the first time I was operational. I would once again use my own name, Joe Moore, but my primary background would be Special Operations, including being a sniper. I would have trained and staged out of Fort Bragg. This time I would be creating separation between who I was and the role I was playing. I'd be going undercover as Joe Moore in name only to keep the darkness from consuming me again.

I showed them a ball cap I intended to wear when I was working undercover that I'd never wear at home around my family. It was embroidered with an American flag on the bill, and would function as a coping mechanism for me—once I took it off, I'd leave the character I was playing at the door and never bring him inside. By doing that, he'd only be inside me when I was operational. I would be playing a role, as opposed to living it. Vaughn and Campbell thought this approach was brilliant, given how much I had learned from my first infiltration. After all, confidential human sources very seldom get a second chance to practice what they learned the first time. It's almost invariably one and done. I was on the verge of becoming the rare exception.

Eight weeks after that initial phone call from Vaughn, and a month after I'd passed my second FBI background check, Jamie Ward called me back. That in itself told me a lot, regarding the fact that whatever Ward had learned about Wayward in the six weeks since I'd first spoken to him hadn't prevented him from reaching back out to me.

"KIGY, Brother Joe," he said.

He asked me to meet him in a parking lot of a Dollar General store in Bronson, the town where the klavern was based, ninety minutes from St. Augustine.

I decided to change things up a bit at the end of the call. "KLASP, Brother," I said, an acronym for *Klanish Life a Sacred Principle*.

I went wearing a wire once again as the first rung of my protocol ladder, Shadow, the lowest step, there only to listen and absorb information.

This meeting never would have happened if Ward had found out how I'd vanished back in Wayward. The fact he had called me back could only mean my story had checked out, and sure enough, he had learned that William Hawley's chapter of the United Northern and Southern Knights had dissolved because of "prayer activity" that had gone bad. I took that to be the result of the whole incident involving the Hispanic driver I'd offered to take care of. I saw the dissolution of that klavern as an accomplishment, a victory, but I kept my focus entirely on this new group. That said, I knew I was facing the possibility of running into some former members in this new group who remembered me from Wayward, which could pose an immediate problem, if not a crisis.

I met Jamie Ward and three other members of the Traditionalist American Knights in the parking lot. Ward made for an interesting study, an entirely different Klan leader from William Hawley. He was much smaller in stature, around five foot nine, slightly built, and bald, but more than made up for all that in terms of his intelligence and, even more, his ambition. I was six one, was bench pressing four hundred pounds at the time, and made an imposing figure with the experience to back it up. I believe I hit it off with Ward as well as I would because he didn't need to be the toughest or strongest man in the room. Because he would have me riding his shoulder, all he had to be was the smartest, which he normally was, as it turned out.

Ward asked to see my driver's license and another form of ID to make sure I was who I said I was. After they were satisfied, they began asking me questions about my background, and I answered them, but asked none of my own as the Shadow I was determined to be initially. The whole time they interrogated me, I noticed them checking the parking lot for any vehicles that stood out or individuals loitering in the area—either members of the press or law-enforcement officers.

"We have a question for you, Brother Joe," Ward asked me. "Are you willing to be naturalized again?"

"I'd welcome it, Brother Jamie," I said to him.

He exchanged looks with the others and flashed a genuine smile. "We're having a barbecue tonight at my house and would love for you to join us."

"That would be great," I told him.

That evening, I went to the meeting, taking on the next stage of my character and the second rung up the protocol ladder: the Gray Man, intending only to answer questions and provide information when prompted. There were about two dozen men and women present, in contrast to William Hawley's Fourth of July bash, and I quickly realized the barbecue had been scheduled in order to fully vet me before a sampling of the membership. I wore my hat to remind myself of the role I was playing, even though I hadn't reached the Character stage in my CIGS ladder; I hadn't even reached the Interrogative stage yet. I was there only to respond. Jamie Ward brought me over to a man named Mike Christopher, and introduced him as the Grand Dragon of the KKK for Florida and Georgia. Ward also mentioned that Christopher was a member of the Kingsmen motorcycle gang.

Christopher and I spoke under a maple tree as the sun bled from the sky, and I could tell that I had a fan thanks to the resources I could bring to the Klan and this Traditionalist American Knights klavern. He had been a Marine in Vietnam and saw a kindred spirit in the Special Operations background my doppelgänger boasted.

Before he walked away, he slapped me on the back and smiled.

"I look forward to you becoming one of us, Brother Joe," Christopher said, paying the respect due me as a fellow Klansman. "I look forward to working with you."

I made a conscious decision not to be among the first to leave the barbecue, so as not to give those remaining a chance to assess meeting me. I was one of the last to depart and made sure that Mike Christopher left ahead of me so we could say our goodbyes.

Shannon was already asleep when I got home, but I noticed the open box of a pregnancy test kit in the bathroom trash. The indicator was missing, and I couldn't resist waking her up.

"Hey, babe," I said as she stirred, making sure she could see I was holding the empty box in my hand.

"Are you mad?" she asked hesitantly.

"Are you pregnant?"

She nodded, clearly concerned about how I was going to greet the news given how deeply I'd thrown myself into my new role. "Well?"

I hugged her tighter than I ever had. "Oh, my goodness, I hope I can do good by this next life. And I hope it's a girl."

▲   ▲   ▲

My second naturalization ceremony took place in the forest, a beautiful, wooded area in Bronson, shortly after I learned Shannon was pregnant. I couldn't tell whether it was private property. Other than the location, the ceremony was virtually identical to what I'd experienced in Wayward with Charles Denton presiding, right down to having my face covered in a dark pillowcase as I was led down a path and told to kneel. When the pillowcase was removed, I found myself directly in front of a table covered by a cloth with a Bible and sword lying atop it, as well as a large cross inlaid with candles rising before me and manned by the chapter's Grand Knighthawk. One big difference, besides being outside, was that the sword looked a lot shinier and sharper. The other difference was that my heart wasn't racing and I wasn't sweating from anxiety the way I had during my first naturalization ceremony. Not only did I know what to expect this time, I was playing a character instead of playing myself. It was a great test of the strategies and coping mechanisms I'd enacted to avoid losing myself a second time. They were working.

This time, I was naturalized alongside a female member. I thought of the November 2008 murder of Cynthia Lynch, just days after Barack Obama was elected president. She had second thoughts and was ultimately shot to death by a Louisiana Klansman leader named Raymond Charles Foster. Even an old-school klavern like the Traditionalist American Knights was not at all averse to initiating women, but they held lower positions operationally and played different roles than the men. They were also addressed as "Sister."

I took my vows as a Knight in the order of the Ku Klux Klan for the second time, and knew there was no turning back. But I wasn't looking for an out. Throughout the ceremony, I felt confident that going back undercover was the right decision, despite the risks. The men who had sexually assaulted me as a young boy never paid the price for that. My time in the army had ended in unceremonious fashion. And then my first infiltration of the KKK ended abruptly, without the resolution that would have given me closure. This second stint as a confidential human source was my chance to finish what I had started back in 2007 and, more importantly, gave me the opportunity to prove I was the man I knew I was.

I felt the blade of the sword brush against my neck, leaving a sting like razor burn behind.

"Rise, Brother Joe," said Mike Christopher, "and welcome to the Traditionalist American Knights of the Ku Klux Klan."

My knees cracked as I climbed to my feet and Christopher said, "You're now one of us."

CHAPTER 12

KNIGHT FLYER

BRONSON, FLORIDA
SEPTEMBER 2013

My second infiltration of a KKK klavern couldn't have been better timed. I witnessed firsthand the uptick in calls to the 800 number I had dialed. At one point, a few months after my naturalization, Jamie Ward told me he had fielded hundreds of calls in the time since we'd first spoken. He stressed that this was a trend the Klan was seeing nationwide. Of course, relatively few of those who contacted the Traditionalist American Knights became card-carrying members. The Klan tends to be cautious and discriminating when it comes to its membership, viewing itself as far too serious a group in terms of tradition and long-term goals to accept people looking to join a social club. As it turned out, other groups more than willing to take those the Klan had rejected were sprouting and flourishing. Groups like the Oath Keepers, the Proud Boys, the Three Percenters, and others were all well known to the FBI back then, but became household names only in the wake of 2021.

The seeds of what I witnessed as a member of the Traditionalist American Knights had been sown in the elections in 2010, two years after Barack Obama won his first term as president. No fewer than twenty-three right-wing nationalists or white supremacists ran for office that year, and five of them were victorious, a trend that steepened further in the presidential election year of 2012.

The 2012 reelection of President Barack Obama was a rallying cry that reverberated across the white nationalist movement, spearheaded by men like John Abarr, a former Klansman who ran for Montana's single House seat. Like the Traditionalist American Knights I had now infiltrated, those groups saw a second term for the nation's first Black president as an ideal organizing and membership recruitment tool. The Klan and other organizations that had adopted their ideology saw it as the death knell for the hegemony of white men in American society. Time was passing them by, and they had to be ready and willing to fight, lest they risk becoming irrelevant, an afterthought in history. The messaging was the most basic imaginable: It's us versus them, without needing to specify who "them" was.

My early months inside TAK were distinguished by two events. First, I was selected to become one of the klavern's Knighthawks, a key position in security. While William Hawley proudly and publicly proclaimed me to be that chapter's hit man, I had never been elevated in Wayward to such a lofty official position. Clearly, though, Jamie Ward, Mike Christopher, and others saw my doppelgänger's Special Operations background, part of the façade of the character I had created for this infiltration, as rendering me tailor-made for that role.

Appropriately enough, a Knighthawk was like a soldier, responsible for protecting my fellow members when they were at a rally, cross burning, or other so-called prayer event. Knighthawks wore the same robes, only they were black instead of white and were cut to three-quarters of the normal length, ending near the knees to facilitate quick movements if we needed to make them. There were also slots concealed in the sides to facilitate the drawing of our firearms. Generally, Knighthawks provided operational security and, if things got messy, were responsible for cleaning it up.

As a Knighthawk, I was also selected for the role of "Keeper of the Fire" at naturalization and other ceremonies. This told me and my handlers that I was being groomed for bigger things in this chapter and perhaps beyond it, and I worked at further gaining the trust and support of Jamie Ward, just as I had with William Hawley.

I quickly ascertained that Mike Christopher was Grand Dragon of this chapter in name only. Although there was a degree of overlap between the Klan and the bikers, Christopher's membership in the Kingsmen motorcycle gang raised questions about where his primary loyalties lay. In my day-to-day involvement with the Klan, I didn't interact with him much at all. Most everything I did was through Ward and it was becoming abundantly clear to me he had risen to become far more than the chapter's chief recruiter. Ward was running things, and was the one who reported directly to the Imperial Wizard of the Traditionalist American Knights nationwide, Frank Ancona.

The second event was participating in what TAK called Night Rides, during which we'd place a one-page flyer in the mailboxes or on the windshields of local residents in areas deemed to be most sympathetic to the Klan's goals and ideals. Avowed racists made up a considerable part of the population in this part of Florida, and Ward's goal with the Night Flyer campaign was to get them to call the 800 number. An unprecedented membership drive was afoot nationwide. The population ratios were thought to be no different than they had been during the Klan's heyday in the 1920s: for every member, it was believed the organization had somewhere between five and ten sympathizers or supporters, like my in-laws. They were considered de facto foot soldiers, who would be there if push ever came to shove, which made them vital components of the Invisible Empire.

It was around this time that I noticed an uptick in members of the law-enforcement community no longer disguising their allegiance and openly joining, especially prison guards, who in the state of Florida are considered law-enforcement officers. Many were either retired or fired cops seeking to supplement their pensions by serving the community behind fences topped with razor wire. Prison guards were also crucial to making sure Klan members and supporters received favorable treatment on the inside. Their allegiance facilitated the ability to get operational messages passed along and allowed incarcerated Klan members to use cell phones for private calls, instead of waiting in line to make a call on a public phone that was likely being recorded. And if someone on the inside needed to be taken out or punished, that message too would come from a guard, likely delivered to a biker prison gang because of that overlap in membership. When such action was required, perpetrators could do so with impunity, knowing that when the target of the assault reached the infirmary, the guards whose loyalties lay with the Klan would make sure no paperwork was generated, meaning that no investigation would take place.

In the spring of 2014, I accompanied Jamie Ward down to Cocoa Beach, an hour east of Orlando on the Atlantic coast and three hours from Bronson, for a meeting with the Imperial Wizard Frank Ancona, who was vacationing there. Because I was providing security for Ward, I was armed, and because I was working for the FBI, I was wearing a wire.

We met at a Mexican restaurant. Physically, Ancona was, like Ward, an unimpressive man, only five six and stocky, with a thick shock of graying hair. He spoke with a slight Southern accent by way of Missouri, and when Ward and I arrived, he was already seated with his wife. To put it bluntly, the first thing I thought upon meeting her was that she was trailer trash, and she spent much of the meal with her head laid down on the table. She wore heavy makeup, jeans, and a T-shirt, and hardly spoke through the duration of the meal, except to address our server. I remember her raising her head to order her meal, but can't recall whether she ever lifted her head to eat it.

Ancona, meanwhile, was the polar opposite, as jumpy as his wife was withdrawn. At one point early on, I stood up from the table to go to the bathroom and said, "Excuse me, I'll be right back."

I could see Ancona's small, beady eyes sweep about the room and, when I was a few yards away, overheard him say, "Where's he going?"

"To the men's room," I heard Ward reply.

When I got back, their conversation had turned to business, starting with something that definitely grabbed my attention.

"We're about to naturalize a lieutenant from a local police force."

"No shit," Ancona commented. "And he's willing to take the oath?"

"He insists upon it. And his department's full of supporters ready to follow his lead."

"That's what I mean when I talk about all these signs our time is coming, Brother Jamie." He leaned in a bit closer to Ward. "So what's the bad news? There's always something bad we need to address, too, isn't there?"

Ward lowered his voice. He spoke so softly, I wondered if my wire would even be able to pick it up. "We've got a problem with Mike."

"What do you suggest we do about it?"

"Move him out. His head's not in it. He doesn't have the group's respect. Hell, he doesn't even know them."

Ancona started getting fidgety again. "Easier said than done. He's got the Kingsmen backing him up and is on good terms with the Outlaws and the Warlocks gangs for good measure. We don't want to risk spoiling our relationship with those bikers." He paused and resumed in a softer tone, "We're going to need them when the time comes. You know, soldiers."

Ancona was alluding to one of the more interesting facts I observed about the link between the Klan and biker gangs. During my infiltration back in Wayward, I had noted the loose alliance the Klan maintained with the gangs. But in Bronson, I saw the mixing of the Outlaws, Kingsmen, and Warlocks when members of all three biker gangs attended Klan meetings. Biker groups are known for their fierce territoriality, especially when it comes to drug dealing, and have gone to guns over something as simple as being in the same Waffle House at the same time. At Klan meetings, though, the members left their vests—their colors—outside with their bikes. When they walked into the meeting, they walked in as Klansmen, not bikers. When the meeting broke up, they'd don their colors and leave in peace. It made me think that the Klan's anti-government goals were probably the only thing this unholy trinity had in common. And thanks to the KKK, these same meetings were attended by members of the law-enforcement community who might have otherwise been arresting the very bikers they were now aligned with.

"I'm only saying we've got a problem in Bronson," Ward reiterated, leaning back in his chair and crossing his arms. "I'm here to tell you the problem's there and it needs to be addressed."

"And you'd be the logical choice to replace him, of course," Ancona said matter-of-factly.

"I'm already running things up there and both of us know it, and so do the rest of the members." Ward looked toward me. "Isn't that right, Joe?"

Ancona looked at me, too, while his wife remained facedown on the table as if she were taking a nap. I knew that my military service—my doppelgänger's, that is—had impressed him. There was enough truth to my story not to doubt the parts I had invented for the role I was playing when I put on that ball cap. And even if he had wanted to, Ancona couldn't check on my background in Special Operations because that information would have been classified at the highest levels.

"Brother Joe," he said, "you have thoughts on this matter?"

"I do, sir," I said, consciously addressing him in a way that made me appear subordinate. "I have observed the way the members relate to Brother Jamie, and how he relates to them, and there's no doubt in my mind he has their respect and they look to him as our leader."

Again, I used "our."

Ancona nodded, weighing his options. "Well, we can't move Christopher out, but we could move him up."

"To what?" Ward asked.

"I don't know. We'll make something up. Make him feel like it's a promotion. Exalted something or other—that ought to do the trick."

Ancona's wife still had her face pressed against the table. I wondered if she was still breathing.

"You know, Brother Jamie," Ancona added, "I'm glad we're having this discussion now, because you know what's coming up."

Ward nodded. "The Klan's hundred and fiftieth anniversary."

Ancona said, "In 2015, dating all the way back to our founding in 1865. I tell you, this Obama has been a godsend to us. Gives us all the motivation we need to make the move that's long been in the making. We can do this—we can replace the current government and take this country over, but we can't do it on the backs of men like Mike Christopher. We need to rely on men like you"—then his gaze turned on me—"and Joe here, men with conviction and the skills to back it up. As I'm sure you've observed, Brother Joe, we've managed to get people positioned throughout all levels of local and state government, for starters."

"Yes, sir, I have."

I had indeed. When I bought that 1989 Jeep Cherokee from Brother Brown in the fall of 2009, he brought me to the Department of Motor Vehicles himself. The line at the DMV was a hundred people long, the wait at least three hours. But we skipped the line and his Klan contact there had me in and out in less than ten minutes. What I'd witnessed in my two infiltrations made me wonder who else the Klan had placed in positions of authority and power. To hear Frank Ancona and Jamie Ward describe it, they had people scattered through all levels of municipal, local, and state governments across the country, concentrated primarily in the South, while maintaining a perfunctory presence in the North thus far. Other members were being elected to public office with increasing frequency, and more were becoming managers for any number of municipalities. These made up a great portion of the Invisible Empire the Klan would be relying on to replace the sitting government when the time came. The members had created an infrastructure that men like Frank Ancona believed could be imposed upon the nation as a whole.

More than anything, that's what separated the KKK from militia groups whose stated desire was to foment insurrection for its own sake, with no knowledge of what might replace the government they intended to overthrow. In that respect, the Klan had evolved from an organization based almost purely on racism to one dominated by ultranationalist desires that made its dogma very appealing to the Christian far right, which was heavily composed of evangelicals. They saw in Klan orthodoxy the same principles they believed in and adhered to.

"I want to make this hundred and fiftieth anniversary into a rallying cry," Ancona continued. "I want to take this opportunity to turn it into the moment the Invisible Empire emerges from the shadows and takes over."

That was a reasonable projection, given the increasing number of Klan supporters and sympathizers, especially in the wake of Obama's election and reelection. When the time was right, the Klan believed they could rely on these people to rally to their side in establishing a new governmental bureaucracy that would cater to the organization's priorities.

"We need a symbol," Ancona resumed, "something that demonstrates just how much this country is headed in the wrong direction. A kick in the ass to tell good people the likes of us that it's time to kick some ass, that things have gone far enough. Obama helped us get the fuse lit, but it's still going to take something more to trigger the explosion."

Little did the three of us know that the "something more" was coming, just months down the road, in the summer of 2014.

CHAPTER 13

FERGUSON

On August 9, 2014, an eighteen-year-old Black man named Michael Brown was shot six times and killed by white police officer Darren Wilson in Ferguson, Missouri, a suburb of St. Louis. Multiple witnesses disputed Wilson's account of the shooting, generally accusing him of killing Brown in cold blood. Insult was added to injury when the victim and his family suffered the further ignominy of having his body left steaming on the hot summer street in full view of passersby for hours before it was taken away.

The community exploded, and the protests quickly spread nationwide in an early harbinger of the Black Lives Matter movement that sent protesters both white and Black into the streets. More progressively minded folks viewed the killing as a rallying cry against the brutality dispensed by almost exclusively white cops assigned to Black areas. The Ku Klux Klan, particularly the Traditionalist American Knights, viewed it as something entirely different: an opportunity.

My own history was diametrically opposed to Klan dogma when it came to race. I attended a junior high school in Florida where white people were in the extreme minority; I even had an English class in which I was the only white person. And my classmates couldn't have treated me better. It made me think about the difference between how Black kids treat a white boy and how white kids treat a Black kid. If the numbers had been reversed, I imagine the class would have had more than its share of racists, like Shannon's stepfather, Rusty, to terrorize that poor kid. As the only white kid on the football team, I well remember that a street gang called the Heights Crew—named after the town of Washington Heights—told my teammates to make sure they looked after me, to treat me with respect and make sure I wasn't ostracized. The team did that and more. And we won a lot of football games, even at away games against predominately white schools, which inevitably featured referees determined to make sure we didn't win.

This experience had broad implications for me in my position inside the Klan, but it also had implications for me as a father. In April, just four months before Ferguson, Shannon had given birth to our daughter, Tia. As with Jordy, Tia was delivered via cesarean section and I was present through the entire process. I almost had to restrain myself from helping the doctor get that baby out. Tears of joy ran down my face. I thought of the purity and innocence of the world she represented, compared to the monsters that were out there. And the fact that she was so small made them seem bigger. I had to dig deeper within myself, because now I had three people I was responsible for. I could either stay home and try to build fences around them, or I could go out and get the monsters who might someday threaten their way of life.

I chose the latter. I now had firsthand knowledge of how dangerous the far right, white nationalist movement was becoming and how fast it was gaining steam. And like a boulder rolling downhill, I wasn't sure if anything was going to be able to stop it. The rise in membership, activity, and resolve that I had a front-row seat for left me wondering just how powerful these groups might become and what kind of world my newborn daughter was going to grow up in.

In that hospital room, though, I could step away from the rest of the world and all the sordidness I had been exposed to. It was just me, my wife, and our newborn child. For the moment, anyway, nothing else mattered.

Just hours after Tia was born, I got a call from Rich Vaughn, asking me to meet him in the hospital lobby. I found him standing there with Lindsay Campbell.

"Congratulations, Joe," Vaughn said.

Then he handed me an envelope with four thousand dollars in cash inside. He and Campbell had already turned and left by the time I looked up to thank them.

Shortly before the events in Ferguson, Jamie Ward had asked to meet with me at a biker bar in Bronson that had once been a convenience store. The 7-Eleven signage was long gone, but the outline of the logo remained imprinted on the front of the building. Inside, a jukebox in the corner played selections for a quarter from CDs instead of those old 45 rpms. In the month or so since we'd met with Frank Ancona in Cocoa Beach, Mike Christopher had indeed been "promoted" to a supervisory position called Grand Giant—which was something like giving retired academics the "emeritus" title. That made way for Ward to take over the entire KKK in Florida and Georgia.

"Brother Joe, are you aware of what happened to Brother John?" he asked me, referring to the TAK member who was the Grand Knighthawk overseeing both states and under whom I technically served.

"I'm not familiar with that, no, sir."

"He pulled a gun on some Black guys who tried to rob him."

I later learned Brother John had taken the wrong route after making a cash pickup, putting him in harm's way and practically inviting the perpetrators to accost him, having not properly observed operational security.

"He's being held in jail and not likely to get out anytime soon, given his record. I don't have to tell you what a vital position this is."

Ward was no stranger to arrest and incarceration. He'd been a nurse in a previous life and was arrested for possession of crystal meth. He was convicted and jailed, only to flee probation upon his release in Georgia. He had been living on the lam in Florida ever since, clever and intelligent enough to avoid all law enforcement other than those beholden to the Klan, who vowed to have his back. He was working at a factory under his real name, making no effort to further disguise himself because he believed the support of the local police and community insulated him from being arrested by Georgia officials on that probation violation and returned to prison.

Beyond that, though, Ward was also intelligent and disciplined. In the months that I had known him, I noticed that even though he was confident he'd remain a free man, he was extremely careful about where he showed himself socially, and he never allowed himself to be photographed for fear that even a single social media posting might jeopardize his freedom. This was a man who was overseeing all TAK chapters in two of the group's most popular states. And he could walk into a high-level Klan strategy meeting as comfortably as he could into the headquarters of a biker gang.

"No, Brother Jamie, you don't," I said, in response to Ward's statement.

"Brother Joe, I'd like to know if you're interested in the job."

I had already gotten the sense in my meetings with Rich Vaughn and Lindsay Campbell, as well as Joe Armstrong in my first infiltration, that I had gotten deeper into the KKK than any previous informant by far. But what Ward was offering promised to take that achievement to a whole new level, assuming that the Grand Knighthawk position meant I'd be involved operationally in all prayer meetings and prayer actions. I'd also be interacting with Klan leaders throughout Florida and Georgia, not just one chapter, and would have access to the databases that the klaverns in both states maintained of their membership rosters on Frank Ancona's private server.

My relationship with Ward, coupled with the background I was using, made me the ideal successor for the job. From an intelligence and psychological standpoint, I felt that men like Ward—who are long on intelligence but short in stature and strength—gravitate to others who are physically imposing, to make up for their shortcomings. It was almost as if, in my presence anyway, Ward could be imposing too. Maybe not physically, but with me as backup, he didn't have to be. And since I had been trained in protective skills in the army, I knew how to behave like a bodyguard.

In addition to being in jail, my predecessor was a known hothead, and there were already rumblings afoot that Ward intended to replace him, since he was a holdover from Mike Christopher's time as Grand Dragon.

I didn't want to appear too eager, afraid of raising any suspicions, so I asked for twenty-four hours to think about it. Attaining such a lofty position would allow me into the innermost sanctum of the KKK's organizational structure and decision-making process, because I'd be in the room when a lot of those decisions were made and planning was undertaken for their fulfillment.

I drove home, excited by the prospects but apprehensive about taking on greater responsibility, which meant being exposed to greater danger. And that turned my thoughts toward my family. I had a newborn daughter at home and my son was going on six. I took off the ball cap I used to get into character and put it on the passenger seat. Then I switched on some calming New Age music, which didn't calm me at all.

Two days later, I met with Campbell and Vaughn in the Jacksonville field office. When I drove there, I was always cognizant of potential tails and utilized what were called surveillance detection routes, or SDR. I'd purposely drive in circles or take odd turns in order to spot anyone who might be following. I had yet to detect any tails in my time with TAK, but I had been forced to abort several meetings back in Wayward when I suspected I was being followed.

No one followed me on this day, but I was extra careful for obvious reasons, given that Ward had every reason to keep a closer eye on me.

Inside the building, Vaughn and Campbell were gobsmacked by my report. I'd been wearing a wire, so they'd be able to hear it all for themselves in good time. Meanwhile, I couldn't make such a move in the organization without their approval. I was serving up promotions for them on a silver platter and both of them knew it. They made a point of telling me in that meeting that my work had been reported up to the "highest levels" of the FBI. They used that phrase several times, and I took it to mean my performance as a confidential human source had reached Director James Comey himself.

They approved me accepting the role of Grand Knighthawk on the spot. This would be a major coup for both the Bureau and the JTTF, given that my new position was about as high up as it gets; after Jamie Ward, the only KKK officials technically over me were the Imperial Wizard, Frank Ancona, and the national Imperial Knighthawk, Brother Fox.

My roles would be many and diverse, from directing security at major prayer events, to delivering messages in person (since the Klan did not trust electronic communications), to overseeing Knighthawks throughout Florida and Georgia, to delivering both drugs and money to the appropriate parties. Additionally, the notion that I had access to the membership rolls for the entire region left the FBI salivating.

In Wayward, I'd learned how little the Bureau actually knew about the inner workings of the Klan and its membership—they hadn't even known William Hawley was the Grand Dragon, or that his klavern was part of the United Northern and Southern Knights until I told them. In Bronson, I was about to assume a position that would allow me to gather intelligence far beyond anything I'd achieved in that first infiltration and beyond anything any confidential human source had ever produced from inside the KKK.

Before I officially stepped into my new role, I had to pass a second written Klan test. I'd passed my initial one-hundred-question exam, dealing with the basic tenets of the KKK, before my naturalization ceremony in 2013. The second one was more elaborate, dealing with Klan history and tradecraft to demonstrate my mastery of the Kloran, essentially the Klan bible, to move up from the organization's K-uno level to K-duo, which was reserved only for imperial and grand positions. Vaughn and Campbell couldn't believe the jump in rank I'd made.

I officially assumed the position of Grand Knighthawk right around the time of Michael Brown's murder.

Not long after I accepted Ward's offer, we paid an unannounced visit to the Outlaws biker gang at their headquarters in a gutted home converted into a clubhouse that sat on five acres overgrown with weeds, brush, and poison ivy. We had come there to settle some business that could have turned unpleasant in a hurry. We exited our vehicle, and Ward noticed a big AR-15 target had been set up at a twenty-five-yard distance; it looked more fit for an archery range.

"Is that any good?" he asked me, sounding a bit intimidated.

"It's crap," I told him, surveying the spray of holes. "At that distance, the target should be the size of a bull's-eye and no bigger than that."

Ward nodded. My assessment seemed to reassure him and strengthen his resolve to complete the business we'd come here for. We were escorted inside and treated as VIPs by the gang's members. Ward was reasonable but tough, leaving no room for negotiation, while I stood between the meeting room and a smoothly finished hardwood bar, scanning the area, secure in the notion I could take everyone out if it came to that. The looks on the faces of the bikers told me they'd come to the same conclusion and weren't about to make any sudden moves.

One of the first things I learned in my position of Grand Knighthawk was how much overlap had begun to take place between the Klan and various militia-style groups, namely the Oath Keepers and Three Percenters, along with several smaller militias (the Proud Boys hadn't established themselves as a force yet). A number of my duties involved ferrying written messages back and forth between the leaders of these groups and Jamie Ward. Acting in that capacity, I learned that Mike Christopher, in his role as Grand Giant, was actively recruiting these militias to adopt Klan orthodoxy and ideology, essentially becoming its foot soldiers so the KKK could remain the Invisible Empire.

The Klan took the "Invisible" part seriously. It had never viewed itself as the engine that would overthrow the United States government. Rather, its foot soldiers, comprised of members of these militias united on a nationwide scale, would handle the heavy lifting, allowing the Klan to emerge from the chaos and anarchy to restore much-needed order by imposing its existing infrastructure on an unsuspecting nation. The organization believed itself to be fully capable of moving in to take over the workings of government in a seamless fashion.

That's why the shooting of Michael Brown by a white police officer in Ferguson, Missouri, in August 2014, for reasons disputed by practically every eyewitness, became the rallying cry Frank Ancona had said was needed for the Klan to take things to the next level.

At that early dinner in Cocoa Beach in April, Ancona had ruminated thoughtfully about the realities of American society and culture he intended to exploit.

"Thirty percent of the country, actually, has always been behind us, when you count everyone," he expounded at one point. "Isn't that right, Brother Jamie?"

"It is, Brother Frank."

"It was that way in the wake of the Civil War, it was that way during the 1920s, it was that way again in the 1940s, and it's even more that way now as we approach our hundred and fiftieth anniversary. Those thirty percent are on our side, but we've never been able to unify them behind a single vision, a single mission. Obama changed all that to a great extent. Now, we need one more thing to bring those people home. Not sure what that is, but I'll know it when I see it."

And Ancona saw it in the wake of Ferguson and mobilized Klan members to the scene of the riots that flared after Michael Brown's murder, while gleefully watching those riots spread across the country. In addition to the Klansmen who took to the streets on the pretext of protecting ordinary citizens, as well as their homes and businesses, Ancona spearheaded a massive Night Flyer campaign in which the following flyer was distributed throughout suburban St. Louis and within the city itself:

The message above was abundantly clear and meant as a rallying cry to draw people to the Klan cause by showcasing the organization as true white knights riding to the rescue of a frightened populace that had no one else to turn to.

Attention: To the terrorists masquerading as "peaceful protestors"! You have awakened a sleeping giant. The good people of St. Louis County of all races, colors, and creeds will not tolerate your threats of violence against our police officers, their families, and our communities. We will not sit by and allow you to harm our families, communities, property nor disrupt our daily lives.

Your right to freedom of the speech does not give you the right to terrorize citizens.

Ancona's vision had basically flipped the paradigm, casting the almost exclusively peaceful protesters as the terrorists and the Klan as the saviors of an orderly society on the brink of descending into chaos. This was made even more ironic by how many national law-enforcement reports by the FBI and others had classified the Klan as a terrorist organization. The tail, so to speak, had begun to wag the dog.

Ancona would appear on any TV news show that would have him and any newspaper or magazine that would interview him to explain the purpose of distributing the flyers and espouse anything that might further his cause. I remember being alerted to an appearance he was making on Chris Hayes's *All In*, which aired on MSNBC on November 12, 2014, and tuned in just as he was being introduced.

"It's interesting that people who are making these terroristic threats don't seem to know that the people of Missouri, they have rights to the guaranteed constitution, a particular law," he said, looking bigger to me on television than he had in person, the stress lines on his face and forehead dramatically evident because he had not donned any makeup. "And it's basically educating them on that law. What their options are because a lot of people seem to not want to live in fear. They don't have to sit back and wait for somebody to throw a Molotov cocktail."

To hear Ancona tell it, the Klan was the only thing standing between people's families, homes, and businesses, and the mob. Support us, join with us, or risk everything you've built being destroyed. To that point, in the wake of Ferguson, armed Klan members mobilized to protect neighborhoods and area businesses from the burning and looting. The more the news was dominated by the spread of the rioting across the country, the more the ideology of the Klan seeped into the lives of everyday Americans who were scared and felt they had no one else to turn to. It didn't matter much to Ancona whether those who bought into his vision rushed to join the Klan or one of the various militia groups that were enjoying an even greater uptick in member sign-ups, because he saw them as the same thing, a single entity with a common purpose. If the election of Barack Obama had lit the fuse, then Ferguson was the powder keg that fuse had ignited. And something else lay in the offing that would threaten to make Ancona's pronouncement a self-fulfilling prophecy.

Something called the "Ferguson effect."

CHAPTER 14

POWDER KEG

ST. LOUIS

NOVEMBER 2014

That fall and early winter, I continued monitoring all the St. Louis–area media. I was especially struck by an article in the *Riverfront Times* that also ran in November 2014.

"Missouri is definitely on fire right now," Frank Ancona told the reporter. "These Ferguson protesters are the best recruiters since Obama. Normally we might hear from ten people a week in Missouri, and now we're hearing from more like fifty people a week. Sometimes, depending on these news stories, we get one hundred, two hundred calls in a day."

For the Klan, "Ferguson" became a brand in much the same ignominious way Charlottesville came to symbolize something much more than what had occurred in a single moment in time during the summer of 2017. And thanks to the Ferguson effect, the trend spread beyond Missouri. Defined as an increase in violent crime and general lawlessness due to reduced policing spurred by communities losing faith in law enforcement, the merits of that argument can be disputed, but not its overall effects. Regardless of the reality, perception was winning out, much to the Klan's delight, thanks to a quantifiable trend that surfaced over the course of the next two years.

"The 56 largest cities saw 17 percent more homicides in 2015 than in 2014—and in 10 of those cities, homicides were up by more than 60 percent," *Vox* reported in May 2016.

> *For people who've been following the debate around police-community relations in America, though, this isn't a surprise. For the past year, defenders of police have been raising the specter of the "Ferguson effect": the theory that protests against police shootings and brutality have made police afraid of doing what they need to do to keep communities safe, which has led to a rise in violent crime. The biggest proponents of the Ferguson effect are conservatives like Heather MacDonald (whose new book on the subject is literally called The War on Cops). But even FBI Director James Comey has put forward a version of the theory (to the administration's chagrin). And while criminologists were originally skeptical, some of them—including one who's doing an analysis for the Department of Justice—are beginning to believe there's more to the theory than originally thought.*

The point is that Ferguson became the catalyst that leaders like Frank Ancona and Jamie Ward had been thirsting for to spearhead their efforts to further their Unite the Right movement.

America seemed to be changing right before our eyes, and the Klan leaders loved what they saw.

As Grand Knighthawk, I was on standby to deploy to Ferguson into the fall of 2014 and had my go bag all packed in anticipation of getting the call. It never came, but I was able to observe plenty in the aftermath that, at the very least, suggested the country could be facing another Klan surge, as in the 1920s, or a white nationalist uprising, as in the 1940s. There were all sorts of Dixie mafia types, rednecks, and Sisters of the Confederacy members whom recruitment efforts openly targeted; if a Klansman walked down a residential street in the suburbs of St. Louis and saw someone hanging a Confederate or yellow Gadsden flag, they'd leave them a flyer or even knock on the door to introduce themselves. Only this time, the perpetrators would be better organized, armed, and committed than previous opportunities permitted, in large part because the Invisible Empire was starting to become more visible, thanks to the likes of Frank Ancona.

White nationalists, as personified by the KKK and other like-minded organizations, want to exploit the often repressed sociological and racial views held by more Americans than we would like to believe. Because I was often tasked with delivering messages back and forth between the Klan and militia groups like the Oath Keepers and the Three Percenters, I became personally familiar with the fact that the overlap in membership between those organizations and the Klan was growing. By the end of 2014, it reached the point where I'd say one third of all TAK members were also members of another similar organization. This was being encouraged at the highest levels of the Klan nationwide, as a means to unite the right around a common purpose. And the more KKK members became part of these militia groups, the more these militia groups would follow the KKK's long-established ideology.

Compelling these organizations to integrate with one another was one of the primary differences in the Klan from my first infiltration to my second. The Klan was actually returning to its roots and the convictions that had spawned its founding.

In 1867, two years after the Klan was founded, Edward Pollard, an editor at a Richmond, Virginia, newspaper, published a book called *The Lost Cause*. Pollard's work sought to reframe the Civil War through a lens of revisionist history. The book was treated like the Bible by unrepentant Southerners whose hearts and minds had never left the battlefield. They might have abandoned their rifles, but not the beliefs that had led them to pick up those arms in the first place. At the time, the South was riddled with illiteracy, which had been exacerbated by the closing of many schools during the war. So when *The Lost Cause* was published, almost none of the followers of the doctrine it espoused could actually read it and were rallied based on secondhand summaries that highlighted only the most divisive issues. Pollard served them up a smorgasbord of rationales to keep them clinging to their principles. He believed that although the war had inarguably been lost, the cause had not. The South may have been defeated, but they could still continue to fight a greater war of ideas, creating the groundswell that allowed the ideology to be perpetuated into the next century, carried there by the Klan after it had been spawned by that very ideology.

In 2014, the Klan was fighting a war of ideas, too, but those ideas were changing, at least on the surface, in order to win that war. That said, the Traditionalist American Knights still had standards for membership, which they took seriously. Take, for example, Johnny Grant, who came over to TAK from the Loyal White Knights, a klavern that lacked affiliation with any of the five major subgroups comprising the KKK nationwide. Grant and two others, David Moran and Charles Newcomb, switched allegiance because they were looking for a more "active" and traditional group. Early on, though, it became clear why the national organization had no interest in incorporating the Loyal White Knights into its infrastructure, especially in Grant's case. He was a loudmouth, prone to spouting off especially when he was drinking, and was especially fluent with the N-word. This in particular got under my skin because under no circumstances would I ever consider using that word, in order to preserve my own humanity. It was one of the lines I just wouldn't cross because of the moral consequences I might face. I could take my hat off at the door, but could never take that word back once uttered.

One night in early January, Johnny Grant, a scrawny, stringy-haired caricature of a wannabe Klansman, was drinking with his girlfriend, Ruby, in a biker bar frequented by the Kingsmen. He had a few too many beers and began boasting to a few of the members about his affiliation with a local chapter of the KKK, through which he'd learned of Grand Giant Mike Christopher being a member of the Kingsmen. He was overhead committing this utter breach of protocol by the Kingsmen's designated assassin, a man named Andre Jenkins. Jenkins was nicknamed "Bear" because he was the size of an NFL lineman and just about as strong, with any number of killings attributed to him on the gang's behalf.

Jenkins's original plan was to dispense punishment that very night, by inviting Grant and his girlfriend to a "private party," where blood would be spilled instead of drinks. Ruby grew immediately suspicious, and instead of heading to the address Jenkins had provided, she and Grant hightailed it out of the parking lot and counted their blessings. When Jenkins realized they'd fled, he contacted Christopher to inform him of Grant's transgression and offered to break several parts of his body . . . or worse. Christopher told him to hold off and contacted Jamie Ward.

The Kingsmen's leader, also a Klan member at the time, was an ex-cop named Bob Bargar, whom I had met multiple times. A week after Grant's run-in with Jenkins, Ward asked me to meet with Bargar. We set aside our usual occasional squabbles between the biker gang and the Klan to settle on the plan that I would handle Johnny Grant, promising Ward and Christopher that they'd never need to worry about him again. For his part, Bargar agreed to send Andre Jenkins on another assignment in upstate New York to take out some rogue Kingsmen who were skimming cash and drugs from the gang's association with a smuggling organization that brought drugs over from Canada. This was an even more serious transgression than what Grant was being targeted for, and one that called for Jenkins's particular area of expertise. While he headed to New York, I contacted the FBI to inform Vaughn and Campbell about both Grant and Jenkins.

They weren't able to intercept Andre Jenkins before he executed the two Kingsmen gang members behind the gang's North Tonawanda chapter clubhouse, but their efforts did help result in his arrest in Georgia, while he was making the return trip on his distinctive yellow Harley. He was convicted of first-degree murder and two counts of second-degree murder. Jenkins was sentenced to life in prison, while the Bureau managed to get Johnny Grant resettled in another state, solving that problem a different way and saving me from ending up with blood on my hands.

In contrast to the way that problem was handled, I recall a situation from the same period, the late summer of 2014, with Brother Merle, one of the TAK Knighthawks who served under me. He was having dinner with his family one evening when his sister announced to everyone that she was gay. Keeping with protocol, Brother Merle reported this to Jamie Ward and was presented with a choice: he had to either renounce his sister or leave the Klan. He chose the latter and was forced to return all his Klan material, including his robes. He had experienced an epiphany and decided he would follow a path of love, rather than hate.

We did meet to discuss Brother Merle's fate, and some at the meeting were adamant that his level of knowledge about the Klan's inner workings made him too dangerous to leave alive. Ultimately, though, it was decided that taking any action against him was contrary to the recruitment activities we had going on. They had become even more important than enforcing Klan orthodoxy on a former member to make sure he never betrayed the brotherhood. A man like William Hawley would have beaten Brother Merle senseless, but the priorities of the KKK were changing. I sat in on a meeting with Frank Ancona, Jamie Ward, and Brother Fox, the Imperial Knighthawk, where active recruitment and uniting the right were not just the highest priorities we discussed, they were the only priorities. This was happening years ahead of the Unite the Right rally in Charlottesville and the January 6 insurrection. At the time, I reported my observations directly to Vaughn and Campbell, who included it in their FBI FD-1023 forms that helped establish the content for several internal FBI reports and memos on the growing dangers of right-wing extremism and that spawned a number of tangential investigations.

One of the confidential memos, based in large part on information I had provided back in 2014 and 2015, was obtained by ABC News in March 2021. "Based on investigations between 2016 and 2020," the network reported,

> agents and analysts with the FBI's division in San Antonio concluded that white supremacists and other right-wing extremists would "very likely seek affiliation with military and law enforcement entities in furtherance of their ideologies," according to a confidential intelligence assessment issued late last month. "In the long term, FBI San Antonio assesses [racially motivated violent

extremists] successfully entering military and law enforcement careers almost certainly will gain access to non-public tradecraft and information, enabling them to enhance operational security and develop new tactics in and beyond the FBI San Antonio region," the document said.

I was a firsthand witness to this. It wasn't just that the Klan was actively recruiting inside the military and, especially, law enforcement; Klan members were actually joining both with an eye toward infiltrating them. All five subgroups of the KKK, on the verge of its 150th anniversary in 2015, could afford to wait a little longer. In addition to TAK, those groups included the United Northern and Southern Knights, the American White Knights, the Brotherhood of Klans, and the Imperial Klans of America, any of which may well have been the subject for that FBI report. A San Antonio–based klavern, for example, would most likely have been part of either TAK or the United Northern and Southern Knights. (Some of these groups maintain chapters in Europe, Canada, and Australia as well.)

The Klan was unique among white nationalist groups not only for its long history but also for its staid infrastructure that allowed it to organize on a national level, instead of in a more disjointed way. The five chapters were in communication with one another and met in person at national conferences and prayer activities. And though I wasn't privy to the kind of meetings Ancona would have attended in his capacity as an Imperial Wizard, he would often relay goals and directives to Jamie Ward, in my presence, that were clearly the result of nationwide strategy sessions among the subgroups. Training and coordination among them were steadily increasing, and with that, the assimilation of other like-minded groups like the militias Mike Christopher was openly trying to bring into the fold.

In early 2015, Ancona issued a new directive to attract more Black and brown members to the Klan. Part of this was misdirection stemming from the penchant of the KKK to disguise its priorities and actual goals, since nothing would have pleased Ancona and the other Imperial Wizards more than to see the Ferguson race riots continue to spread across the country and become more violent. Indeed, while the Klan was trying to bring in more minority members, at the same time it was circulating subversive videos—like a Black man chasing an old white lady out of a grocery store—across social media that had nothing to do with Ferguson or any race riot.

In the Klan's mind, who else would traditional white America turn to for protection and help when they had to board up their homes and businesses? Who else was out there promising to keep their families safe? In Ancona's mind, getting that 30 percent of the country he believed was there for the taking into the Klan fold was now an achievable goal.

Something, though, was about to get in the way of all that, leading to a precipitous downfall nobody—not me, and definitely not Ancona—saw coming.

CHAPTER 15

HOT TIN ROOF

Johnny Grant was out of the picture, but the other two Loyal White Knights with whom he was naturalized into the Traditionalist American Knights were coming into sharper and sharper focus. I'd met both of them at their naturalization ceremonies in early 2014. In my capacity as Grand Knighthawk, I was also Keeper of the Fire, which meant it was my responsibility to don an ornamental black glove and light the fire that had been a staple of the Klan naturalization ceremony since its founding.

The first, David Moran, was a prison guard at the Florida state prison known as Raiford, after the town in which it was located. Interestingly enough, Moran was Native American, a member of the United Houma Nation hailing from Terrebonne Parish in Louisiana—a tribe that actually fought for the Confederacy during the Civil War. In the war's wake, the tribe wasn't disbanded, like the rest of the Confederate units, or resettled, like the vast majority of Native American tribes of that era. So in that respect, the Klan and die-hard contemporary Confederates consider the Houma tribe as the last remaining active Civil War unit; at least, that is the KKK's perspective.

That would have been enough on its own to warrant membership for Moran, even though he was not white. But Moran also served as a perfect example of the KKK's desire to rebrand itself as more of a political organization and less of a racist one. Virtually from 1865 right to Barack Obama's election, the Klan's very existence has been based pretty much solely on a hatred of Black people, along with other minority groups, like Jews and Hispanics, to a lesser extent.

The overarching goal to unite the right, though, had increasingly led the organization to make a conscious effort to abandon their racist roots in favor of their anti-government ideology and recruit more minorities into the ranks. Moran was a poster child for that trend.

Across the country, the idea of a "new Klan" came to light. In 2014, John Abarr, a top-ranked recruiting officer for the KKK, started a new klavern in Montana called the Rocky Mountain Knights. Abarr claimed it would be all-inclusive, reformed, and no longer discriminate against anyone because of race, sexual orientation, or religion. Abarr reportedly said of his new organization, "The KKK is for a strong America. White supremacy is the old Klan. This is the new Klan."

Unlike Moran, the second new TAK member, Charles Newcomb, was unabashedly old Klan. He'd been a patrol cop in Tennessee until, he boasted, he was fired for excessive violence around a decade before, which by his own admission ended his career in that part of law enforcement. From Tennessee, he moved to a town called Keystone Heights, in the Bronson area, and joined the Klan, while also getting a job as a prison guard at Raiford—where he'd met Moran and brought him into the Loyal White Knights around three years before. That group, though, held almost all their meetings online and never committed to the kind of prayer meetings and prayer events that had led Newcomb to join the Klan in the first place—out of a desire not only to, quite literally, see the country burn, but be one of those holding the match.

So Newcomb switched his allegiance to the TAK, and Jamie Ward was all too happy to have him. It's a fairly common occurrence and consists of nothing more than a Klansman informing his former group that he's being naturalized into a new klavern. Ward let Newcomb retain the Exalted Cyclops (klavern leader) title he held in the Loyal White Knights, and allowed him to serve as the Bronson chapter's de facto mayor while Ward remained governor, freeing him to focus his efforts on running all TAK chapters through Florida and Georgia, as well as coordinating his efforts more with the national organization under Imperial Wizard Frank Ancona.

Interestingly enough, if the FBI knew any more about Newcomb than what I had told them, they didn't share it with me. I assumed they didn't want any preconceived notions to interfere with my path of fact-finding. While that's entirely different from what they would have done with an active agent as opposed to a confidential human source, it allowed me a blank slate with which to work, while also exposing me to more potentially dangerous situations for lack of background information.

Newcomb was five foot six but thick with muscle, cutting a raw-boned figure, with oversize cheekbones and piercing blue eyes that never seemed to blink. He was the kind of guy whose shorter stature made you look down upon him, but at your peril. He had a thick neck and short hair that was graying on the sides. When I first met him at his naturalization ceremony, it was impossible not to compare him to William Hawley—except Newcomb immediately impressed me as being considerably more dangerous. Hawley might have been a Klansman first, but he was also a respected member of the Wayward community, in large part because of his affiliation. Although he had helped organize an assassination attempt on then candidate Barack Obama and okayed the revenge murder of a Hispanic truck driver, I never observed him commit violence himself with the exception of that man he beat up in the woods shortly before my naturalization ceremony. And Hawley was as comfortable running prayer meetings as he was hosting his annual Summer Bash.

But from the first time I met Newcomb, I couldn't envision him doing anything of the sort. His capacity for violence was exemplified by a harsh stare that he'd once used to challenge prisoners under his authority when he'd worked as a correctional officer, and I pegged him as the kind of stone-cold killer often labeled a psychopath. After a few more encounters with Newcomb between his naturalization and December 2014, I was convinced that he lacked any semblance of a conscience and saw people who didn't share his skin color as members of a substandard race no better than insects to be crushed under his boot if the opportunity came about.

Nine months after Newcomb's and Moran's own naturalization ceremony, they recruited Thomas Driver, another Raiford prison guard, into the TAK fold. I was away on Klan business, delivering messages between Jamie Ward and the trio of motorcycle gangs, during Driver's naturalization ceremony two weeks after his recruitment, which I otherwise would have helped preside over as Grand Knighthawk and Keeper of the Fire.

Moran and Newcomb were actively soliciting new members from inside the law-enforcement system, and Driver was the first they'd brought in. Without making too much fuss about it, I spoke to some klavern members who had championed his membership about the kind of man he was. According to them, Driver feasted on abusing the weakest inmates—those not affiliated with any gang that might have offered protection. And I was about to hear his story firsthand.

The klavern held a cross burning—a regularly scheduled event staged as a rationale to bring the members of the klavern together for a common purpose—a few weeks before Christmas in 2014. It was for naturalized members only, all outfitted in the white robes that defined Klan regalia. I would be presiding over security that evening and drove out to the site in north Florida thinking of all the Christmas shopping I still had to do. It comforted me to think about pleasant, mundane tasks because that grounded me in the man I really was and reminded me that the reason I had committed myself to this role was so simple traditions like that could be preserved.

I roamed the outskirts of the crowd, alert for trouble of any kind. The Outlaws motorcycle gang had men posted around the perimeter for operational security under my supervision. Only gang members who similarly belonged to the Klan were allowed to participate in the event; the rest of the gang were considered to be "ghouls," the label given to the nonnaturalized who provide material support for the organization. Very few, if any, of these men were considered to have enough character to become members, but they had plenty enough of it to work security. Among them that night was Charles Newcomb's personal bodyguard, Jim Heart, who doubled as a Klan ghoul. Like Moran, he was a Native American from the same Houma tribe in Louisiana. Though small in stature, only five foot four, he was known to have an extreme propensity for and history of violence.

At one point during the evening, a biker who strayed inside the perimeter attacked me without provocation. Maybe he was drunk or, more likely, was trying to make his bones with the gang by taking down a Knighthawk—in my case, a Grand Knighthawk. If this was the Old West, he'd be some quick-triggered kid looking to challenge a gunfighter who rode into town. Those shoot-outs never ended well for the kid trying to make his mark; nor did things end well for the biker who rushed me.

It wasn't hard to pick me out of a crowd because Knighthawks wore black robes. I still put him down pretty easily, stamped on his neck, and disarmed him. I returned his firearm to the gang leader but couldn't help but wonder if the attack had a deeper basis. Had my cover been compromised somehow? Was word, at least rumor, potentially spreading through the Outlaws that the Grand Knighthawk for Florida and Georgia was working for the FBI?

So I was already on alert when Charles Newcomb approached me later in the evening.

"Brother Joe," Newcomb said, "could we speak privately?"

"Of course, Brother Charles," I said back. "Let's step over here."

When we were out of earshot of anyone else, barely grazed by the fading firelight, Newcomb lowered his voice. "I was wondering if you might be willing to speak with Brothers Moran and Driver. They have something they'd like to talk to you about."

"Does this pertain to Klan business, Brother Charles?"

"It does, and I can tell you I've already spoken with Brother Ward, who's given his blessing and referred the matter to you as the Grand Knighthawk. Would that be agreeable to you?"

I don't believe in coincidence. First, I get rolled by a punk biker and now two recent inductees, both members of the law-enforcement community in Florida, had a problem they wanted to talk to me about. I began to wonder again if my cover had been blown or rendered suspect somehow. I told myself to remain calm and stay in character.

"It would, Brother Charles," I told Newcomb. "Why don't you bring them over?"

Newcomb did, and hung back while I shook hands with David Moran and met Thomas Driver for the first time. Driver was of average size and build, unremarkable save for a pair of hollowed-out holes in his earlobes, fit for gauge earrings he hadn't donned that evening.

"An inmate named Warren Williams tried to kill me, Brother Joe," Driver started. "We got into a fight, but he didn't fight like a man. This monkey, he's got all kind of diseases and he bit me and scratched me. I had to have all these tests for HIV and hepatitis and go on leave until the results came back and I was cleared. HIV, Brother Joe, can you believe that shit?"

"A damn shame," I said, remaining in character.

I'd learn the actual story at an FBI debriefing a week later. Warren Williams, a Black man in his late twenties, was a nonviolent drug offender who'd somehow ended up in Raiford's maximum security section because he had struck a police officer in the midst of the mental health crisis that had precipitated his arrest. All inmates in this section were assigned a "counselor" to keep them informed of what was expected of them and to be responsible for dispensing punishment in the event they stepped out of line. Unfortunately for Williams, he was assigned to Thomas Driver. This afforded the guard plenty of opportunity to make Williams's remaining time inside miserable. Complaining would only make the treatment worse, until the day when Williams finally snapped.

He had only a few months left to go on his sentence when Driver took to blowing smoke from a vape into Williams's face inside a cellblock hallway. Williams tried to hold his breath and, when he couldn't any longer, sucked in a breath laced with the toxic smoke. As soon as he was done coughing, Driver did it again.

"Stop," Williams said, as other inmates looked on and laughed.

Driver blew more smoke.

"Stop!" Williams said louder.

Driver blew yet more smoke, and the inmates nearby were now hooting and hollering, hurling all kinds of expletives and insults at Williams for letting a guard get the better of him.

"I said STOP!"

With that, Williams, considered soft and effete by the prison population for writing poetry, lunged at Driver and launched a full-scale attack that included scratching and biting, until Driver gained the upper hand and brutally beat Williams up to the moment other guards broke up the fight.

Williams ended up getting months added to his sentence, but Driver felt his punishment was even worse. While the prison and prison system failed to discipline him, he had lost face, having been bloodied by an inmate held in no regard at all by the inmate population—the ultimate dishonor for a prison guard that Driver still carried with him after Williams was released from Raiford.

"The monkey's been out for a few months, free as a bird when he should still be inside for trying to infect me and murder me," Driver said. "He should've gotten years tacked on for what he did, assaulting a cop."

I studied Driver and Moran, then Newcomb, who was still hovering behind them.

"We got a picture of him right here," Moran offered, handing me a one-page sheet with a picture of Warren Williams on the top and all kinds of biographical information beneath it.

"So," I said to him and Driver, "do you want somebody to go talk to him?"

"No," Moran answered.

"Do you want somebody to beat him up?"

"No," Driver responded this time.

"Do you want him six feet under?"

Driver and Moran looked at each other.

"Yes," said Driver.

"And do you want to be a part of the operation?"

"I can't myself because I'm too obvious a suspect," Driver offered.

"But I'm not, and neither is Brother Newcomb," Moran said.

I looked from one to the other, needing to choose my next words carefully to leave my options open. "I'm going to need to get back to you on this, so hang tight."

Charles Newcomb, who was standing ten feet away, slid back toward us and addressed Moran and Driver. "So we good?"

They both nodded, their expressions indicating that they were satisfied with my response.

"I just need to discuss this with Brother Jamie before we do everything else," I added.

Moran and Driver nodded again and then slipped off with Newcomb between them, his heavy arms laid over each of their shoulders.

When they drifted out of sight, I took some deep breaths, trying to appear contemplative and calm. What were the odds that maybe an hour after I get attacked by a biker, a couple of recent members who were prison guards at Raiford, members of the law-enforcement community, would be asking me to kill somebody? My defenses were revving in the red over the fact that this might be some kind of setup, either to smoke me out as a confidential human source for the FBI or maybe to usurp Jamie Ward's power by finding a way to remove me from the scene.

At the end of the night, just as the event was starting to break up, I approached Ward about my conversation with Charles Newcomb and Moran and Driver's plan of action.

"Brother Jamie," I started, "Brother Newcomb approached me about taking some potential action and said you had given blessing."

"I felt it was necessary, given Brother Newcomb's status." Ward hesitated, leaving it there, which was enough to tell me he wanted me to comply with the request to kill a man. "I leave everything else, all the details, to you." His eyes flashed in the spill of the full moon. "While we're talking, I was wondering if you could help me out with something else."

"Of course."

"I have a semiautomatic rifle I'd like to convert to fully automatic. Is that something you could help me with?"

"I'm sure I can be of help there."

Ward smiled. "I greatly appreciate that, Brother Joe."

"KLASP, Brother Jamie," I said.

"KLASP, Brother Joe."

I was always anxious leaving a Klan meeting, but as I got in my car and started driving away, it took everything in me not to step on the gas and get far from those people as quickly as possible. I counted to ten in my head, forced myself to drive within the speed limit, and gradually calmed myself down using my breathing techniques. But I couldn't stop thinking that not only had I been randomly attacked and then pulled into a murder plot, it seemed possible my cover was blown.

I called Rich Vaughn on my way home, being extra cautious to use a surveillance detection route to make sure I wasn't being tailed.

"I have vital information to share with you," I told him. "Can we meet tomorrow?"

I could tell right away from his voice that he was in a harried state of mind. "I'm tied up with something for the next couple days. This will have to wait."

I was dumbstruck. Had things finished out in Wayward the way we all expected they would, the FBI and JTTF would have had William Hawley and other klavern leaders on a conspiracy to commit murder charge. Now we were in a similar position here in Bronson with an equally dangerous group that maintained tighter ties to the national organization than William Hawley's klavern. I was in a position to begin making a case for a similar conspiracy that included not only three members of the law-enforcement community but also the Grand Dragon for Florida and Georgia, someone who reported directly to the Imperial Wizard—and this was going to have to wait? I was utterly flabbergasted.

"Should we set something up now?"

"No. Give me a few days and I'll call you back."

Vaughn hung up before I'd even had a chance to tell him what this was about. He'd sounded like I wanted to meet to issue a routine quarterly business report or something of that nature. In point of fact, a man's life was on the line, and I drove home thinking about my three operational priorities: first, protect the public, which in this case meant Warren Williams; second, attach myself to the unholy trio of Newcomb, Moran, and Driver to make sure they don't end up hurting somebody; and, third, maintain operational integrity inside the klavern, since I had deep concerns that I might be in danger.

When I pulled into the driveway of my home, I took off my tan ball cap and steadied my nerves with my 4-7-8 breathing exercise, which was kind of like an injection of oxygen. I sucked in my breath for four seconds, held it for seven, and then let it out over eight. I practiced this technique several times until I felt sufficiently calm to enter my home. I felt confident I hadn't been tailed, but my defenses were still on high alert. If they came for me here, I had to be ready to protect my family.

I wasn't about to go inside until I was certain that it would be my one-year-old daughter's father who stepped through the door, and not the character I was playing, which meant I needed to unzip that persona, so the real Joe beneath the costume could be revealed. I sat behind the wheel of my car and pictured myself unzipping my costume from my head, my arms, my chest, my torso, and my lower body, to leave all that behind me as soon as I stepped out of the vehicle to go inside where my children were waiting.

Shannon knew something was wrong right away.

"Where are you at right now?" she asked me, after I'd checked on Tia and Jordy.

"Sorry, babe, I was off somewhere and need to click back in."

I couldn't tell her anything about what had happened in order to preserve operational security. And I had to think hard about every word that came out of my mouth to make sure I didn't indicate that something serious was going on. I felt overwhelmed by the nature of the task before me, like I alone was responsible for keeping the KKK at bay. I had to find a way to keep my composure.

I sat down in a comfortably worn, dark-brown leather chair in our living room and went through my breathing exercises again, as well as the mental unzipping of my persona, because neither had fully worked the first time. These were tried-and-true techniques that had succeeded in helping me battle my bipolar depression and had similarly succeeded in my first year inside the Traditionalist American Knights. But I started to fear that being asked to kill a man was putting me back in a place I'd sworn to myself I'd never go again. Was I on the verge of losing myself? What if this time I couldn't find my way back?

"Don't stay up too late. You need to go to bed."

Shannon went upstairs before me, further exaggerating the deep sense of loneliness I was experiencing. I finally joined her, but something woke me up in the early morning hours. Anxious and unable to fall back asleep, I removed my pistol from its gun safe and headed downstairs to the family room, sitting by the window that overlooked the front of the house. If someone was coming, this was the way it would happen.

It was an unusually warm December evening. After a few minutes, I heard a storm start to roll in, with thunder rumbling in the distance and lightning flashing overhead. The rain hit the hot tin roof, making a sound not unlike a heavy machine gun spitting out rounds.

I decided to do what I often did on nights like this, when insomnia sets in, in the early-morning hours. I grabbed my Jackson electric guitar from the corner, went outside under my covered porch, and plugged in my amp. With my pistol wedged in my waistband, I propped a foot up on a crossbeam beneath the railing of the porch and started picking. A mist coated my face as I began to play a song I wrote for my family called "Arpeggio to You," feeling my heart pick up a bit when I got to the part where the tempo increased and always got Jordy and Tia dancing. Sometimes, on nights like this, if my wife woke up and realized I wasn't in bed, she would find me outside and watch me play. But if she had done so tonight, I would have chased her back inside the house, leaving me alone on the porch in the coal-black darkness.

I wasn't much for writing lyrics, just instrumentals. But if I'd penned words for this particular song, they would have started, *The good times we have as a family* . . .

Music always recentered me, and this night was no different. As I played, I thought of my kids, asleep and safe in their beds, and reminded myself that no matter how difficult the next few weeks would be, losing myself wasn't an option. I switched to playing the opening chords of "Bad Moon Rising" by Creedence Clearwater Revival, singing out loud this time, "I see the bad moon a-risin' . . ."

CHAPTER 16

THE THREE AMIGOS

My meeting with Rich Vaughn and Lindsay Campbell took place two days later at the FBI field office in Jacksonville, again in Campbell's private office.

I got straight to the point, and told them that Grand Dragon Jamie Ward had given his blessing to the murder of Warren Williams at the behest of Charles Newcomb, David Moran, and Thomas Driver, making him party to a conspiracy to commit first-degree murder.

"Wait a minute," Rich Vaughn said, interrupting me, "could you repeat that?"

"Jamie Ward blessed the action," I said. "And I was about to tell you he also asked me to modify his semiautomatic assault rifle to full auto."

Vaughn was still looking up from the pad he always took notes on during our meetings. That meant we'd have Ward on another federal offense, making more prison time a certainty when he was convicted. The FBI could have scooped him up anytime they wanted on a felony fugitive charge, or alerted the local authorities with jurisdiction to his whereabouts. But Ward was more valuable to this operation in place and would be looking at far more serious federal charges that could put him away for a very long time, not to mention the treasure trove of information he could provide on the Klan if he decided to make a deal with the Justice Department. In that respect, the Bureau was essentially shielding Ward from arrest and an immediate return to prison, because they were after something much more important and didn't consider him to be a flight risk.

In the FBI's storied history, from its founding on July 26, 1908, very few high-profile arrests of KKK ranking members have been made, and even fewer cases have been successfully prosecuted. Even the "Mississippi Burning" case of 1964 succeeded in gaining guilty verdicts against only seven of the eighteen defendants. And the highest figure on that particular totem pole, lead conspirator Edgar Ray Killen, got off when a single juror obstinately refused to join the eleven in voting to convict because she couldn't believe a Baptist preacher could be guilty of such crimes. Fortunately, justice would eventually be served when Killen was convicted of manslaughter forty-one years later, in June 2005. Small consolation for the three young civil rights workers who were murdered and hardly enough to erase the stain of the government's inability to produce the requisite convictions a case of this magnitude called for.

More recently, in 2014, Steven Joshua Dinkle, a former Exalted Cyclops of a purported KKK chapter in Ozark, Alabama, was tried, convicted, and sentenced to serve twenty-four months in prison for his role in a cross burning. I say purported because this particular chapter claimed affiliation with the International Keystone Knights of the KKK. Like the Loyal White Knights Newcomb and Moran had been members of, Dinkle's chapter was not recognized by the Klan's national hierarchy and did not fall under the domain of any of the organization's five Imperial Wizards. Dinkle himself was only twenty-eight and hardly qualified for such a lofty position inside the KKK. I call that kind of knowledge, gleaned mostly through research on the internet outside my undercover work, "situational awareness," which I defined as educating myself as deeply as possible on every aspect of the Klan's history and operational methodology. I could learn only so much through observation alone.

So as I related the events of the cross burning in painstaking detail for Vaughn and Campbell, they were practically salivating at the thought of where this operation might lead. A successful prosecution of Grand Dragon Jamie Ward and Exalted Cyclops Charles Newcomb on conspiracy to commit murder charges not only would be a feather in Vaughn's and Campbell's caps, but it would also be a win for the FBI and the Joint Terrorism Task Force in their war against domestic terrorists—of whom the Klan remained Public Enemy Number One.

After catching up on his note taking, Vaughn said, "We're going to need to get federal wiretap warrants on these three amigos so you can record them. The good news is that we won't need to follow Foreign Intelligence Surveillance Act guidelines, which means that process shouldn't take very long at all."

The three amigos became the way we referred to our targets internally, drawn from the comic film of the same name, starring Steve Martin, Chevy Chase, and Martin Short.

"How long is not very long?" I asked him, leery of the kind of stalling that risked drawing too much attention to myself.

"A week or so, give or take a few days. We just have to be a bit patient here."

Easy to say that when you're not dealing with psychopaths on a regular basis, I thought as I was leaving the office. I used that week to get a temperature check on Newcomb to make sure he didn't get antsy and attack Warren Williams on his own instead of letting the process he'd started with me play out.

A few days after my meeting at the FBI field office in Jacksonville, I met with him briefly to let him know we were a go and that the planning for how best to take Warren Williams out was underway. I got the sense he was being deferential to Jamie Ward in this respect, not about to do anything that might run afoul of a legitimate Klan organization he saw himself as part of for years to come. Besides, he was now the Exalted Cyclops, effectively Ward's number two and the klavern's de facto leader whenever the Grand Dragon was off on the greater business of the Klan.

I had my own Klan-related business to attend to at this time, mostly making deliveries of drugs, money, and messages, none of which were necessarily germane to what was a counterterrorism investigation. One of these jobs was delivering a written message to the Kingsmen for Mike Christopher. I arrived at their headquarters and was ushered into a back room, where I handed the sealed envelope to Bob Bargar, the gang's leader. I could tell from his expression that he didn't like what he was reading and must have been expecting it, because three armed gang members entered the room.

"What makes you think you're gonna be alive to deliver my response?" he sneered.

I'd already pulled my jacket back to expose my pistol, ready to draw. "How 'bout because I'll drop those three guys behind me before they get their guns out?"

He sneered again and shook his head. "Just like a fucking Grand Knighthawk," he said, then handed over some cash for me to take back to Mike Christopher, which the message I'd delivered must have demanded.

I lost count of how many laws my doppelgänger, the guy in the tan ball cap, was breaking in the process of moving drugs and money between groups and individuals. This was generally classified as "authorized illegal activity" and occupied a great deal of my time while undercover during this period. Every task I performed ingratiated me further with those I needed to maintain contact with on a regular basis, while continuing to win their trust. Newcomb, too, had his own logistical issues to deal with, namely, Moran's and Driver's respective shift schedules at Raiford. Driver needed to be on duty when the hit was performed on Williams to give him an alibi. And that shift couldn't overlap with Moran's, since he'd be participating in the murder along with Newcomb.

I was reassured by the fact that Newcomb had come to see the Williams murder as no different from a lynching, in that it was being conducted under Klan auspices. I imagine he was shrewd enough to realize that offered him a layer of insulation against arrest and prosecution, since law enforcement would be more interested in pursuing the organization's role than any individual's, in the event it came to that. I also had the sense that Newcomb had other things on his mind, although I didn't find out precisely what until the operation was approved.

A week after my meeting with Vaughn and Campbell, the FBI got the warrants, and I was authorized to take the next steps. First among those was a meeting with Newcomb at his home in Keystone Heights, for which I was wearing two recording devices to make sure not a single word he uttered would be missed. Driving up for the first time, I couldn't help but compare the property to William Hawley's compound in Wayward. Newcomb's was similarly isolated and also surrounded by a fence, as well as equipped with an electric gate at the entrance. The property was only two acres; Hawley's was considerably larger. It lacked the target ranges and, as near as I could tell, the hidden weapons and ordnance bunkers as well.

But there was one addition, invisible to the eye, that Newcomb would soon be proudly showing me.

The electric gate opened and I was met inside the property by Jim Heart. I left my car right there inside the fence and walked with Heart toward Newcomb's house. On the way, I noticed a small mobile home parked in a rear corner under the shade of pine trees and took that for Heart's residence here on the property. As Newcomb's bodyguard, Heart spent much of his day when Newcomb was present patrolling the property, either on foot or on an ATV. Whenever Newcomb left the property, Heart would accompany him and serve as driver.

Newcomb's home was a simple ranch house, plain-looking from the outside and so small I wondered how they'd even squeezed in three bedrooms. It was a kind of cookie-cutter home, totally unremarkable except for the fact that all the trees and brush had been removed from around it in order to deny places of concealment for any law-enforcement body that stormed the property.

Newcomb emerged from the home as soon as he saw us approaching, the angle making it look like his stout frame filled the entire doorway. I was already aware that he lived here with his wife, nineteen-year-old daughter, her boyfriend, and his twenty-two-year-old son. He'd had another son who'd passed away at the age of sixteen after contracting a deadly disease back in Tennessee.

"Nice to see you, Brother Joe," Newcomb greeted me, and shook my hand.

"KIGY, Brother Charles."

"KIGY."

"I'm glad we're finally able to get together on this," I said, picturing the recording devices doing their job. "And I appreciate your patience."

Newcomb flashed a crooked smile. "Of course. Williams isn't going anywhere anyway, except six feet under, right?"

I forced a smile to match his. "Right."

"And I appreciate you permitting Brother Moran and me to assist you."

"The more the merrier, so long as the merrier know what they're doing, Brother Charles."

He flashed the same smile again, only tighter. "I've already killed four men, Brother Joe, and look forward to adding another to the tally."

I didn't press him for any specifics, because that kind of probing can be a dead giveaway of someone working undercover. Deep-cover confidential human sources in place for extended periods need to let suspects volunteer information and not push them for it. Men like Newcomb would almost always give themselves up without much prodding, if you choose your words carefully or, sometimes, not at all.

"Let's take a walk," Newcomb said.

I was reminded again of the tour William Hawley had given me of his sprawling property that morning I showed up to buy his rifle. No such tour, though, awaited me today. Instead, Newcomb guided me around the rear of his home to a rectangular formation of cinder blocks poking out of the ground a hundred feet from the house.

"I get the feeling you're a man who's seen some things in his time, Brother Joe."

"I have indeed."

"You were in the army."

"I was."

"Special Operations, I heard told."

I remained silent.

"Did more than a share of your time at Fort Bragg, I imagine."

Again, I remained silent.

"I'm not asking for specifics, Brother Joe."

"And I couldn't give them even if you did, Brother Charles."

He flashed that tight smile yet again. "My point being you've put your share of men in the ground, which is why I think you'll appreciate seeing this."

We'd reached the cinder-block structure that surrounded what I first thought might be some kind of bunker, not unlike William Hawley's. On second glance, though, I realized this couldn't be anything like that at all; the contours were too small, and if it was an escape tunnel of some kind, Newcomb wouldn't have surrounded the entrance with cinder blocks to advertise its presence. I saw a flat steel door with a locked latch. For some reason, I thought of backyard leaf-burning incinerators and began to get a pretty good idea of what I was looking at before Newcomb resumed.

"This is where we can put the likes of Warren Williams and other scum. It's a bottled gas incinerator, my own personal crematorium to dispose of those who need disposing. Generates thousands of degrees of heat and leaves nothing behind but teeth. Just for disposing of dead bodies, of course, but I'd be lying if I didn't admit the thought of firing it up with a scum like Williams inside screaming for his life didn't cross my mind."

Newcomb's smile lingered this time, his eyes seeming to twinkle at the sight of the incinerator. I realized I'd lost track of Heart's deadly presence, a potentially fatal mistake if this had been an adversarial encounter as opposed to a friendly one between like-minded individuals.

"We need to take out the trash, Brother Joe," Newcomb continued. "We need to pop the cherry on this here contraption and, once that cherry's popped, we need to keep the flow going. Get my money's worth out of this thing, if you know what I mean."

I felt it was the right time for me to interject something. "I believe I do, Brother Charles."

"No shortage of men who deserve that fate, Williams being one of many. There's this guy from India with a face blacker than night who works at this convenience store my wife and me stopped in. He looked at her all wrong. A man gotta pay for looking at a white woman that way, don't he, Brother Joe?"

I may have nodded, but I don't remember for sure. I was too busy thinking of how much that reminded me of the twisted reasoning behind the murder of fourteen-year-old Emmett Till in Mississippi in 1955.

"There's a place for him in that heat too. Then there's a sexual predator living just down the street a ways. I don't know exactly what he did, but if he's on that list, it can't be good. Two thousand degrees would suit him just fine."

I learned later that the fourth man Newcomb mentioned as being worthy of placement in his bottled gas incinerator was a former boss he'd run afoul of in the repossession world, where he now made his living. Even in that business there were rules to abide by, and it was abundantly clear to me that Newcomb was a man who preferred making up his own. I looked at that proclivity as something I might be able to take advantage of by demonstrating to Newcomb that I was of the same mind.

I needed to stall Newcomb for as long as possible while the FBI got a plan in place to deal with the Warren Williams situation. Such operations took time to enact and a whole roll of red tape to work through. While this was happening, I continued to stick close to Newcomb.

As it turned out, he made that easy.

Jamie Ward called one day about a week after Newcomb showed me his incinerator.

"Brother Charles is in jail," he said when I met him in person at his home. "Apparently he used one of his old police badges to repossess a car and got arrested for impersonating an officer."

"That's a hefty charge in these parts, Brother Jamie."

"Explains the bail it's going to take to get him out. But we take care of our own, Brother Joe, and I need you to collect the money."

I immediately contacted Vaughn and Campbell, who confirmed Ward's facts were correct, and I got their permission to do as Ward asked me. I paid visits to the homes of several Klan members, raised the amount—around a thousand dollars—needed to spring Newcomb, and delivered it to his wife.

"I'll head over to the jail first thing in the morning," she said after I handed her the cash.

"They open at eight," I told her, "but you can't get prisoners out on bail until nine."

She nodded. "We all appreciate your help, Joe. You're a true friend."

While I continued to wait for Vaughn and Campbell to get the pieces in place for how we were going to deal with the planned killing of Warren Williams, I caught another break in terms of stalling Newcomb, Moran, and Driver. I was asked to help oversee security for a Klan rally being held in Cedar Key, home of the marina where William Hawley and his son had taken me fishing. Sometimes, the KKK schedules these rallies to bait the local municipalities into denying them the required permits, so the Klan can take them to court for being denied their First Amendment rights. In this case, Cedar Key didn't fight the permit at all and the rally went forth as planned.

There were about ten Klansmen present and maybe a hundred and fifty people in the crowd for our presentation. There were no counterprotests, and the sheriff's department beefed up patrols in case there was trouble. Vaughn and Campbell informed me they'd be in the crowd wearing disguises, which must have been good ones, because I never spotted them from my position providing security for the TAK participants.

All in all, it was a peaceful event during which several dozen of those in attendance approached Klan members to request additional information about becoming involved. A few might end up being naturalized, while still more might become ghouls. But the Klan was just as interested in building its roster of sympathizers and supporters. When push came to shove in the country, as the KKK definitely believed it would, these supporters would prove vital to the cause. The organization had definitely come around to the fact that there was strength in numbers, and the numbers of like-minded individuals who openly avowed Klan ideology continued to rise steadily. Barack Obama's second term remained the driving force behind the desperation members of the extremist right felt over the country they believed was slipping away from them, and desperation makes for the greatest recruiting tool of all.

As for me, I couldn't help but cast my gaze toward Cedar Key Marina, just a few hundred feet away, wondering what I'd do if William Hawley happened by while pulling his boat and noticed the rally.

CHAPTER 17

RECON TRIP

ST. AUGUSTINE, FLORIDA
DECEMBER 2014

Christmas, you might say, came early that year when William Hawley didn't show up at the rally in Cedar Key. The actual day marked Tia's first Christmas, but it was Jordy who stole the show.

Earlier that week, he decided he wanted a baby brother for Christmas and, instead of asking Santa for one, he approached the stork directly by writing a letter stating his request. I wrote Jordy back in the guise of the stork saying that if he kept putting up good grades and was a good boy, before long the stork would grant his wish. Then, on Christmas morning, Shannon and I drew little stork footprints in the kitchen right around where we kept the cookies and milk we put out for Santa Claus. The footprints led straight to the tree, under which all the gifts he'd asked for, save for a little brother, were waiting for him.

It turned out our little family—Shannon, Jordy, Tia, and I— enjoyed a peaceful Christmas. Even with the stresses and inherent risks of my work undercover, I did my best to stay in the moment and savor these precious, fleeting moments of normalcy.

That peace lasted through the holidays, then abruptly ended in early January with a call from Charles Newcomb. Thanks to the bail money I'd raised, he'd been able to enjoy Christmas and New Year's Day at home, and was now ready to get back into action.

"We're having a little get-together Sunday for family and friends, Brother Joe. I'm wondering if you might want to attend. It'll just be a small gathering."

"As long as your wife's a good cook, Brother Charles, count me in."

"She makes a great fried chicken. And if that doesn't suit your fancy, I'll have hot dogs roasting on the grill."

"The fried chicken sounds great."

The more Newcomb felt comfortable in my presence, the better I'd be able to do my job, so I accepted the invitation knowing that the FBI would approve, and drove out to his property in Keystone Heights on Sunday. I pulled in halfway between the fence line and the house, where other cars had been parked, and saw around two dozen people milling about outside. The next thing I noticed was Thomas Driver climbing out of his car.

"KIGY, Brother," I greeted.

"KIGY, Brother," he said back, lowering his voice as he approached me. "I'll get my schedule for the next few weeks when I go into work tomorrow."

"Keep us informed."

"I will, sir. And I appreciate everything you're doing. It's a righteous thing."

"We're a family, Brother."

I extended my hand, and Driver shook it gratefully. We approached the festivities together, passing Jim Heart on the way, who greeted me with a nod I returned in kind. I noticed him pay attention to the way I was carrying my firearm and rehearsed in my mind the actions I'd take if he asked to search me, which would almost surely reveal the wire I was wearing. But he didn't say a word.

Charles Newcomb approached me straightaway, nodding to Driver as he steered me away from the crowd. The look on his face was different from any I'd seen on him before, softer and bordering on appreciative. I noticed his cheeks and thick neck were red, maybe from getting overheated after standing over the grill too long. I could smell charcoal in the distance. I observed that the men, all Klansmen, were seated at one large table, while the women and children sat separately, crowded around smaller tables set back a bit to free the men to talk without being heard. This was typical of the Klan's antebellum, patriarchal society, in which women played a subservient role. Newcomb didn't ask his wife to do something so much as command her in a way that was clearly demeaning. I also noticed that the men's table was positioned closer to the kitchen door so they could get first crack at any platters of food that emerged. If the barbecue's attendees had been wearing different clothes, this could have been a scene straight out of 1865, when the KKK had been founded.

"Thank you for your efforts, Brother Joe," he said, shaking my hand.

"KLASP, Brother Charles. It's nothing you wouldn't have done for me."

"Let's go inside," he said, angling that way. "There's something I'd like to show you."

Inside the house, the air-conditioning was making little dent in the heat and humidity. Newcomb led me to a glass display case that rose maybe five feet off the floor with several shelves inside, all holding an assortment of knives.

"I don't show this to a lot of folks," Newcomb said, obviously proud of his collection.

"Impressive," I noted, even though it was anything but.

The knives were all shiny and new, most of them with the outline and features of the Confederate flag forged into the steel at the thickest part of the blade, near the hilt. The assortment of folding knives had the same Confederate flag design carved into the handle. As someone trained in knife fighting, it was clear to me these were only for show, ordered from some redneck version of the Knife of the Month Club.

Newcomb didn't bother opening the case to let me handle any of them, saving me from feeling how poorly weighted these knives were certain to be. Instead he directed me to a mantel where a sword I recognized as the kind used in Klan naturalization ceremonies hung.

"That's the real thing, Brother Joe, tested in battle and having drawn blood almost for sure," he said proudly. "We're going to be using it when we naturalize someone from this point forward."

I pictured myself, as the Grand Knighthawk, playing the role of the Keeper of the Fire while Newcomb, as the Exalted Cyclops, presided, with that sword laid out on the table between us. Then I thought of William Hawley handing me the Walther P38 he expected me to use to pop that truck driver. The contrast between Hawley and Newcomb was striking when you consider Hawley's car collection, vast stores of weapons, and respect of the community. While Newcomb occupied a similar position in this chapter of the Traditionalist American Knights to Hawley's in his United Northern and Southern Knights klavern, the differences in resources and reputation were dramatic. I wondered whether this was emblematic of the Klan as a whole, their nationwide expansion rooted in the willingness to accept more violent loners into the ranks and promote them to positions of leadership, just as the TAK had with Newcomb.

"We should go get ourselves a look at Warren Williams's home in Palatka, Brother Joe. You know"—he smiled, as if about to share something between us—"do some recon."

"That would be you and me?" I said.

"And Sarge," Newcomb said, referring to Moran, whose nickname came courtesy of his prison guard rank. "We'll do our recon while Driver is at work."

By this time, I had informed the FBI about the additional three targets Newcomb had mentioned to me during my last visit to his property.

"Joe," Vaughn had told me at a regularly scheduled meeting, "we're not going to move these people or put any men on them. We're relying on you to dig deeper within yourself to keep these people safe."

In that moment, I could hear my own heart pounding in my chest, along with a tingling on the back of my neck as beads of sweat built up on my forehead from the stress of having more added to my plate.

"Yes, sir."

The Bureau's focus, meanwhile, was all on Warren Williams. The challenge the Bureau and the JTTF faced was that this would actually be prosecuted as a state case and not a federal one, since murder wasn't a federal crime. So Vaughn, Campbell, and company needed to work closely and cooperatively with Florida state prosecutors, which required a lot of coordination behind the scenes. No way the Bureau could risk working with local prosecutors, since my intelligence had already identified several who were beholden to the Klan. Bringing in anybody whose loyalty to our cause was not absolute could pose a big problem in the event the recon of Warren Williams's home occurred before they had an opportunity to get everything in place.

As things turned out, Driver's and Moran's schedules lined up perfectly one week in mid-February, and I got a call from Newcomb.

"We're on for the day after tomorrow, Brother Joe. Be at my house at eight in the morning."

His authoritative tone unsettled me a bit, because it indicated he was placing himself in the lead instead of continuing to show deference to my position as Grand Knighthawk. The good thing was he had provided enough notice for the FBI to get my Kia Sportage wired up with devices to record and transmit everything Newcomb and Moran said during our drive. My instructions were to make sure we took my vehicle, and I wondered if I'd need to come up with some way to disable Newcomb's in the event he insisted on driving.

I dressed in church clothes for the recon, a Gray Man technique that made it appear I was not armed, because the fuller cut of the shirt allowed me to wear a shoulder rig that concealed my pistol under my armpit. I was still confident I could get the gun out and fire in a timely fashion, especially in a confined space like the inside of a car. Newcomb claimed he'd killed four men, but I seriously doubted either he or Moran had ever been involved in a close-quarters shoot-out. My advantage lay in the fact that I had.

I arrived at Charles Newcomb's home right on time on a Tuesday morning to find Jim Heart patrolling the property on an ATV. I was grateful he wouldn't be accompanying us, although he did cast me what passed for a friendly wave as I climbed out of my car right alongside Newcomb's home. Moran, who'd gotten there ahead of me, gave me a similarly friendly wave from the truck he was leaning on and then pocketed the cell phone he'd been on.

Newcomb emerged from the house toting a fishing pole and a tackle box. Taking the initiative, I moved to the back of my Kia and raised the rear hatch to indicate I'd be driving.

"That supposed to be our cover if we get stopped?" I said, nodding at his fishing gear, to distract him from my effort to use my car.

I held my breath when he placed the rod and tackle box inside, afraid he might notice some sign of an FBI recording device. One of them, tucked inside my tool bag, looked like a pipe bomb with an antenna rising from one end. I could picture Newcomb looking at me quizzically while posing the question, *Why do you have a pipe bomb with an antenna?*

He was looking at me, though, instead of the tool bag on the carpeted cargo area. "No, sir. Come inside and I'll explain better."

He led me into the kitchen, where he plucked a pair of glass vials from the refrigerator.

"This here's insulin, Brother Joe. We happen to see Williams and scoop him up, all we have to do is inject him with this. It'll kill him quick and there won't be any sign how he died."

My stomach dropped as I eyed the vials, but I forced my expression to remain neutral.

"What we do is take him to some secluded fishing spot, shoot him up there, and dump his body in the water," Newcomb went on. "By the time they find the fishing gear and his body, there won't be much left, and even if there is the autopsy won't show a damn thing. It'll look like an accident."

I almost asked Newcomb, *What if Williams doesn't fish?* But I didn't pose that somewhat obvious question because I was preoccupied with this new development. As far as I knew, this was supposed to be a reconnaissance trip. Now Newcomb was talking about going operational this morning, should the opportunity present itself. How did I know Newcomb and Moran might not take violent action on Williams? How did I know they wouldn't storm the house? I knew I might have to gun them down if that came to pass. At least, though, the Bureau would be aware of all our impending actions, thanks to the listening devices in my vehicle.

I showed no surprise and posed no questions about the apparent change in plans, not about to risk doing anything that might make Newcomb suspicious. I shouldn't have been surprised, but then again, until that point he had paid deference to me when it came to planning the murder.

Newcomb climbed into the passenger seat of my Kia, Moran into the back, and we set off on the one-hour drive to Palatka. We made small talk along the way, nothing coming out of my mouth to suggest anything was amiss, other than to pose some questions about the plan and the insulin in order to alert the FBI that things might not be unfolding exactly as per the plan. The FBI would be listening to the entire episode on a live feed; I just needed to choose my words carefully to keep them informed, while saying nothing that might make Newcomb and Moran suspicious.

When we pulled off the highway and reached the outskirts of Warren Williams's neighborhood, I could see Moran's eyes scanning about, clocking the number of people on the sidewalk or outside their homes.

"What are all these people doing outside hanging around on a Tuesday morning?"

"Most of 'em don't work, Sarge," Newcomb said. "You know how these people are. Rather pick up an unemployment check than do an honest day's labor. Maybe you should recruit them to work at Raiford," he finished, joking.

"Nah, these n—— are too stupid to pass the written test."

We took a turn that put us on Williams's street. He lived with his mother in a small, well-kept home pretty much identical to all the others on the block, squeezed together with small yards at front and back. They were tract homes of a sort, layered in amid an impoverished section of the state that was riddled with unemployment. Right away I noticed unmarked police vehicles, including a van and a truck, were parked everywhere. I tensed up behind the wheel. I figured the

On September 13, 1926, approximately thirty thousand Klan members marched down Pennsylvania Avenue from the Capitol Building toward the White House.

(Courtesy of the Library of Congress)

Another view of the September 13, 1926, Ku Klux Klan gathering, with the Capitol dome in the background.

(© Bettmann/Getty Images)

The first flag used by the Confederate States of America.

Although the Confederate battle flag never represented the Confederate States of America, it was used by the Klan to stress the fact that the South would someday rise to fight again.

The glove I wore to hold the torch to light the cross, in my capacity as Grand Knighthawk at cross burnings during my second infiltration of the Klan, which began in 2013.

Me, at the age of six, in
1977, holding a
toy rifle.

Me and my sister, aged eight and four.

Graduating from army
basic training in 1996, at
Fort Benning in Georgia,
in my dress uniform.

My recon platoon, including snipers, in 1998. I'm in the front, lower left.

A Barrett M107A1 .50-caliber sniper rifle like the one I trained on, which the Klan was planning to use to assassinate Barack Obama during a Kissimmee, Florida, campaign stop on October 29, 2008.

Mug shots of (*left to right*) Thomas Driver, David Moran, and Charles Newcomb, taken April 1, 2015, following their arrests.

A typical KKK cross burning. The figure cloaked in black, second from the left, is the chapter's Knighthawk.

(© William Campbell/Getty Images)

Klan Imperial Wizard Charles Denton (aka "Cole Thornton") in June 2005 outside a Mississippi courthouse, where Edgar Ray Killen was tried and convicted of having arranged the murders of three civil rights workers in Philadelphia, Mississippi, in 1964.

(© Erik S. Lesser/EPA/ Shutterstock)

Then presidential candidate Barack Obama, with former president Bill Clinton in the background, on October 29, 2008, in Kissimmee, Florida. The Klan planned to assassinate Obama after this event.

(© Martin Field/UPI/Alamy Stock Photo)

Klan Imperial Wizard Frank Ancona at a cross burning in Missouri.

(Frank Ancona, via YouTube)

ABC's George Stephanopoulos interviewing me for the December 2022 Hulu documentary film *Grand Knighthawk*.

(ABC News)

Maintaining my skills on a Florida shooting range in 2022.

(ABC News)

My wife, Shannon, and me on our wedding day.

On a Florida beach with two of my kids after catching a redfish.

My wife and me at the beach in Jacksonville, Florida, in December 2023.

FBI had arranged for enough of a law-enforcement presence to dissuade Newcomb and Moran from taking any action independent of me, without giving me any advance notice. And as if that wasn't bad enough, almost immediately an unmarked highway patrol car, recognizable from recessed lights in the grille, showed up and pulled in right behind me. It followed us past Williams's house, recognizable from the number on the mailbox, all the way to the end of the block.

I noticed Moran was looking out the rear window. "You see that car behind us?" he asked.

"Suspicious," Newcomb acknowledged.

"Looks like an unmarked police vehicle," Moran said.

"Yeah."

I remained silent and drove around the block twice. The unmarked police cruiser never left our tail. Newcomb let out a breath of exasperation, and I thought I heard him swearing under his breath. I needed to keep one eye on Moran, one eye on Newcomb, and one eye on the road.

But I only had two eyes.

I had to keep myself under control. *Breathe, focus, observe . . . Breathe, focus, observe . . .* I had to assume the worst, that the unmarked cruiser was going to make a move on us and this was going to go to guns. In preparation for that, I eased my hand up to my sidearm, feeling my heart thudding against my chest, ready to tear back my shirt to grab my gun, as I turned back onto the highway. Just when I thought we'd hit the point of no return, the unmarked patrol car pulled over and made a U-turn. I thought to myself, *Thank God*, but Newcomb remained suspicious.

"Weird that they were right there waiting on something," he said.

"Yeah," Moran agreed, "strange."

And that's when my phone rang with Rich Vaughn's phone number lighting up in the caller ID, listed under a fictitious name. I knew I had to answer it so as not to arouse any suspicion, but I couldn't believe he was calling me at this moment. Didn't he know what was going on? By calling now, he was putting me in an extremely dangerous position that could have resulted in a shoot-out.

"Hey, babe," I greeted, pretending it was my wife, and knowing this would get violent if Newcomb insisted on confirming it was Shannon on the other end of the line.

"Have you left the area?" Vaughn asked me, and I could only hope his voice was soft enough so Newcomb and Moran wouldn't hear him.

Fortunately, they were paying more attention to what was behind us to see if any more cars pulled up on our tail. I assumed Vaughn wasn't in contact with the highway patrol and must have been too far out of range for the listening device to reach him.

"Everything's good, babe."

Vaughn got the point that I couldn't talk. "Okay, I'm gonna ask you a few questions you only need to answer yes or no to. Are you still in the neighborhood?"

"No."

"Are you headed back?"

"Yeah, babe, we're headed to Brother Charles's house right now."

"So you're not headed back?"

I realized he was referring to the neighborhood. He wanted to make sure we weren't going to get down the road and then go in search of Warren Williams again.

"Call you when I'm on my way home," I said, aware the call had gone on for too long already. "Love you, babe."

Looking back, in my mind this entire scenario could have been staged to leave me no choice other than to kill Moran and Newcomb, in which case everything would have ended then and there. There would have been no need to stage Williams's murder and then make a case that would have to go to trial. And you can't try men who are dead. Though I never confirmed this, or even inquired about it, the more I recall the circumstances, the more I think it may have been me who was being set up to execute our targets.

The rest of the drive back to Newcomb's passed without incident, with not a lot of words exchanged until we pulled onto his property.

"What now, Brother Joe?" he asked me, his voice deferential again.

It was abundantly clear to the FBI in the wake of that trip that these guys had every intention of killing Warren Williams. What we needed to do was come up with an alternative to prevent them from taking independent action.

"I'm not sure, Brother Charles. Let me think on it a bit," I said, to buy myself some time.

CHAPTER 18

THE PICTURE

KEYSTONE HEIGHTS, FLORIDA
MARCH 2015

Two weeks later, with the approval of the FBI, I met Charles New-comb on his property. He and Jim Heart were doing some yard work when I arrived, and Newcomb took off his gloves and stowed his tools to walk to one of the few shady spots his property offered.

"You got an update for me on where we stand with this thing, Brother Joe?"

"I do, but I still can't make hide or hair of all that surveillance around Williams's house."

"Looked like they were waiting for us," he said, but I didn't detect any suspicion aimed at me in his tone.

In point of fact, all that police surveillance had inadvertently served up a plan I could go forward with that would implicate our targets without involving them in the actual murder. That unmarked police car gave me the excuse to get things handled on my own, cutting the three amigos out of the process.

"No, sir," I said. "If that were the case, they would've scooped us up. They were waiting for somebody. Could be Brother Thomas isn't the only enemy Williams made on the inside."

I could see Newcomb's eyes flashing as he considered that. "Makes a good deal of sense, Brother Joe. So where's that leave us?"

"Well, Brother Charles, it's too dangerous for this to have Klan fingerprints on it, so I'm gonna be handling it myself through a certain hit man I'm familiar with," I said, hinting that the hit man might be me. "I need for you to keep Brother David and Brother Thomas patient. I'll be informing all of you when the deed is done."

Newcomb nodded approvingly. The FBI had blessed this notion because it was the surest way to keep the three amigos from acting on their own. Instead, they were waiting for me to do so.

Newcomb, Moran, and Driver needed to know Williams was dead, without participating in the act themselves. The solution to that problem was to make it appear that the deed had been done when, in fact, Williams remained very much alive, by staging his murder. Thankfully, it was actually the FBI, in conjunction with local and state authorities, who ended up handling that staging, not me.

Two weeks after my meeting with Newcomb, Vaughn and Campbell arranged to meet me outside the Jacksonville field office to give me an old-fashioned snapshot of Williams lying (apparently) dead on the floor in his underwear, having been murdered. He had been positioned with what appeared to be gunshot wounds to his chest visible. Then they moved Williams and his mother into protective custody in a nearby hotel under guard.

"You need to get them on tape blessing the action, Joe," Vaughn told me, clearly aware of what a heavy lift that was. "You need to get them to tell you they're satisfied in order to make their culpability clear. And you need to get them to admit this was what they intended, what they wanted to happen. Otherwise, we haven't got enough to arrest them. That comes straight from the attorney general's office."

I had to show three men who'd been fully prepared to commit murder a picture of their intended victim, with a story that I'd gone ahead and set it up on my own to keep them out of harm's way. I wasn't as worried about them buying the second part of the story as the first. What if they realized the photo was a fake? What if they realized I'd set them up? One thing was for sure: I needed to meet each of them separately, get them to say what I needed them to say, and then get gone.

When that time came, the FBI would rig my vehicle with a video camera for the three meetings. My life would be in danger during all three, four including the stop at Jamie Ward's to implicate him for illegal possession of a firearm. These men had already proven their desire and intention to kill. If any of them suspected the truth, if they spotted the camera or wire I was wearing, it was going to get ugly in a hurry. I wrote out a note to Shannon and the kids and placed it inside our bedside safe, saying how much I loved them, in case anything happened to me.

If everything went according to plan and my work secured the evidence needed to obtain indictments, Ward would be arrested on a federal firearms charge and local felony fugitive charges. Newcomb, Moran, and Driver would be subject to state charges on conspiracy to commit first-degree murder.

I knew I needed an excuse for the anxiety I'd be unable to totally hide, just as I knew I needed to direct their attention away from the photo, so they wouldn't notice anything awry or pose questions I wouldn't be able to answer. So to throw the three men off their normal thought process, I smeared some powder on my face to make me look pale and sick, a distraction I hoped would lead them to pay more attention to me and less to worrying about what they were looking at and get them to accept the photo at face value. I wanted to look tired and exhausted as I handed each of them the picture. I even rigged an intravenous port of red Kool-Aid to make it look like an IV infusion going into a vein to pump me full of medications to ward off whatever sickness I was suffering from.

The morning in mid-March that I was to pick up the rifle from Jamie Ward and then show that picture of the "murdered" Warren

Williams to the three amigos was cool and crisp. Before leaving the house to first have my car wired with that surveillance camera, I gave Shannon my customary three kisses on the lips, at which point she couldn't help but notice my makeshift disguise.

"Do you know what you're doing?" she asked, clearly more concerned than she normally was.

"Not really, but I'm doing the best I can."

"I'm afraid for you. Be careful out there, babe," she said, patting me on the back.

As I got in the car and pulled out of our drive, I thought to myself, *That's the woman I want to come back to.*

The comfortable temperatures and low humidity didn't last long. The heat—along with the tension—built throughout the day as I met with all four of our targets to implicate them in their respective crimes beneath a cloudless sky that allowed the sun to roast me through my windshield.

With my car now wired, I arrived at Jamie Ward's mobile home at ten o'clock in the morning. It was located in a nice neighborhood dominated by families and within view of Bronson Elementary School. The school was set behind a fence line maybe two hundred yards from his property. All I could think of was Ward fleeing the FBI and taking refuge in that school full of potential hostages. And that made me think, What if my own kids were in that building at the time?, which strengthened my resolve to see this through.

For obvious reasons, I made a mental note to include that in the schematics of the surrounding area I was assembling for the FBI for his coming takedown. Jamie Ward was expecting me, and I saw him waiting outside his mobile home when I turned the corner onto the street. I pulled up to where he was standing and rolled down the window; I needed to remain in the car in order to capture him on video and audio giving me the gun. And by not getting out he was far less likely to notice my makeshift disguise.

"KIGY, Brother," I greeted.

"KIGY, Brother," he answered, and handed me the weapon.

He thanked me for making the arrangements to convert the assault rifle to full auto, and I drove off to deliver it to the drop point where Rich Vaughn was waiting. To preserve operational integrity and properly secure the evidence needed to obtain indictments, I would return to that drop point for debriefing after each of the three successive meetings, spaced hours apart, at around noon, two o'clock, and five o'clock. At the initial meeting, I handed over the gun to Vaughn, who took hold of it while wearing plastic gloves so as not to disturb the chain of evidence. That way, the only fingerprints on it would be Ward's and mine. Any other latent prints would be dismissed in court as moot.

David Moran was next on the list, right around noontime. That left me some time to get into character, think about what I had to do. I knew Moran was an extremely dangerous man known for beating prisoners within an inch of their lives. I met him in a Lake Butler parking lot that housed a barbecue restaurant and watched him approach my Kia with my heart trying to pound its way out of my chest.

"Okay, good Brother," I said when he opened the passenger-side door, "have a seat."

Moran climbed in and closed the door behind him. "How you doing, Brother Joe?"

"I want you to see this to make sure it's all clear."

I had no idea how he was going to react when I held the picture out for him to see. I didn't bother explaining the manner in which I'd handled this, because that would have led to more questions. Keeping it simple was definitely the best strategy, but I wondered if he could hear my heart.

His expression as he regarded the photo was one of glee, pure delight. I tried not to let the disgust I felt show, and to maintain my composure and stay in character.

"Is that what y'all were wanting?" I asked him.

"Yeah," he said, beaming. "Yeah."

"Okay. Call Brother Thomas and make sure he knows I'm gonna meet him next."

"Yeah, I know. I will call him as soon as I . . ." His voice trailed off, and his smile broadened. "Do you know how happy this makes me? Love you, Brother!"

"KLASP," I said, realizing he'd bought it.

"KLASP, Brother!"

He climbed out of my car and walked away with a spring in his step, freeing me to collect myself while he called Driver and confirmed my next meeting.

After meeting with Rich Vaughn at a second drop point, I headed to my meeting with Thomas Driver. I set it up in the parking lot of a shopping mall in Lake City, forty-five minutes from Lake Butler. Since the whole case had started with Driver, getting his stamp of approval was the most important task of all. If Driver had said something to the effect that he hadn't really wanted Williams dead, the whole case would fall apart then and there.

"KIGY, Brother," I said when he came up to my window.

"How you doing?"

"All right. Have a seat in the car. I don't want anybody noticing us." I watched him come around the front of the vehicle and climb into the passenger seat, just as Moran had. "I know how emotional this all was to you, what that guy did to you and all, and I thought you might want some closure."

I handed him the photo.

"Let me know what you think."

His eyes widened. "That works."

"That what you wanted?"

"Oh, yes."

"That's what you wanted to see."

"Yes, sir." He gave the photo back to me and opened the door. "Take care, Brother."

He smiled the way a man might in the company of his best friend, and I suppose that's what I was to him, at least for today.

When I drove off, a huge wave of relief spread through me. It didn't last long, though. I still had one more meeting ahead of me, and Charles Newcomb was not only the ringleader but the most dangerous of the conspirators.

I called him when I reached our meeting spot. "KIGY, Brother. I just wanted to see if you're on Southside Boulevard yet."

"Almost there now."

"I'll wait for you here, Brother."

He arrived five minutes later. Newcomb used to be a cop, so I knew he'd be the most likely of the three to ask questions, maybe not take the photo at face value, and maybe challenge me on who else I had involved in the effort. I was standing outside my car to meet him, in the hopes of looking more welcoming and inviting.

"KIGY, Brother," I greeted him.

He stopped before me and gave me a long look, appearing concerned. "You all right?" he asked, giving the fake IV tube in my arm a long look. "That don't look too good."

Neither Moran nor Driver had noticed my sickly looking complexion or the fake IV, or if they had, they didn't say anything, maybe out of deference. But I knew that wouldn't be the case with Newcomb, and I had donned this whole getup specifically to throw him off.

"I'm fine. Just a little under the weather. Get into the car. I don't want anybody else to see this."

I was afraid he was going to ask me where the body was, or why there wasn't anything about a guy getting murdered on the news. Because of his police training, he was more likely to ascertain any inconsistencies in the scenario that had been concocted to get him to implicate himself, as Moran and Driver had done.

"You all right?" he asked again, taking it.

Breathe, focus, listen . . .

"'Cause you look kinda weak, Brother Joe."

Breathe, focus, listen . . .

He was studying the picture. "Is it all right?" I asked him.

"Yeah." He chuckled and handed the photo back to me. "N——even pissed himself. Hey, good job, Joe."

And then he climbed out of my vehicle and cast me a smile. Solace like nothing I'd ever felt before washed over me. Newcomb had bought the story; all three of them had. The plan had worked.

But we still needed to arrest them.

CHAPTER 19

HOME AWAY FROM HOME

ALACHUA, FLORIDA
MARCH 2015

"How was your day?" Shannon asked me when I stepped through the door. "Anything you wanna talk about?"

"No, I'm good."

She looked down at the discolored patch where I'd taped the fake IV. "How'd it go?"

Shannon knew I couldn't answer, so I just hugged her tight. I knew this had been a very successful operation, but I knew from my experience that looming summits could prove to be false. And as well as everything had gone until that point, there was still ample opportunity for something to go wrong, just as it had back in Wayward. Jamie Ward had given me a single assault rifle to convert to fully automatic, but he had a multitude of other firearms stored in his home. The records of both Moran and Driver, meanwhile, were peppered with complaints from prisoners about the use of excess force. And I'd reported Charles Newcomb's claim that he had killed four men to the FBI, so they were aware of the dangers he posed.

Vaughn summoned me to the Jacksonville field office on a damp, gray morning a week after I showed Moran, Driver, and Newcomb the photo of Warren Williams. Even though it was a weight off my shoulders to have gotten through those meetings not only unscathed but with the evidence the FBI was looking for, I hadn't gotten much sleep the night before. Tia, just short of her first birthday, had been up coughing through the night. And even if she hadn't, the measure of the work ahead of me—helping the FBI with the arrests—weighed heavy. Worrying about another potential false summit, I knew I wouldn't feel truly at ease until I was certain we had gotten to the top. Maybe worst of all, I couldn't share any of this with Shannon, because that would violate operational security.

Entering an overly bright conference room with a TV monitor still switched on from the last meeting held inside, I once again noted the absence of Lindsay Campbell, just as I had noted the absence of Vaughn from any number of the meetings I'd had with Joe Armstrong. I took this as more process than anything else, since Armstrong had been my official handler then just as Vaughn was now. But we had never reached this level with the first infiltration.

"State prosecutors met with a judge yesterday," Vaughn said, right at the start. "The judge agreed that the evidence was overwhelming and issued arrest warrants for all four subjects on the spot. You've done an incredible job, Joe. Just like the first time, you've given us everything we need to prosecute. I'll let you know when we secure the warrants and are ready to move to the next stage."

There was something in his gaze and his tone that told me there was more.

"You could have told me that over the phone, Rich," I prompted him.

His expression tightened. "Priority number one now becomes keeping you, and your family, safe until the arrests are made. So we're officially moving you into protective custody."

"What's that mean exactly?"

"We've already chosen the hotel. Look at it like a vacation."

"You didn't answer my question, Rich."

"We're going to move you out of your home today. Agents will be waiting when you get back. We're going to take your vehicles and give you a new one. You can pack one suitcase for each family member—that's it. You take with you only what you can carry."

"When do we come back for the rest?"

Vaughn was trying to remain unruffled. "You don't. Whatever gets left behind stays behind. Standard procedure, Joe, and this all happens today. I want you and your family settled into your temporary new home at the Embassy Suites by dinner."

I knew there was no point in arguing, wasting time better spent getting back to my family and packing up whatever we could. True to Vaughn's word, four FBI agents were waiting when I got home. Two would be driving my vehicles away. A rental car was already parked at the curb.

"What's going on?" Shannon asked, opening the door before I could grab the knob.

"We've got to leave. For our own protection."

"Were there threats? Are we in danger?"

"Nothing like that. The FBI called it standard operating procedure."

"What do you call it?"

I looked down, then back up. "We can only take what we can carry. Everything else stays behind. Everything else is gone."

I thought of my children's toys, especially Jordy's collection of Elmo dolls. It was his pride and joy, but there was no way we could squeeze all those stuffed animals and figurines into a suitcase crammed with clothes and possessions. Nor could we squeeze in all of my mom's pictures that were scattered throughout the house, keepsakes that helped keep my memories alive. And I had so many documents and commendations I'd accumulated over the years. I thought of the modest furniture we'd pinched pennies in order to fill the house with. So much I was used to, so much that had become part of the fabric of our lives. Whatever we left behind, we'd never see again, and that amounted to quite a lot.

"How's Tia?" I asked, as much to change the subject as anything.

"I thought she was a little better. Now I'm not so sure."

The fact that all her material possessions, including the clothes and shoes she'd accumulated over the years, were gone for good—I could see all the pain and angst from that reality all over her taut expression. She was trying not to get angry or frustrated, and put on as brave a face as she could for me and the kids. We hadn't done anything wrong, yet we were the ones who were suffering.

When I checked on Tia, I saw that she had gotten worse since last night. So amid the chaos of FBI agents entering our home to supervise the packing process, what we could take with us and what we couldn't, I rushed my daughter to the hospital, leaving the rest of my family behind.

At the emergency room of University of Florida Hospital, doctors diagnosed her as suffering with RSV, or respiratory syncytial virus. They began antibiotic treatment immediately, gave me a prescription, and told me I had nothing to worry about after three tense hours by my daughter's side.

I was relieved that Tia would be okay, but I knew I still had plenty to worry about once I got home. I stepped inside to find not only the FBI present, but also an official from the Department of Children and Families in the company of a local sheriff's deputy.

Shannon pulled me aside before we got around to introductions. "I called my parents to let them know Tia was sick and you'd taken her to the hospital."

Uh-oh, I thought. *What did you do that for?* I wanted to ask, but stopped short, given how much stress my wife was already under.

"Anyway, someone called in an anonymous complaint to DCF, the Department of Children and Families," she resumed. "They tried to find you in the hospital, but you'd already left."

"Complaint about what?" I asked, my blood starting to boil over what was clearly my father-in-law's sordid attempt at payback.

Shannon swallowed hard. Tears welled up in her eyes. I'd never seen her look this guilty over anything.

"Whoever called in the complaint accused you of physically abusing her."

Although I was never actually able to confirm it, I suspected this represented Rusty's long-awaited opportunity to seek revenge on me—not very surprising on its face, though the timing couldn't have been worse. Here we were with a family room occupied by FBI agents, DCF, and a deputy thrown in for good measure. The suitcases my wife had managed to get packed while I was at the hospital with Tia were sitting in the middle of the room, and the FBI agents present couldn't intervene. So I called Rich Vaughn.

"Everything good on the home front with packing up, Joe?" he asked me, never expecting what I was about to tell him.

"Far from it," I said, and told him about our uninvited visitors.

"Put the sheriff's deputy on," Vaughn instructed.

I handed the phone to the deputy and could only hear his side of the conversation, which wasn't much. Vaughn was obviously giving him his marching orders and saw no reason to let him get a word in edgewise.

"Yes, sir, I do," the deputy said. "Yes, sir, I will."

With that, he handed me back my phone and turned to the woman from the Department of Children and Families. "We're leaving. Nothing happened here. We're not filing a report."

I was so angry at my father-in-law for causing a ruckus at such an inopportune time, I showed neither the deputy nor the woman from DCF out, nor remember them leaving. We put on a brave, happy face so as not to upset our kids, telling them we were going on a vacation, that it was going to be fun. Jordy was thrilled, seeing this as an adventure. Tia had fallen asleep.

The FBI got us settled at the nearby Embassy Suites under a different name. My wife and I claimed the bedroom and turned the living room area of the suite into our kids' bedrooms and playroom, although there weren't many toys we were able to bring for Jordy to play with. I had no idea how I was going to break the news to him that he'd never see his Elmo collection again.

It made no sense to me why the FBI couldn't place the rest of our stuff in storage to reclaim later, once they moved it out. This all caught me totally by surprise. There had been no forewarning about what this stage of the process would be like. It wouldn't have changed a thing about my commitment to bringing down the Klan, but it would have been nice to be given some advance notice nonetheless. I'm sure such standard operating procedure involved not wanting to have those under FBI protective custody or witness protection possess anything that might connect them to their former lives. Resettlement was about embarking on brand-new lives, starting from scratch. That made a degree of sense, but I couldn't help feeling some bitterness that my payback for laying my life on the line for the FBI was to have them strip away items I truly treasured, like a number of letters and pictures, including one from a great army friend who'd lost his life in Iraq. There were also my medals, awards, and my scholarship letter from Florida State, even my sniper school certificate. There was a document that officially commended me on the work I had done undercover for the army's Criminal Investigation Division that had resulted in the arrest of sixteen drug dealers. All told, those possessions felt to me like Jordy's Elmo collection felt to him. We couldn't keep my Kia Sportage or the Mazda sport coupe I'd just purchased for Shannon. Whatever we left behind, we were never going to see again.

It wasn't unusual for me to be out of communication with the klavern hierarchy for stretches at a time amounting to days or even weeks, given the multitude of duties I performed as the Grand Knighthawk for the region. Of course, Ward and Newcomb were both well aware of the murder I'd apparently facilitated, so lying low for a while would make perfect sense to them.

Then, a week after we'd taken refuge at the hotel, I contracted severe tonsillitis and had to go into the hospital to have my tonsils removed. I made a point of contacting both Ward and Newcomb prior to that, and in a raspy voice that was every bit real, told them I was going to be out of commission for a stretch. I remained in the hospital for four days. Shannon and the kids visited me there every day, creating a false sense of normalcy that would slip away when I returned to the hotel that was a vivid reminder of what had already transpired and what was about to come to pass: the simultaneous takedowns of all four targets the day after I was released from the hospital.

▲ ▲ ▲

I felt like I was in the center of a tornado, swept up in all the moving parts of what was about to go down. Every time I thought I was done, it turned out there was another mountain to climb. My life had been dominated by my work inside the KKK for so long, even in the period between the two infiltrations, that I just wanted it to be over for the sake of my family.

A week before the takedowns, I met with Vaughn and the FBI SWAT commander at the Jacksonville field office. Lindsay Campbell did not attend that meeting. In answer to my inquiry about her absence, Vaughn told me she was responsible for coordinating our efforts with the state prosecutors out of Attorney General Pam Bondi's office. The SWAT leader was right out of central casting: six foot two, ruggedly built, and bald. I was never introduced to him by name and addressed him as "Commander."

"We're gonna do this next week on April first," he told me. "That was a strategic choice, because it's a day when Thomas Driver will be coming off shift at the same time David Moran will be coming on. That gives us the opportunity to swoop them up together. We know they'll be armed, but we intend to come at them in force with a tactical team. Whatever move they try to make, they won't get to finish."

He left it there, and I remained silent.

"That brings us to Jamie Ward," the commander continued. "Agent Vaughn tells me you've got some intel on his place of residence, where we'll be picking him up."

I eased a notebook from the backpack that had been thoroughly searched when I entered the building lobby and opened it to pages filled with notes, schematics, drawings, and maps that all pertained to Ward's home and yard.

"You did all this yourself?" he said, flipping through the pages.

"Yes, sir. You'll see on the maps I indicated the precise positioning of routes of egress both in the front and rear of the home. The colored circle in the middle is a hatch that leads to a crawl space beneath the house, like an escape route. I wanted to make sure you knew about that."

The commander just stared at me.

"The other thing I wanted to mention," I said, turning to a set of two pages that mapped out the surrounding area and pointing out a large building I'd drawn, "is Bronson Elementary School, which is located here, approximately two hundred yards away diagonally from the rear of Ward's home."

I didn't bother to mention that I'd been thinking of my own kids the whole time I was drawing out these schematics, doing everything I could to make sure Ward never got anywhere near that school.

"The takedowns are going to occur in the morning," the commander said, "which means we'll need to cover the school."

"What about evacuating it?" Vaughn asked.

"That will take too long and attract too much attention. We'll assign four men and a K-nine unit to the school on the remote chance Ward slips away and shows up there to take hostages." Then the commander looked back at me as he took my notebook. "Impressive work. Which brings us to you."

He reviewed my role in the April 1 operation, which he explained would include a hundred SWAT commandos. Those men had been culled from the Jacksonville Sheriff's Office, Gainesville Police Department, Columbia County Sheriff's Office, and Bradford County Sheriff's Office, with others providing support. Approximately eight different agencies were involved, attesting to the magnitude of the operation, which would begin with a briefing in the Alachua Police Department parking lot at four o'clock in the morning under the spill of floodlights.

"We're going to put twenty-five men on Ward, twenty-five on Driver and Moran at the prison, and fifty backing you up in the Home Depot parking lot." The commander's expression had been serious and stern from the get-go, but I watched it tighten even further. "Now comes the most important question of all: Do you expect Charles Newcomb to put up a fight?"

"Well, Commander, I can tell you he's told me on several occasions that if the police ever tried to take him, he'd shoot his way out to the death."

He nodded, clearly not surprised. "That's why we're allotting fifty men to the parking lot."

CHAPTER 20

TAKEDOWN

ALACHUA, FLORIDA
APRIL 1, 2015

Let me see your hands!

The FBI SWAT team commander had prepped me for this moment. I was the tip of the spear for the most dangerous part of the takedown operation, given Charles Newcomb's proven capacity for violence. At this point, the takedowns of David Moran, Thomas Driver, and Jamie Ward would be underway, but my focus was rooted squarely on this parking lot and the fact that upwards of fifty guns were trained my and Newcomb's way. With that many guns, something could easily go wrong, especially if Newcomb resisted in any way. Once the first shot was fired, a barrage was likely to follow, with me as potential collateral damage.

I raised my hands in the air, while Newcomb left his by his side. We turned together, and I found myself facing an M4 assault rifle six inches from my face, the finger of the FBI SWAT team member in full body armor starting to curl over the trigger.

At that point, I had to resist giving in to instinct, since in training I had disarmed any number of men pointing a gun at me in almost the identical positioning.

Breathe, focus, execute . . .

I steadied myself with my breathing and managed to restrain my instincts, clasping my hands behind my head instead.

"Down on the ground!" a voice ordered.

I lowered to my knees and then lay on my stomach. I felt SWAT team members bring my arms together in order to fasten handcuffs to my wrists. Out of the corner of my eye, I could see that Charles Newcomb had not complied with the order to hit the ground and was being cuffed in a standing position instead.

"Come on, brothers," he said, with surprising calm as they confiscated a backup firearm he was carrying, "we're all friends here. What's this about?"

These men were protecting my identity and preserving operational security by making it appear that I had been swept up in the takedown I had been responsible for initiating. I later learned that the arrests of Jamie Ward at his home, as well as Thomas Driver and David Moran at the prison, had gone off similarly without a hitch. The overwhelming show of force and attention to every last detail had combined to leave the suspects no choice but to surrender.

I was placed in the back of one state of Florida highway patrol vehicle, staged to look as if I was being taken into custody, while Newcomb was placed in the other. It would be the last time I saw him until we faced each other in a courtroom.

After my "arrest," I was transported to a separate police station from Charles Newcomb so he wouldn't be able to observe me being treated differently. The cops left me in the back of the squad car, with my handcuffs still in place, and said someone from the FBI would be coming out to get me. I recognized him as soon as he emerged from the building:

It was Joe Armstrong. He smiled as he removed my handcuffs. I hadn't seen him since the unsavory end to my first stretch undercover.

"Long time, no see," I said, greeting him with a smile.

Armstrong grinned back. I realized he was holding his ever-present plastic cup, a personal spittoon, with a wad of tissue stuffed in the bottom to catch juice.

"You did an awesome job, Joe. You're still a rock star. You've always done everything we've ever asked you."

We didn't speak any further about Wayward.

"When we're done here, I'm going to take you and your family to your new home," he said instead.

The new home Armstrong was referring to turned out to be a two-bedroom apartment in Jacksonville. The complex was secure enough and featured a pool and a gym. There was also a Dave & Buster's almost directly across the street. Not a bad place to call home temporarily, since we wouldn't be staying there long, right?

Wrong.

Over the course of the next month or so, nobody would give me a straight answer to the simple question, *How does this work?* Even Vaughn and Campbell, who I'd come to trust and rely on, were being evasive. I could only guess that was due to the fact that they didn't really know themselves. The wheels of justice, as they say, turn slowly, and my family was at the mercy of the interminable time it often takes before a case moves from arrest to prosecution. All four suspects were considered flight risks and a danger to the community, so their bail was set at figures too high for any of them to meet. The longer they stewed behind bars, though, the higher the chances they would reach out to a Klan member or ghoul to track me down and exact their revenge.

That reality made the next few months feel like we were living in a particular kind of purgatory. Neither my wife nor I was allowed to work, and my son, who was supposed to be entering first grade the following fall, wasn't allowed to attend school. We weren't allowed to socialize, which meant Jordy couldn't have any friends. That would have been okay for a few weeks, but when those weeks stretched into months, the experience began to take its toll on us. We were nowhere near the beach in St. Augustine anymore and would never again see our home of seven years, the only home Tia had known. We'd come to love that place, and now it was gone. It might as well have been burned to the ground.

One June day near the onset of summer, two months after the move to our "new home" in protective custody, I was taking my son to the pool when he just broke down.

"Why can't I have any friends?" he cried.

Try explaining to a six-year-old the meaning of protective custody. You can't. The best I could do was play Marco Polo with him in the pool and let him stand on my back and pretend I was a motorboat. He was fine by the time we went to Dave & Buster's to play video games later the same day, but I started getting antsy every time one of the arcade consoles flashed GAME OVER. The message was just too on point. We had replaced all his lost Elmo toys with new ones, but he'd often whine that he missed the old ones because the new ones weren't the same.

Something I could relate to all too well.

Our rent was covered by the FBI, who also provided limited funds for other living expenses like food and clothing, on top of my VA benefits. Meanwhile, our bills for credit cards, car payments, and the like were suspended through the duration of protective custody; that didn't mean we wouldn't have to pay them, only that our creditors weren't able to send us any because we were "ghosts" now. Not paying those bills because we weren't receiving them destroyed our credit, and even though we would be provided with new identities by the FBI, we had to keep our old social security numbers, meaning once this was over we'd have to rebuild our credit from scratch. It would be years before we could get a credit card again, and during this period we would have to rely on cash. Not to mention the legal fees of hiring counsel to execute our legal name changes in court to obtain new driver's licenses and birth certificates. We had basically ceased to exist, but the world kept right on going without us. We were living entirely off the grid, the way federal fugitives do. Even Jamie Ward, who had escaped from prison, had enjoyed more freedom than we did.

When you agree to become a confidential human source, nobody tells you what the aftermath is going to be like. Apparently, the more successful you are, the higher the price you pay. And the more time you're alone and exposed, the more opportunity there is for something bad to happen. I'd lie awake nights thinking that my payback for the most successful infiltration of the Ku Klux Klan in FBI history was losing my house, almost all my possessions, my friends, and by all accounts, my future. This was what I got for my years of service? All that was missing was the gold watch and answers to my questions. No matter how often I reminded myself of the importance of what I'd accomplished, not only putting dangerous, hateful men behind bars but also providing an unprecedented amount of information to the FBI about the hierarchy and inner workings of the Klan, it was difficult to stomach the immense cost my family was now paying.

I didn't think things could get much worse, until they did. Later in June, my wife called her mother and stepfather to inform them of our status without giving them any specifics. So Sharon and Rusty took to calling everyone from the Bureau, to the U.S. Marshals Service, to the office of the presiding judge, to badger them for more information. All they learned was what they had already been told. But that didn't stop them from harassing anyone and everyone inside the system, who, in turn, would contact us to ask us who the hell these people were. It was psychological torture, with no idea of when it was going to end. Our whole world felt like a fishbowl we were living in, prohibited from even tapping on the glass to let anyone know we were there.

Things escalated further almost immediately, when a journalist named Nate Thayer contacted me, having somehow come into possession of my phone number. Thayer, it turned out, had close ties to white supremacist groups and the movement in general. He had once been a highly respected investigative journalist best known for scoring an interview with the murderous Khmer Rouge leader Pol Pot in the jungles of Cambodia in 1997, for which he was ultimately rewarded with a prestigious Peabody Award.

From what I read and heard about Thayer, he had developed alcohol and substance abuse problems and suffered from a myriad of health issues, many stemming from shrapnel damage caused by a landmine a truck in which he was riding drove over in Cambodia in 1989. I uncovered a GoFundMe campaign that was launched on his behalf to purchase a wheelchair-accessible van for him. (It was later reported in the *New York Times* that over thirty-five thousand dollars had been raised on his behalf.) Broke and desperate, he swapped his award-winning coverage of left-wing guerrilla groups for championing the work of right-wing fringe groups that included white supremacist and Christian nationalist movements.

Thayer, for whatever reason, appeared to hate the FBI. When we finally spoke, off the record over the phone, he informed me that he had a source who appeared to know me well and had provided him with a laundry list of terrible lies I was helpless to disprove. I didn't want to talk to him, but if I didn't, I knew he would just run with the story. I had to try to salvage my reputation and the case. He was quick to dismiss the most salacious accusations leveled against me, but he had detailed knowledge of the mental health issues I had experienced, and it was clear he was going to use those facts against me in his article. It was just as clear that he saw me as an FBI tool fit for skewering. Thayer's hatred for the government, especially the Bureau, together with his embrace of groups like the Ku Klux Klan, meant his hit job of a story would serve the dual purpose of destroying the FBI's case while allowing the Klan to emerge unscathed. Without me, after all, there was no case. And if I walked away from the whole thing, or lost my credibility as the only real witness against the perpetrators, the case would go away with me. Thayer's only concession was a promise that he would hold off publishing his story until the trials began.

But that wasn't my only problem. Around the same time, Rusty took to Facebook and posted a picture of himself brandishing a rifle on a dirt road that cut through the woods with the caption, "Take him down the road."

In the South, that phrase describes what you do when you decide to shoot your dog. Maybe it was paranoia on my part, but was he making his true intentions toward me clear? Was he trying to intimidate me? Because he hadn't mentioned my name, though, there was nothing Rich Vaughn or Lindsay Campbell could do when I showed them the post. Still, my paranoia made me wonder if Rusty might pass my name to parties that had every reason to want me dead.

I was meeting with Vaughn and Campbell regularly for updates, but there really wasn't anything they could update me on. Every meeting or phone call was the same—there was never new information, so we just kept repeating the same conversation, with me posing the same questions.

How much longer until we get to court?
How much longer will my family have to live this way?
What was being done to protect my family?

All naturalized KKK members take a blood oath: If you disclose Klan secrets, you will pay with your blood and your life. I knew better than anyone that these weren't empty promises. I had no idea who might be out there gunning for me—somebody who wanted to make their mark in the organization by taking me out. I just wanted to pack my family up before it was too late and say, *You know what? Screw this. We're done.*

But I knew that wasn't an option. Leaving would mean that everything I'd endured undercover over two operations would be forfeited. I had infiltrated the Klan a second time to finish the job I hadn't the first time. How could I up and walk away now, especially when I wouldn't be walking, I'd be running?

Rusty's attempted intimidation made me wonder if he was provoking me so I'd take action against him myself. Getting arrested for assault, though, would destroy my credibility as a witness; it was the equivalent of walking away, except I'd still be exactly where I was. So I ignored the bait, since to do otherwise would leave him the winner. I would be playing right into his hands.

I thought of the morning after I'd met with Rich Vaughn in 2013 when I told Shannon at the kitchen table that the FBI wanted me to go operational again.

"You don't have anything to say, babe?"

"I know if you want to do it, you're going to, no matter what I say."

She was right: I would. In moments of frustration like this, though, I wondered if I'd made the right decision.

CHAPTER 21

FISHBOWL

NORTH FLORIDA
JUNE 2015

I had no idea how long my family would have to remain in protective custody. After two months, though, our kids were starting to get antsy. Jordy and Tia loved going to look at fish, the bigger the better, especially Jordy, so we decided to get out of town for a few days to pay a visit to the South Carolina Aquarium in downtown Charleston.

In my ongoing process of monitoring right-wing websites, what I came to refer to as the society of ideologues, I came across a lot of disturbing chatter and posts about shooting up a Black church, given there would be multiple unarmed targets unlikely to mount any resistance. I informed the FBI of what I had surmised and left the rest to them.

On the multiple occasions that we visited the aquarium over the course of our trip, we must have driven past the Emanuel AME Church in Charleston, a famed Black church, five or six times. They say snipers sometimes develop a keen intuitive sense that borders on clairvoyance, but I can't say I felt anything odd when passing this historic landmark other than to remark to Shannon that wherever we drove, we always ended up driving right past its beautiful, ornate exterior. My warning to the FBI pertained to the multitude of Black churches across the country, not one church or city specifically.

Then, barely a week after our visit in the spring of 2015, a young man named Dylann Roof shot the place up and murdered nine innocent people who had welcomed him into their midst. He may not have been a naturalized member of the Klan, but he followed the ideology in becoming a fringe accelerationist—a lone wolf motivated by the kind of tenets and dogma embraced by the KKK. He was probably looking at the same sites I had been and followed the suggestion left on numerous chat boards. It was like somebody had wound Dylann Roof up and pointed him in the right direction. This was what happens when someone like that young man goes kinetic.

By the time I was six months into a life that wasn't much of a life at all, though, the repercussions of my infiltration and the arrests it had led to had left the Klan critically wounded from coast to coast, according to information I had gained from right-wing websites that followed KKK activity in the aftermath of the arrests. I had brought down two major KKK figures in Grand Dragon Jamie Ward and Exalted Cyclops Charles Newcomb, not to mention drastically reducing the efficacy of Frank Ancona, on whose watch it had all occurred, and who mused about reinventing himself. No one was sure exactly how much I knew or what other leaders I could name. Chapters all across the country began to wonder if they, too, had an informant in their midst. Klaverns stopped holding cross burnings and general meetings. Klan brothers turned against their leaders and sought refuge in militia-style groups like the Oath Keepers, Three Percenters, and Proud Boys, which had become a rising force in the world of ultra-right-wing fanatics.

As the months kept passing, Vaughn would inform me that depositions had been scheduled, only to be postponed; then rescheduled only to be postponed again. It was like that Samuel Beckett play *Waiting for Godot*, in which two hoboes meet under the same tree every day to await the coming of a man who's going to give them jobs, but he never shows up. I could only do my best to hope that my family wouldn't meet the same fate, that the trial would happen soon. But with each passing day, it became harder and harder to believe we would ever see the other side of this.

The holidays rolled around, and we were still in protective custody, but we made the most of it. Even though we had been relocated to Jacksonville, St. Augustine, where we'd been living, had this great tradition of lighting up the whole town for Christmas, which they called "Nights in Lights." People actually came from all around the world to see it, and for us, viewing the town festively aglow helped vanquish the darkness into which our lives had descended, even if only for a brief time. Watching Tia's eyes widen at sight of a thirty-foot Christmas tree wrapped in ornaments was one of the happiest moments of my life. That was also the first year she sat on Santa's lap, and I listened as he asked her what she wanted for Christmas.

"A home," my twenty-month-old daughter told him.

Our seventh wedding anniversary that same December of 2015 came and went, as did our kids' birthdays. Shannon was keeping as brave a face as she could, though I could tell how much the strain was wearing on her. We took trips to other aquariums, in Tampa and New Orleans, among others, to break the monotony, but there were only so many we could reach by car and only so much time we could spend staring at fish. At my regular meetings with Vaughn and Campbell, I pushed as hard as I could for answers. Their response was always the same: *Be patient. It won't be long.*

I lost count of how many times I heard that, and finally I'd had enough. I stopped being patient, because it had been too long.

After more than a year in protective custody, with no end in sight, I finally paid a visit to the nearest satellite office, like a drop-in center, for Florida senator Marco Rubio, without informing the FBI. It was located in a downtown Jacksonville office building with a secure entrance that barred admittance absent an appointment. I had called ahead, so they were expecting me and buzzed me in through the door as soon as I announced myself.

I found myself in a cramped reception area, manned by a female receptionist. I could see offices down a short hallway, but wasn't escorted toward them. Instead, the receptionist offered me a seat in front of her desk.

I explained my situation to her. She seemed utterly befuddled, even scared, but agreed to put through an official request that the senator look into the matter and intercede if he could. I had the sense that I had unsettled her and that she wanted me out of the office as quickly as possible; she asked no follow-up questions and didn't jot down some of the pertinent personal information I was providing. My protestations weren't quite being met by deaf ears, only ears unwilling or unable to grasp the totality of what I was trying to explain.

A few weeks later, I got a call from the senator's assistant, a woman named Mercedes.

"Is this Joe Moore?"

"Yes."

"Mr. Moore, this is Senator Marco Rubio's office calling."

"Thank you, thank you for getting back to me."

Her tone turned curt. "Mr. Moore, I'm afraid we have a problem. You put this office in danger. You should never have done that."

I was dumbstruck. All I had requested of the senator's office was to help us get on with our lives. Was that really too much to ask? Was this treatment my reward for risking my life every day for my years inside the KKK?

That call from Senator Rubio's assistant was followed swiftly by one from Rich Vaughn.

"That was a mistake, Joe," he told me. "You don't need Senator Rubio's help."

"Well, my family needs somebody's help," I said, trying to keep from raising my voice in anger, "since the FBI doesn't seem interested in helping us."

"We're doing everything we can."

"Then maybe I should hire a lawyer to see if he can do more."

I had already retained a lawyer to handle our identity changes and wondered if he could help with this as well. Before I was done, I was out of pocket thirteen thousand dollars for his efforts.

Then Rich Vaughn called in May 2016, more than a year into our life in limbo.

"Joe," Vaughn said, "Lindsay and I need to see you right away. There's been a development."

When Vaughn and Campbell arrived at our apartment, they served me with a subpoena to appear for depositions in two weeks. The subpoenas had been issued by the defense attorneys for Moran, Driver, and Newcomb, but couldn't be served in the traditional manner because I was under protective custody. So the FBI told the defense lawyers that the Bureau would provide service.

Getting the depositions scheduled was the biggest step so far in advance of the looming trial, fourteen months after the FBI had arrested the four men in question. Jamie Ward had already pled out on the gun charges and his case was federal, not state, as the others were.

I was picked up by the FBI on three consecutive mornings—June 3, 4, and 5—and transported to the Jacksonville field office. I was relieved to see the drivers using surveillance detection routes to make sure we weren't being followed. Inside the conference room where the deposition process would take place, my own lawyer was waiting, along with a state attorney from the attorney general's office. Supposedly, they were there to protect my interests, but you wouldn't have known it from the way things went.

Individual lawyers for all three defendants took turns hammering away at my credibility, both personal and professional.

"Could you describe Thomas Driver for me, please?" Driver's attorney asked me.

I described his physical appearance, making it a point to mention that he was wearing large earrings, called gauges, in both his earlobes.

"You thought he had gauges?" the lawyer followed up, pouncing.

"Yes, because he did."

"And what if I told you he does not wear such gauges? How did you come up with that? I think you need to describe who it is you're actually talking about, because Thomas Driver does not have gauges in his ears."

It turned out that when Driver's attorney saw him, Driver wasn't wearing the gauges and the lawyer never noticed the large holes in his earlobes that had been drilled to accommodate them. During a break, I explained this to the state attorney, who tried to clean things up when he questioned me. But the exchange had left me rattled, which might have been its purpose in the first place.

The lawyers asked me about everyone in my family, one at a time. There was no investigative value to these questions. They were posed just to unnerve me. And it worked.

They kept dredging up my past to weaken me, including my bouts with mental illness to impeach my character. They produced a copy of my military records and pointed to an area that was redacted.

"What is this, Mr. Moore?"

"Redacted material in my military records."

"Would you have any idea what it was?"

"No, I have no idea because it's been redacted. I've never seen my records before, although I suppose it could contain classified information, something like that."

I expected the lawyer who'd posed that question to drill down deeper into that, but they didn't want to get into the specifics of my service because they needed to avoid making me a hero; it didn't suit their narrative. The lawyer implied that the redaction contained something negative, and I was not in a position to correct him.

Then the state attorney got his turn.

"Mr. Moore, did you save the lives of two soldiers under your command in action?"

"I did, yes."

"And did you receive the Army Commendation Medal for that specific feat?"

"I did."

"And did you receive an honorable discharge?"

"Yes."

Another of the lawyers, Newcomb's, I think it was, jumped in on that train of questioning.

"You claim to have served as a sniper during your service in the army."

"I was a sniper, as well as a section leader—"

"That being the case," he interrupted, before I'd finished, "can you describe the weapons that you would most commonly use in your duties?"

"The M24 sniper system, which is a bolt-action twenty-four-inch rifle. We also carry the M4 rifle, which is a fourteen-point-five-inch, magazine-loaded, gas impingement select fire system that takes five-point-five-six millimeter bullets in fifty-five grain cartridges that travel approximately three thousand and fifty feet per second with a point range at five hundred meters and an area range at six hundred and fifty meters."

The lawyer remained silent for a long stretch, before finally yielding the floor to another of the defense attorneys.

"Let's talk about your mental health issues, Mr. Moore. Could you describe them?"

"I'm receiving veterans disability payments for a major depressive disorder and PTSD that was service connected."

"Isn't it a fact you suffer from schizoaffective disorder?" he asked, referring to a condition that produces delusions.

I could see where this was going. "No, sir, I do not, and have never been diagnosed as such."

"Are you sure about that, Mr. Moore?"

"Yes, sir."

"So would I be wrong if your medical records include mention of schizoaffective disorder?"

"You would be, yes."

"And if I produced those records for you to see, what would you say?"

"That they must belong to someone else."

The defense lawyer chimed in again. "Is it not a fact, Mr. Moore, that you were the one who suggested killing Mr. Warren Williams, after the defendants approached you?"

"No, sir, it's not a fact. Not at all."

"Let me ask the question again," he said, raising his voice slightly. "Were you not the one who suggested killing Warren Williams?"

"No," I shot back, my voice raised more than slightly.

"You suggested killing Warren Williams to my client, is that not a fact?" he practically yelled at me.

"No!" I barked back. "It's a lie!"

"One more time, Mr. Moore, did you not tell my client that Warren Williams should be killed?" he said, his voice breaking because of its volume.

"One more time," I shouted at him in the conference room, "I . . . did . . . not, no!"

I had spent fourteen months in hiding, the bulk of my life put on hold, awaiting the time when I could just tell the truth. And now I was getting carved up by a trio of lawyers who only wanted to make me look as bad as they possibly could. To hear them tell it, I was a mentally unstable man who had embellished his service record and then proceeded to feed a story I'd concocted to the FBI. Nothing they were suggesting about me was even remotely true, and no matter how many times the state attorney objected for the record, it didn't matter. Because I wasn't able to get any in-person treatment for my depression and PTSD while in protective custody, my temper was shorter—I started feeling more like the man they were painting me as than the man I really was.

After the depositions were over, part of me wanted to go back to the apartment, pack up my family, and take off. Everybody else could go to hell, which was where I'd been living for fourteen months now. Sure, my patriotism was strong and my faith was unwavering, but I had reached a point where it felt like I had lost everything. I wasn't sure I could take any more of this.

But I told myself I was a soldier and a leader. If I can lead men in battle, I can lead my family through this. If I could survive the things I had survived in my deployments, I could survive this. If I walked away, the case would fall apart, those three men would never stand trial, and that would all be on me. I swore an oath to protect the Constitution—and the Ku Klux Klan presented as great a threat to it as any enemy I had faced overseas. I couldn't walk away from my country then, and I couldn't walk away now.

My wife and I had joined a gym that was right near the apartment complex, and after the final day of depositions was over, I went straight there and just pounded the heavy bag. No gloves, no tape—just bare hands pounding and pounding so hard I could feel the room shake. I just let loose on that bag until my hands ached so much I had to stop.

That was only the first of a whole bunch of times I pounded that bag. The deposition stage had ended, but the actual trial was nowhere in sight. Not a single hearing had been scheduled, and my family's life remained in a perpetual state of limbo. Worse, the long delay that had followed the arrests had left us vulnerable, with targets painted on our backs for every white supremacist in the country to aim their crosshairs at. I learned that law-enforcement officers associated with the Klan from two states, Florida and Oklahoma, had tried to locate me. Fortunately, they'd been unable to access the system, and their efforts were flagged by the FBI. I had no way of knowing, though, how many similar attempts across the state and country had not been flagged, which meant a cop from anywhere associated with the movement my testimony could bring down might be coming after me.

That reality made us virtual prisoners in our temporary home, pretty much confined to the neighborhood. No more aquarium trips, no more driving any more than a mile or so from the complex. If we needed groceries or anything else, Shannon or I would go alone, never together as a family, because we had been left in too vulnerable a position to take the risk.

Our plight worsened even beyond that when Shannon's mother filed a missing person report that was all lies, starting with the fact that she claimed she'd heard from her daughter, who insisted that she and the kids were being held against their will. Procedure dictated that the FBI had to investigate, and Rich Vaughn showed up in the company of a team of agents who specialized in that kind of domestic case. I suffered the indignity of having to wait in the apartment building hallway with another agent while my wife and children were interviewed inside to ascertain whether there was any validity to the report.

Sharon and Rusty's hatred for me had known no end ever since, in their minds, I had taken Shannon away from them. This was just another attempt to make my life as miserable as they could in return and perhaps even win Shannon back in the process. But they underestimated her strength and my resolve. While not card-carrying KKK members themselves, they represented the mindset I was committed to destroying, and in June 2017, after more than two years in protective custody, I finally got that chance in the form of a call from Rich Vaughn.

"Joe," he said, "we've got a date to meet with the judge to finalize your name change. You're going to need to get all the paperwork in order before you leave."

"Leave?"

"A trial date has been set for September, so we're going to relocate you somewhere else to ensure your safety."

What Vaughn was getting at was the fact that now the trial date had been set, the Klan would redouble their efforts to come after me, and we had to take extra measures to ensure my family's safety. To their credit, the FBI asked us to select where we wanted to live, any place in the country, with no restrictions. After some research and careful thought, we chose Boise, Idaho. Not only was the city considered to be the jewel of the Northwest, it had a historically low crime rate and was the most geographically remote city in North America. And I felt anyone who came to Boise with bad intentions would have to go through a lot of trip wires before they got to me. While rural Idaho is considered by many to be a hotbed for right-wing activity, the city of Boise was like the state of Florida—pretty much fifty-fifty.

The FBI found us a beautiful town house, complete with a garage, in an upscale community. The managers of the complex received us as "ghosts" of the FBI, a necessary step since we otherwise wouldn't have been able to pass their stringent credit check. With the trial set to start around two months from then, on September 7, 2017, I began to breathe easier, feeling safe and hopeful that there was finally an expiration date on the nightmare that wouldn't end.

Shannon hadn't been feeling well through much of the drive to Boise.

"Should we go see a doctor?" I asked, once we were settled into our town house.

"No, I'll just go to the drugstore and get something."

She came back with a pair of pregnancy tests, figuring that's what might explain her symptoms. Sure enough, both tests came back positive, and a visit to an obstetrician confirmed she was already four months pregnant with our third child. I couldn't have been happier. That was more than enough to wash away the misery of the past two-plus years in protective custody. I was about to become a father again at the same time I was on the verge of giving testimony I hoped would result in a safer world for all my kids. The fact that we had another on the way was like the cherry on top of a sundae. We'd given up our families when we'd left Florida, but that felt okay, because we had our own growing family now. And our third child would be a symbol of the future we would build for ourselves, a cleansing baptism into our new lives.

Then Nate Thayer's articles started appearing on right-wing sites across the internet. The second article that popped up splashed my new name for everyone to see. It was like hanging a welcome sign outside my new home, inviting the KKK to take a shot at me. That article also included Shannon's new name, as well as the names and ages of my kids, which clearly compromised the safety of myself and my family. So with the long-awaited trial set to begin, I had to hope I managed to live long enough to take my spot in the witness box.

CHAPTER 22

THE WHOLE TRUTH

COLUMBIA COUNTY COURTHOUSE
SEPTEMBER 2017

We'd been in Boise for two months when Rich Vaughn called and said it was time to come back to Jacksonville. Shannon, who was six months pregnant, had to accompany me because the FBI believed she would have to testify as well. So the four of us boarded a plane and flew back to Florida. I had paperwork that allowed me to check my gun in a lockbox inside our checked baggage, so I'd be able to arm myself as soon as we retrieved our luggage in Jacksonville.

The FBI picked us up at the airport and brought us to a rental car agency, where we picked up a car they had arranged for us. Then we were escorted to a suite hotel under our new names, which had been revealed online by Nate Thayer. We entered the hotel and I immediately recognized the manager behind the reception desk as an old acquaintance. I handed him my ID, he looked at it, looked at me, and his jaw dropped. I could tell he'd recognized me and was confused, even scared—I could see his hand was shaking.

"Christian," I said, remembering his name, "it's me—Joe."

Then I handed him a document from the FBI.

"Oh my God," he managed, "we all wondered what happened to you."

We had FBI protection from that point forward until the trial started eight days later, after a six-day postponement. The morning the trial was set to commence, the FBI came to our room and knocked on the door. Then they entered the room to make sure we were all okay. I left with one of the FBI agents, got into an unmarked vehicle, and drove ninety minutes to the Columbia County Courthouse in Lake City, Florida. I felt comfortable that the Bureau had things under control and my family would be safe.

As we approached the courthouse, I noticed lines of reporters gathered outside. But I was more interested in observing the surrounding building sight lines in order to determine where, if someone were going to take a shot at the car, it would come from. We drove around the corner, the agent driving made a call, and we pulled into a sally port. A huge garage door opened, we drove through, and the door closed behind us.

I had already prepped my testimony with the lawyers who'd be prosecuting the case. They had informed me that Thomas Driver had recently pled out, leaving Charles Newcomb and David Moran as the remaining defendants I'd be testifying against. At the courthouse, I was taken to a holding room. I felt extraordinarily calm because I was both very well prepared and centered, thanks to my tried and true, battle-hardening breathing techniques that would help me stay in control until it was time for me to take the stand. When word came down that the moment had arrived, county deputies escorted me up a set of stairs and into the courtroom through the same side door through which the judge entered.

I heard murmuring start immediately from the jam-packed seats. And as I entered the courtroom, I heard someone close to the front mutter, "That's him!"

The witness stand was to the right of Judge Wesley Douglas and the defense table was to the left, so I had to walk past Newcomb and Moran. I made a conscious effort not to make eye contact, but I wasn't nervous. I felt prepared and determined. For ten years, my association with the Ku Klux Klan had dominated my life. This was my chance for closure, a chance I didn't get in my first infiltration.

▲   ▲   ▲

"Place your right hand on the Bible and raise your left hand in the air."

I did as the bailiff instructed.

"Do you swear to tell the truth, the whole truth, and nothing but the truth?"

"I do."

"Be seated."

The moment I had waited two years for had finally arrived. My heart was thudding in my chest as the prosecutor, Cass Castillo, rose from his chair. Castillo was a thin, bespectacled middle-aged Hispanic man with dark hair. He had actually retired as a prosecutor in 2014 to go into private practice, but had been called back on a special basis for this case because of his prosecutorial prowess and reputation.

Castillo had an assistant prosecutor named Kelsey Bledsoe working with him. She was in her midthirties and resembled Jodie Foster with glasses added to the ensemble. She had vast courtroom experience and was considered a rock star in prosecutorial circles; she had long drawn the highest-profile cases, like this one. They were the ultimate professionals, leaving me with the sense that they had my back and would be looking out for my best interests through the course of my testimony.

"Mr. Castillo," the judge signaled.

Castillo moved out from behind the prosecution's table to a lectern set halfway between the table and the witness box.

"Is your name Joe Moore, sir?" Castillo began.

"Yes," I answered.

"How old are you, Mr. Moore?"

"Forty-six."

"Are you married?"

"Yes."

"Have any children?"

"Yes."

"Mr. Moore, have you ever served in any branch of the United States Armed Forces?"

"Yes."

"Which branch?"

"U.S. Army."

To maintain my sense of purpose and remain centered, I focused on the courtroom the way I would a battlefield engagement, with detachment, objectivity, and dispassion. It was a large space, and there was even a second floor, like a balcony, that was also packed. I noticed there were no windows. In the very back row, I saw my mother-in-law, Sharon, sitting next to none other than Nate Thayer. I thought that was odd and wondered if they knew each other.

I wasn't angry, because I was focused on the vital task at hand. All I could think in the moment was that these two very small people in the back of the courtroom were mistaken if they thought their presence was going to have an effect on me.

The early boilerplate questioning focused on my years of service and where I'd been stationed. Interestingly enough, the prosecutors and I had rehearsed answers actually alternative to the truth, since the classified nature of my deployments made them impossible to confirm.

Even if I had told the truth, it would have opened a whole can of worms with the defense, who could demand corroborating evidence I wouldn't be able to provide.

"Now, have you ever shot anybody, Mr. Moore?"

"No."

"Had you ever seen combat during the time that you were in the service?"

"No."

"Ever serve in Special Operations in any capacity?"

"No."

The questioning continued for about an hour, during which we covered all the issues in my personal life that had sprung up during my two and a half years serving as a recruiter.

"Explain to the jury what kind of treatment did you get while you were still in the service," Castillo prompted me.

I turned to face the twelve men and women of the jury. "I was referred to a mental health counselor, who saw me a number of times in regard to the depression set on by duties as a recruiter."

"You mentioned that you separated from the army in 2002. What type of discharge did you receive?"

"Honorable."

I was baring my soul, covering some of the most painful times of my life in response to Castillo's questions. He had no choice; if he didn't get these issues out front right away, the defense attorneys would. They were certain to hammer me on a great deal of my past anyway. At least this way, the jury wouldn't be surprised by anything they heard. It would just be information that had already been covered, and hopefully they'd be able to see right through what the defense was doing.

Then we came to a part I had planned for, but that was unsettling nonetheless.

"Now, do you know who a man by the name of William Seaton is, Mr. Moore?"

"Yes."

"Who is he?"

"He is my father-in-law, my wife's stepfather."

"And what is his wife's name?"

My eyes sought out my mother-in-law in the back of the courtroom, next to Nate Thayer. I held her stare briefly and expressionlessly. She broke it first, turning her gaze downward, where it lingered. I pulled my focus back to Castillo.

"Sharon Seaton," I replied.

We had to bring this out as well, because we'd learned that Rusty was going to be testifying later in the trial in a desperate attempt by the defense to impugn my testimony and defame my character. Under Castillo's direct examination, we went through a blow-by-blow description of how I'd suspected my wife's mother of abusing my one-year-old son, and the aftermath of that, including the need for us to relocate to St. Augustine after Shannon's parents evicted us.

Then we moved on to how Joe Armstrong and the FBI had recruited me to go undercover in the Wayward chapter of the United Northern and Southern Knights, where William Hawley served as the Grand Dragon. We went through the details of those months as well.

"Now, did you perceive that what you were doing for the FBI in terms of infiltrating the Ku Klux Klan in the Gainesville area to be a dangerous endeavor?"

"Yes."

"That your life may be in danger?"

"Yes."

"Your family's life might be in danger?"

"Yes."

"Now, Mr. Moore, did your work with the FBI cause you to be away from home for periods of time?"

"Yes, it did."

"Now, did you tell your wife that you were working with the FBI?"

"Yes, I did."

"Were you the first to reveal to Mr. Seaton that you were working with the FBI?"

"No."

"Who did so?"

"My wife."

Shannon regrets doing that to this day, but I don't blame her at all. I think part of the reason why she'd told her parents was to warn them she was protected now, no longer dependent on, or subservient to, them.

We covered the circumstances that led to the end of my first deployment inside the KKK and moved on to Rich Vaughn spotting me at the gun range, which led him to ask me to come back in.

"What did [the FBI] propose that you do, Mr. Moore?"

"They wanted me to look at—look for other KKK organizations in the area and report back to them any information I had on those organizations."

We continued in more detail from there, on how I'd made contact with Jamie Ward and later met him in the parking lot of a Dollar General in late spring of 2013. I answered questions about both Ward and Mike Christopher to set up my ultimate testimony about what transpired at the cross burning and all that followed.

Then we started covering the barbecue that had taken place later the same day I'd met Jamie Ward.

"Mr. Christopher pulled me aside and wanted to talk to me about the military and tell me what he had specifically done in the military [as a Marine]," I said in response to another of Castillo's questions.

"Did you use the fact that Mr. Christopher was interested in the military and had experiences in the military as a way of endearing yourself to him?"

"Yes."

"What did you do?"

"I inflated my military background and claimed that I had more experience than I did. I told him I was in an elite unit, a Special Operations unit, and I truly was not, and I told him I had been to various combat theaters and I had not."

The FBI was aware of the nature of my military service, just as they were aware I was gagged by official government agencies that prohibited me from disclosing it.

Castillo went on to cover how I first became acquainted with Charles Newcomb, David Moran, and Johnny Grant after they'd come over to the Traditionalist American Knights from the Loyal White Knights. Then we finally came to the night of the cross burning, when I was approached by Newcomb and Moran, in the company of Thomas Driver, about "dispensing justice" on Warren Williams.

"Mr. Newcomb," I testified, "took me to where Mr. Moran was standing on the property, and Mr. Driver, who I'd never met previous to that evening, was standing next to him. Mr. Moran states that Mr. Driver has a situation and wanted to talk about it and tells Mr. Driver to tell the story. Then Mr. Driver pulls out a picture with some information on it."

Castillo held up the picture in question.

"Now, Mr. Moore, this picture, had you ever seen it before?"

"No."

"Do you remember what the information said on this photograph?"

"It had a name and some other biographical information."

"What do you see on the photograph, besides the writing? What image did you see on that?"

"I see a picture of an inmate."

"And what race was he?"

"Black."

"Had you ever seen that individual before?"

"No."

Castillo took me through the remainder of my conversation with Driver and Moran in painstaking fashion, making it plain what they wanted and were asking for my help in doing. Next, it came time for the defendants to implicate themselves in the recording I had made thanks to the wire I was wearing.

"And do you know who Charles Newcomb is, Mr. Moore?"

"Yes."

"And do you see him in the courtroom?"

"Yes."

I pointed Newcomb out, looking at him for the first time since entering the courtroom. He was looking straight at me, his expression utterly devoid of emotion.

"And do you know who David Moran is, Mr. Moore?"

"I do."

"And do you see him in the courtroom?"

"Yes."

I pointed David Moran out for the court. He was looking down, taking notes, but suddenly he looked up. Our eyes met briefly, but long enough to reveal a rage that told me he wanted to launch himself at the witness stand. But I also saw something in his eyes I'd never seen before: fear.

"Thank you, Mr. Moore. Could you please listen to the following recording?"

Castillo then hit a button on a laptop resting on the lectern, and the recording I'd made at my meeting with Newcomb after the cross burning played over the courtroom speakers:

I've already looked at the map and looked at where [Warren Williams] is at, but, you know, tell me the likely scenarios that you—you would feel comfortable with, Brother Joe.

I tell you I feel comfortable with just doing recon and make sure where he's at. One night we find him out there and I could walk right up and put him out of his misery.

Okay. It's that simple.

Newcomb spoke that last line matter-of-factly, as if he had no regard for human life at all. Castillo stopped the recording there and addressed me.

"'Where are we at looking at the church over in Palatka?' you said at a later point in the recording," Castillo asked, stressing the word "church." "What did you mean by that?"

"'Church' refers to the target."

"And that would have been Mr. Williams."

"Yes."

He switched the recording back on.

Did you get what I asked you the other day, Brother Joe?
I went to get that special ammo you asked for.

And then this from Newcomb:

If we can grab him up, throw his ass in the car, and take off with him somewhere and we'll just inject his happy ass with a bunch of insulin and let him start doing his flopping.

It felt like Newcomb was testifying against himself. My response resounded through the dead quiet of the courtroom.

Let's ride, Brother.

That was for the reconnaissance we did in Palatka the morning the Florida highway patrol car crawled up our tail and chased us out of the neighborhood. Then the conversation on our way back home played over the speaker, Newcomb postulating on how we were going to snatch Williams up.

The next question is how are we going to pull this son of a bitch out when he's living in the projects?

All we need to do is step up to his front door, have a pizza delivered, Brother Charles.

What pizza place delivers over here? They ain't allowed to come over here to the projects.

It was right about then on the recording that Newcomb noticed our tail. He said to Moran:

See that red car back—to the back left?
Yeah.
I seen him back there.
Is he still back there?
He stopped at the red light, but now he's coming up on us again.
This is just a strange car that he's not seen in the area before, two white guys sitting in the front.

Next came the recording I'd made getting Driver to establish motive and concede his culpability.

I don't know what it is he's got, but he's dirty and he tried to pass it to me. When he realized he couldn't get the better of me, he bit me. I had to go through fricking like nine months of blood work, you know. They had told me that I had Hep C from him and everything. Come to find out, you know, luckily it was a false positive. I had to go through all that shit because of him. I'm going to tell you like this. If it was me personally and I had another chance at him, I'd stomp his larynx closed after I kicked his teeth out so he wouldn't never bite nobody again.

That was followed by the recordings of me showing Driver, Moran, and Newcomb the picture of Warren Williams, apparently shot dead in the chest. My initial testimony that morning was to establish the timeline and confirm the veracity of the recordings, starting with David Moran. I heard myself say:

Have a seat. I want you to have a chance to see this and make sure it's all clear.

Oh, shit. Ha-ha, oh, shit. Ha-ha, oh, shit. I love it. Fucking pissed on himself. God fucking—good job, Brother Joe.

Is that what y'all wanted?

Yeah. Hell, yeah.

All right. And you're happy with that?

Yeah.

Okay. Because, you know this was a group effort.

Hell, yeah.

All right.

Brother, I love you, man.

Call Brother Thomas and make sure he remembers to meet me. I am going to meet him next.

I love you, brother.

I love you, brother.

God bless.

CHAPTER 23

CROSS-EXAMINATION

COLUMBIA COUNTY COURTHOUSE
SEPTEMBER 2017

"I remind you, Mr. Moore," the judge said the next morning when I retook the witness stand, "that you're still under oath."

"Thank you, Your Honor."

Judge Wesley Douglas looked toward the defense table at Robert Rush, who was representing David Moran.

"Mr. Rush."

He rose, looking like a shorter version of former secretary of defense Donald Rumsfeld without the glasses. He was an older man, in his sixties, very thin, and he carried himself in a way that made him appear feeble. Instead of coming out to take his place at the lectern, he remained standing behind the table. I watched him consult the notes he'd made on a yellow legal pad, before his focus turned to me.

"Good morning, sir."

"Good morning."

"You have been working for the FBI basically spying on American citizens, right?"

"Yes."

"And you were paid to do that, right?"

"Yes."

"You were paid very well to do that, weren't you?"

"I'm sorry," I said, "I don't understand what you mean by well."

"Well, you've been paid over a hundred thousand dollars, haven't you?"

"Yes."

"I mean, you get all of your expenses paid for, right?"

"The last two years, yes."

I'd been anticipating this moment for those last two-plus years of living as ghosts on the fringe of society, the moment when defense counsel would throw everything at me they could to defame me and besmirch my character. I was, essentially, the state's only witness. If Rush and his co-counsel representing Newcomb poked enough holes in my testimony, as well as myself, the case would blow apart.

As Rush continued, I reminded myself that I was on the stand today because these defendants were part of a movement that wanted to start a civil war. They wanted to divide the country in two. I looked at my testimony under cross-examination as the means to hold it together.

To salvage something from this experience, for any of the hell I endured to be worth it, I needed to carry the case all the way to guilty verdicts for both defendants. I couldn't buckle under what I knew would be relentless questioning, meant to bait and provoke me. Nothing would be off-limits, but I knew I was ready. So much so that I made sure the jury could see me staring straight at the defense table, face-to-face with my inquisitors. I don't think either Moran or Newcomb ever looked my way during the cross-examination, as if afraid of what they might see. They kept their gazes fixed downward or straight ahead.

Rush hammered me on the money thing for a long stretch, badgering me with questions that suggested I had done what I did just for the money, while also insinuating that I had either inflated or manipulated certain events, like the hit on Warren Williams, to keep fleecing the FBI. It sounds absurd on its face, because it was, but it was a prime component of the only defense he could muster. At times, I didn't know what he was after besides trying to rattle me to make my emotions get the better me, or maybe spike my temper.

Breathe, focus, stay on subject . . . Breathe, focus, stay on subject . . .

"Mr. Newcomb did not know where Warren Williams lived in Palatka, right?"

"I don't know that, sir."

"You don't know if he knew it?"

"No, sir."

"And Mr. Moran certainly didn't know it, did he?"

"I don't know that, sir."

"Well, Mr. Moore, you know that from the recording when he keeps asking questions about what's going on, right?"

"Again, I don't know that, sir."

I addressed him as "sir" to show false deference in the face of his aggression. I was maintaining an even tone, fighting the temptation to raise my voice to counter his approach. It got harder to do that when the subject became more personal—my mental health struggles.

"You also were having hallucinations, weren't you?"

"I don't recall any—no, no hallucinations, sir."

"You were in a paranoid schizophrenic manic phrase when you went to the hospital, were you not?"

"No, sir, I don't know that."

"Well, why were you hospitalized then?"

"I went to get help. I was not feeling well and I followed the directions of the medical staff and sought help for whatever they thought I needed help with, sir."

Rush might have been scoring a few minor points with the jury, but I could tell their observations of me didn't match up with the man defense counsel was describing. He then tried to score some more points by rehashing the incident when I reported my mother-in-law for allegedly abusing my year-old son. I don't regret doing that at all; I wish someone had done it for me when I was being molested as a little boy.

"[Mr. Seaton] came over that night to have a violent altercation with me, sir."

"And that was what it was about, your false accusation that [the Seatons] were sexually molesting their grandchild, right?"

"He came over to kick us out of our home, sir."

"Wasn't it because of the false accusation of child sexual abuse? Isn't that why Mr. Seaton was at your house?"

"I did not make an accusation, sir," I said in a measured tone. "I let the deputies listen to [the tape] themselves. They took things from there."

Rush flipped past some pages, as if changing his mind about the line of questioning he wanted to pursue. I was getting the sense that I was rattling him, instead of the reverse.

"Okay," he said, after collecting himself. "Now I think you said on direct that one of the admonishments the FBI gave you is you weren't supposed to tell people you were working for the FBI, right?"

"No, sir, that is not an admonishment."

Rush's gaze narrowed. I seemed to have caught him off guard. "You mean you were allowed to tell people that you were working for the FBI?"

"No one ever told me that I was not allowed to tell someone that."

"Really? Agent Joseph Armstrong of the FBI, he never admonished you that you're not to represent to people that you were working for the FBI?"

"That you're not to represent yourself as an agent of the FBI," I corrected pointedly.

"Okay. So it's your testimony that Agent Armstrong did not tell you that you should not be telling people that you're working as an informant, as a spy, as an operative for the FBI?"

"Agent Armstrong told me in an admonishment that I'm not to tell people that I am an agent of the FBI."

"But you can say that you work for them?" Rush posed, starting to sound exasperated.

"No one ever told me that I could not disclose that."

Rush flipped through some more pages, then flipped back again. His questions became more meandering and less focused, as if he himself didn't know what he was trying to get me on or how exactly he intended to trip me up. Things weren't going as he expected. Based on yesterday's direct examination, I think he saw me as an easy mark,

Ku Klux Klan
Blood Oath

███████████████████████ on this 13th day of the 10th Month
in the 2013 Year of the Lord, do before God, and my brethren, do solemnly swear, That I
dedicate my life, my honor, and my service to the sacred order of the Ku Klux Klan, I do so willingly,
without duress, and of my own free will, do swear. I fully recognize that this is a vow of Blood, Life,
and Honor.

I swear that all things I say and do shall be in accordance of the Klan Craft, Kloran and Konstitution,
I solemnly swear to obey the word and commands, without hesitation or contempt of the Supreme Officer
of this order, my Imperial Wizard.

I swear to be faithfully. Solemnly uphold allegiance to our sacred order, and to be Klannish in all things,
to accept, the life of the Brotherhood of Service, to regenerate our country and to the white race and maintain
the white blood and natural superiority with which God has enabled it....

I swear to devote myself to Chivalry, Patriotism, Honor and Brotherhood of service in the Sacred Society.
In sound state of mind without persuasion or cohesion. All to which I have Sworn. By this oath, I seal this
oath with the signature of my willing hand and the blood which gives me life.

Be thou My Witness, Almighty God
So help me God.

██

██

This agreement shall be enforced under the laws of the state of Florida .
This allegiance shall be binding forever without time limitations.
Attested By: Witness: ████ Date:
Signature: _____

██

The actual "blood oath" document I signed on October 13, 2013, upon
being "naturalized" into my second Klan chapter in Bronson, Florida.

someone disingenuous who was prone to embellishing his record and accomplishments. That's why he'd just hammered me on my mental health. Make that front and center in the minds of the jury and my credibility would take a severe hit. Right now, though, it was he who was starting to sweat, based on the sheen I saw glowing on his forehead.

I was studying the jury while watching Rush, and it was pretty clear his questions weren't landing with them at all. I didn't see anyone jotting down anything on their notepads. He kept badgering me, but it was like trying to punch holes in a cloud.

"Mr. Moore, you receive a VA service-connected disability that pays you about thirty-two hundred dollars a month. Is that correct?"

"Yes."

"You receive a social security payment of eleven hundred dollars per month?"

"Yes."

"And this is all while you've been working for the FBI, right?"

"Yes."

"You still get paid for those disabilities?"

"Yes."

Rush dropped that line of questioning without making any substantive point. I thought I caught one juror actually shaking her head, as if trying to make sense of his scattershot cross-examination that had failed to impeach my direct testimony or credibility whatsoever. He moved on next to a detailed expense report, and out of the corner of my eye I spotted a juror or two yawning. Maybe they were just tired from the late-summer Florida heat. Then he dug deeper into the expense report, and that, too, was received with a resounding thud. Generally, he was throwing everything he had at the wall in the hope something would stick.

Finally, Castillo objected.

"Your Honor, this has been asked and answered several times, so I would object to the repetitive nature of this line of questioning."

Rush jumped in before the judge could speak. "It's not repetitive. I'm going into another matter."

"Do you need to approach?" the judge asked.

As Rush and Castillo did just that, I observed two or three of the jurors actually rolling their eyes. The sidebar with the judge went on for several minutes. When I ultimately read a transcript of it, I rolled my eyes too, because the whole issue was about, yet again, the FBI paying our living expenses.

Finally, Rush retook his place behind the defense table and brought his line of questioning to the incident involving Johnny Grant, the former member of the Loyal White Knights who had joined the Traditionalist American Knights alongside Newcomb and Moran.

"You created an appearance that you were a very dangerous person, right?"

"Yes, sir."

"You can make people disappear, right?"

"I don't recall saying that, sir."

Rush looked suddenly flustered. Now his cheeks were shiny too. "Well, isn't that—do you know who Johnny Grant is?"

"Yes, sir."

"Isn't that somebody that you pretended to make disappear from the group?"

"No, sir, I did not make him disappear. Did not say that I made him disappear, sir."

"What did you say?"

"I told people that the issue was dealt with. In accordance with whatever they gleaned from that, that was up to them."

"So you didn't tell anybody what you did to Johnny Grant, right?"

"I do know that I did not tell people that I made him disappear, sir."

Again, Rush couldn't let it go and just kept at it, to the detriment of his case. Another long sidebar followed that was toxic to the way the jury was regarding Mr. Rush and, thus, his client.

After lunch, he did his best to impeach my testimony about the fabricated murder of Warren Williams, but it felt like he was merely restating the facts of the case and repeating my own testimony without reducing its impact at all.

When nothing else worked, Rush circled back again to my mental state, specifically the conditions I was being treated for and the medications I was taking.

"Now you still have—suffer from hallucinations, don't you?"

"No, sir."

"You suffer from flashbacks that include hallucinations, don't you?"

"No, sir, I don't have hallucinations."

"Okay. When you have a flashback and you are imagining things that are not real, would you not call that a hallucination?"

"Like a dream, you mean?"

"Like seeing things that are not real."

"No, sir, I don't have those."

The problem for me here, of course, was that since I couldn't get into the circumstances of my military service that had caused severe PTSD, the jury wasn't getting a full and accurate picture of my mental state. They were only getting a portion of the story because that was all the classified nature of my service allowed me to provide. Rush had no idea about my service either, so he just kept hammering and hammering, even though the nail had bent and wasn't going any deeper in the jury's mind.

And then it got heated.

"Wasn't there an incident where you—in 2014, where you were pretending to be a sniper and shooting at imaginary objects?"

"Absolutely not."

"You were laying down in a front yard and somebody said he's out there?"

"When and where?" I challenged, aware I had raised my voice for the first time. "That is false."

"And you then had a visit to your doctor to check on medications after that?" Rush demanded, just short of shouting.

"No, sir," I said, even louder.

"And that's all in your medical records, aren't they?" Rush shouted this time.

"No, sir. That is not in my medical records," I shouted back.

In that moment, a hush fell over the courtroom. Jaws dropped. I noticed that all the jurors were looking straight at me, a clear message carried in their eyes. I believed in that moment they were wearing the ultimate verdict on their expressions, and I knew it was over.

Rush had nothing, so this was what he was coming at me with. I did some breathing exercises to steady myself, not wanting to appear anything but composed to the jury.

Rush finally gave up and yielded the floor to Moran's lawyer, Wilson. Incredibly, Wilson started regurgitating the same information and chronology that Rush already had gone over repeatedly. A bunch of jury members looked like there was someplace else they wanted to be, any other place really. A few didn't even appear to be paying much attention, their eyes drifting over the walls as if in search of nonexistent courtroom windows. We had strayed so far from the facts of the case, I was surprised that Castillo wasn't objecting. Then again, why stop opposing counsel from digging their own grave?

Wilson came back to my infiltration of William Hawley's klavern in Wayward.

"Okay. And so no one was ever convicted from that?"

"No."

"All right. Well, let's talk about that. You said you had to leave for personal reasons. I believe you said that your involvement ended because you said you had to move?"

"Yes, our in-laws had kicked us out of our home."

Finally, it was Castillo's turn at redirect to clean up whatever confusion Rush and Wilson may have left in the jury's mind.

"I think both Mr. Wilson and Mr. Rush asked you about the trip to Palatka."

"Yes."

"Now, how was that trip arranged? How was that put together?"

"The weekend prior, Mr. Newcomb had conversations with us stating that he was thinking about having that ride the following weekend. The night before the Palatka ride, we had phone conversations where he asked if I was going to come over for that ride."

"Was Mr. Moran to be a part of that as well?"

"Yes."

"Now, was there a location that was agreed upon to meet?"

"Mr. Newcomb's."

"His home?"

"Yes."

"And did you travel there in your personal vehicle?"

"Yes, I did."

Castillo was doing a great job of getting the jury's focus back on the facts of the case, instead of the extemporaneous fodder the defense counsels had fed them. He finished his redirect examination of me by clearly demonstrating I had risked my life by infiltrating the KKK as a confidential human source.

"Mr. Moore, why did you believe that the blood oath that Mr. Wilson asked you about was a threat on your life if you revealed the Klan secrets?"

"I was told by the leader [at the time], Grand Dragon Mike Christopher, that that blood oath actually meant that they would enforce it with death because they don't put their secrets in documents, not that kind of secret."

Castillo turned toward the bench. "Judge, I don't think I have anything else for Mr. Moore. Thank you."

CHAPTER 24

THE VERDICT

JACKSONVILLE, FLORIDA
SEPTEMBER 2017

Castillo and Bledsoe couldn't have been happier with my performance on the stand.

"You were brilliant," Castillo said afterward.

"Outstanding," Bledsoe added.

There wasn't a single thing they had a problem with. That marked my final appearance in the courtroom, so I wasn't there when Rich Vaughn took the stand. But I knew he would make for a great witness who wouldn't give defense counsel any quarter at all. I later learned that he had corroborated everything I said, which must have ruined that day of the trial for Rush and Wilson, not to mention their clients, who by this point were probably wishing they had copped a plea like Thomas Driver had.

The following day, though, my testimony would face its biggest test when my father-in-law testified. Rusty was the last hope the defense had to punch holes in my credibility, which was the only way Newcomb and Moran were going to avoid significant jail time. I knew what was coming because many of the questions Rush and Wilson had posed in their cross-examinations were based on inaccurate information Rusty had provided them and outright lies he had told, all of which he repeated under direct examination by the defense. Then Cass Castillo got to cross-examine him, and Rusty revealed his true nature and his reasons for testifying for the defense, those being his antipathy for the United States government in general and me in particular.

"Mr. Seaton," Castillo began, "you have some very intense feelings of resentment and hostility toward Rich Vaughn, don't you?"

"No."

"You don't? Haven't you called him a piece of shit in the past?"

"That's not hostility."

"That's not hostility?"

Rusty shook his head.

"Why did you use that reference then against him or in reference to him?"

"Just a figure of speech."

"It wasn't meant to describe how you feel about him?"

"No, just for the moment."

At this point, I knew Castillo must have felt like a hunter who had successfully cornered his prey.

"Do you consider it a compliment, Mr. Seaton?"

"No."

"Isn't it true that you thought or you believed that Rich Vaughn is responsible for the separation of you from your stepdaughter and grandchildren?"

"That's what I believe, yeah."

"That's what you believe," Castillo echoed. "And you don't like that, do you?"

"Not a bit."

"Because you have gone to the extreme of contacting Pam Bondi, the FBI, Nick Cox, the statewide prosecutor, the U.S. Attorney's Office, Alachua Police Department, the Columbia Sheriff's Office, anyone that would help you get your daughter back from the FBI?"

"To tell us where she was."

"And have you gotten, at least in your judgment, no cooperation, isn't that true?"

"None at all."

"And you have very intense dislike for Mr. Moore, don't you, Mr. Seaton?"

"No, not dislike. No."

"Didn't you call him a turd and a piece of shit before as well?"

"Figure of speech."

"And that, again, was not designed to be a compliment, was it?"

"Not at the time it wasn't."

"And isn't it true, Mr. Seaton, that you feel that Mr. Moore is the one that is responsible for you not having any contact with your daughter and with—along with the FBI, but he's responsible for the separation of you and—"

"Along with the FBI, yes, sir."

"Both of them?"

"All of them."

"All of them together?"

"All of them."

"And you don't like that at all, do you?"

"No."

"And how would you describe, Mr. Seaton, how the FBI and Marshals Office responded to your request for assistance? How would you describe that?"

"I didn't get nowhere. We don't know where she's at."

"Did the response make you angry?"

"Not angry. We just—we don't know where she's at."

"Have you said, Mr. Seaton, that they all told you to fuck off?"

"Pretty much. Yep."

"And again, Mr. Seaton, that response really indicates how angry you are at Mr. Moore and the FBI and everyone else in this case?"

"No, not angry, we're just—we don't understand where she's at. We don't know where her and the babies are."

"And in [a Facebook] post you used some very insulting language when referring to the different agencies you contacted for help, didn't you?"

"I could have."

"Did you not post it?"

"Yeah, I posted it."

"It was very insulting language that you used about all of them."

"Saucy."

"Saucy? Would you consider calling them sons of bitches to be insulting?"

"No, salty."

"Salty," Castillo repeated. "Again, does that language really convey, Mr. Seaton, how intense your hatred is for everyone that's connected with this case?"

Everyone meaning the United States government. Rusty had shown his true colors, exposing himself as the man I had judged him to be from the very first time I met him. The damage had been done, and instead of destroying my credibility, he left the stand having destroyed his own. For all intents and purposes, the trial was over.

The following day, I received a call from an FBI agent named Sean, who oversaw all confidential human sources for the Jacksonville field office.

"Hey, Joe, the verdict's in."

I waved Shannon over and put the phone on speaker so she could hear the result.

Sean went on to say that the jury, composed of all whites, two of whom were military veterans, had taken all of thirty minutes to come back with a verdict, less time than it took for the judge to give the jury its final charging instructions.

"Moran and Newcomb were both found guilty of conspiracy to commit first-degree murder," Sean continued. "They were each sentenced to twelve years in prison."

The sentence would have been twenty-five years, but a Florida statute automatically cut in half any sentence doled out to law-enforcement officials within the state. Pleading out had left Thomas Driver with a sentence of only seven years, the same handed down to Jamie Ward for the federal crimes he had pled to.

I felt an enormous sense of relief wash over me and nearly dropped the phone.

I looked at Shannon and said, "It's finally over." I barely recognized my own voice. It was like an out-of-body experience.

She broke down and cried, and I hugged her so tight and close our happy tears mixed together. All those false summits we'd experienced had finally resulted in one that was real. Even though we knew this would never be completely over, knew that we would be looking over our shoulders for the rest of our lives no matter where we went, at least we could move on.

PART III

Injustice anywhere is a threat to justice everywhere.

—MARTIN LUTHER KING JR.

CHAPTER 25

MY OWN PRIVATE IDAHO

BOISE, IDAHO
CHRISTMAS 2017

On September 14, two days after the verdict came in, my family and I went back to Idaho. After the intensity of the trial, we spent a lot of time outdoors to regroup. It was beautiful and clean, full of bright colors. It had been so long since I had allowed myself to appreciate the stunning landscape—or much of anything else.

My wife gave birth to our third child, Willie, five days before Christmas, the best present I could possibly imagine. Christmas featured the first snowfall of the season and the first white Christmas we'd ever experienced. I'll never forget sledding in these majestic snow parks with our three children. It felt like I had been gifted an entirely new life, an opportunity to build a home and happy memories with my family. We came to love the french fries fashioned from genuine Idaho potatoes and, initially anyway, got used to people noting our tans and saying, "You're not from around here, are you?"

It was a safe and comfortable community, and we let our kids play in the street without any worry at all.

One day, in a moving box, I found that grungy tan ball cap with the embroidered American flag I'd worn only when in my undercover guise. The hat was dirty and riddled with sweat stains and discoloration in patches, particularly where the fabric got corroded from the sniper pin I always wore on the bill. I was ready to throw it in the trash, but then changed my mind. The hat wasn't just a reminder of the stress and anxiety I'd experienced in my years undercover, in protective custody, and then testifying in court. It was also a reminder, as well as a symbol, of my service to the country.

Stuffing it away in the darkness was like putting the stress of the past ten years on the same shelf. I genuinely believed I had helped change the course of history and felt an enormous sense of pride over that.

In our new, peaceful life in Idaho, nearly everything felt different. We were living under our new names. I didn't go by Joe Moore anymore and told people that I was retired from the government, which seemed true enough. We knew we'd miss family, settling that far away. My parents were aging, as were Shannon's grandparents. In the wake of the trial, she had severed all ties with Rusty and Sharon and began thinking about reconnecting with her birth father and his family for the first time since we had gone into protective custody more than two years before. By going all out in support of the Klan, her mother and stepfather had crossed a line that couldn't be uncrossed, although that wouldn't be the last time we heard from them.

As for the Klan, my testimony and the guilty verdicts had rocked the organization on a national level. From my monitoring of that community, I was aware of any number of the members I'd come into contact with running for the hills, disavowing their Klan membership even as they sought to join other like-minded organizations. I specifically uncovered examples of former Klan members moving to militia groups like the Oath Keepers, the Proud Boys, and the Three Percenters, which had collectively adopted Klan orthodoxy and ideology hook, line, and sinker, and with whom the Klan had already enjoyed a strategic alliance.

Stormfront, the neo-Nazi website that had become a haven for right-wing extremists, reported on the trial, the subsequent convictions, and the long-term damage to the Klan. Their coverage was very critical of the defendants for doing untold damage to their treasured movement by pursuing a personal quest of revenge that had led to the Klan's virtual downfall. That coverage was also extremely critical of the Bronson klavern for letting an outsider not only into their midst but into a position of power. Stormfront openly speculated on how many other klaverns across the country might have been similarly compromised.

From a statistical standpoint, the long-term damage of the trials to the Klan was quantifiable. In 2017, the Southern Poverty Law Center reported that the number of Klan chapters fell by almost a third, from 190 groups in 2015 to 130 in 2016. It was a drastic shift from the steep rise in membership of the previous years, when the number of groups more than doubled from 2014 to 2015, from 72 to 190. The Klan was experiencing decimation on a scale not seen since the 1940s, when the government took down the group by making tax evasion cases against their leaders, as well as against high-ranking naturalized members. In the case of the weakened Klan of 2017, the convictions were just the icing on the cake. Had the prosecution failed to make its case, though, or if there had been no case made at all had I walked away through that long period of limbo, the Klan could have emerged stronger and more emboldened.

I like to think—in fact, I know—that my infiltration of the Traditionalist American Knights and the resulting case we made against a Grand Dragon, Jamie Ward, and an Exalted Cyclops, Charles Newcomb, was greatly responsible for that. We aren't talking about run-of-the-mill Klan foot soldiers, ghouls, or supporters. We're talking about godfather-level takedowns that sent a seismic shock through the oldest and largest white nationalist group in the history of the country, to the point that they could no longer assemble even a thousand members in one place at one time.

In February 2017, while monitoring the internet for white nationalist and supremacist activity, I came across the shocking news of the murder of Frank Ancona, Imperial Wizard of the Traditionalist American Knights, and the face of the Klan from Ferguson onward. Ancona was shot to death by his wife, the woman who had accompanied him to that restaurant in Cocoa Beach, Florida, when she learned he was on the verge of casting her aside. While the incident might ordinarily be dismissed as personal, the truth was I don't think she would have dared commit such a brazen act had Ancona's power not have been so severely diminished by the decimation of the flagship chapter of the TAK in Bronson, Florida.

The overall movement in general, though, was far, far from dead or even in decline. While I was living in a surreal limbo for over two years between the arrests and the trial, an unprecedented event almost no one saw coming changed the face of America and brought white nationalism to the forefront of our geopolitics: Donald Trump's election as president in November 2016.

"A surge in right-wing populism, stemming from the long-unfolding effects of globalization and the movements of capital and labor that it spawned, brought a man many considered to be a racist, misogynist and xenophobe into the most powerful political office in the world," the report from the Southern Poverty Law center concluded.

The Trump campaign did many things to garner the support of those who'd previously been shunned and renounced by politicians for generations, but one in particular stood out in the mind of white nationalists who had their eyes trained on the Republican candidate for president who was openly espousing racist views. During one of his rallies in February 2016, Trump spotted a Black man being led down an aisle to be ejected, to a chorus of boos.

"Punch him in the face!" Trump exclaimed, and the boos were replaced by raucous cheers.

Observers, pundits, and politicos at the time failed to realize how important a moment that was in garnering the attention and support of white nationalists both inside and outside the Klan. Later, the future president of the United States refused to denounce David Duke, the avowed Klansman who was a fixture in Louisiana state politics; he couldn't, he said, because he didn't know who David Duke was, a claim that was demonstrably false.

Over the course of his campaign, the more Trump gained the support of what his opponent Hillary Clinton accurately referred to as "the deplorables," the more he sought it. Movements that had been reviled and ostracized for decades emerged from the shadows to greet their champion. They had found their voice, a mouthpiece for all their grievances. It didn't matter that these were the kind of people who would be stopped cold at the entrances to his hotels or golf clubs. It mattered only that his spewing of hatred and longing for an America long gone gave them hope that instead of facing irrelevance, they were at long last being heeded.

The election of the nation's first Black president had set the stage for its first demonstratively racist president since Andrew Johnson, who had ushered in the post-Reconstruction movement aimed at returning the South to prominence by basically reconstituting the Confederacy in principle. Even today, go south below the Mason-Dixon Line and the Civil War is known by a different moniker: the War of Northern Aggression.

This was the audience that propelled Trump to power, even as it similarly empowered white nationalist dogma and its supporters, who had been disavowed since the Civil Rights era. It marked a giant step backward for the United States, which was just what this movement wanted.

Once elected, Trump populated his administration with the likes of Steve Bannon, Michael Flynn, and Stephen Miller, whose expressed views represented a closeted form of white nationalism that was more avowed as time went on. Although Flynn didn't last long in the administration, due to having been accused (and later convicted) of lying to the FBI, his appointment as national security advisor was part and parcel of an administration that was effectively tossing the radical right a life preserver when it was on the verge of going under. And if that "Punch him in the face" moment marked the figurative beginning of the movement, then another event confirmed the rise of its efficacy: Charlottesville.

I was in Idaho in August 2017 when news broke of the Unite the Right rally that served as a major turning point for the white nationalist and supremacist movements. Klan members were responsible for taking out the permits for that now infamous rally. On its face, it was a desperate move meant to preserve some level of efficacy in the face of the KKK's precipitous drop in membership, while so-called rival hate groups were surging. But that apparent trend was misrepresentative on its face, since where did sociological analysts think those new hate group members were coming from? The fact that the marchers were wearing khaki instead of white robes was all that separated Charlottesville from the kind of rally the Klan had been famous for in years past. Anyone wanting more proof of that need only count the Confederate flags, long a dominant Klan symbol, proudly on display. Dressing uniformly made for an unspoken message that these previously disparate groups that had never interacted with one another had indeed united in common cause, the precursor and ultimate harbinger of what went down at the Capitol Building on January 6, 2021.

When Trump refused to denounce the white nationalists who'd roiled Charlottesville streets and the University of Virginia campus, saying, "There were good people on both sides," it was more bullhorn than dog whistle to the far right. I watched in abject disgust as the then president of the United States took a seat at the table right next to the likes of Nathan Bedford Forrest, the KKK's first Imperial Wizard. Forrest had helped birth a movement that Trump embraced and ushered into the twenty-first century. If Forrest taught members how to walk, you might say Trump allowed them to run.

Think of the white nationalist movement, as defined by the Klan, as a three-legged stool. Membership and ideology are obviously the first two things that are required to build the Invisible Empire, but the third runs hand in hand with those: influence, in the form of the clerk at the DMV, the patrol cop, the town manager, and dozens more such positions. The notion of the Invisible Empire required them to perform the kind of quiet work in support of the Klan and like-minded organizations, which saw a massive surge of energy thanks to the tacit, wink-and-a-nod support of the Trump administration.

I was listening to NPR in the wake of the Unite the Right rally, when Ian Solomon, a former official in the Obama administration, aptly warned that Charlottesville had lit a fire under the white nationalist movement and drew members out of the dark corners they'd long inhabited.

"Are the pro-democratic forces and pro-democracy movements going to prevail or not?" I listened to Solomon say. "There's no inevitability to this democratic experiment. One of the things about that weekend of 2017 was it revealed, it reenergized, it revived in many people's minds the reality that anti-democratic forces are ascendant in this country, that hate is quite brazen, to show its face proudly, confidently, with encouragement from elected officials."

The key phrase in Solomon's words that struck me was "with encouragement from elected officials," namely the president of the United States himself, an occurrence previously thought to be impossible in this day and age. The Klan and others now knew they had a friend in the White House, who similarly wanted to turn the clock back to a neo-antebellum period when women were second-class citizens, Blacks weren't full citizens at all, and the Bill of Rights applied only to a certain class of people. Americans sometimes forget that the notorious Jim Crow laws that disenfranchised Black voters in the post–Civil War era were named for James R. Crowe, a founding member of the KKK back in 1865.

Thanks to the church we joined in Boise, we made friends on both sides of the aisle, both liberal and conservative. Fortunately, the city was no haven for the KKK and was far from the hotbed of white nationalist–type activity I had witnessed in Florida. A few people who'd read Nate Thayer's articles outed our new identities and then steered clear of us, either because of their politics or because they didn't want to be subjected to outside danger when around us.

Still, my family exercised caution when we were out in public. As had been the case while in protective custody in Florida, we divided possible threats into three levels of assessment: low risk, contact possible, and contact imminent. So whenever we had reason to suspect contact may be imminent, either my wife or I would say our code word, "Fumble!" At that point, we'd go through our protocols for getting the family to safety. We created a game we called "Follow

Daddy," where our three kids got in a line and followed me to a se-cure place, where we were able to cold-call for reinforcements. This process was straight out of my military training, which counseled to always prepare for the worst possible scenario. Although I never thought I'd have to rely on it after my service was over, I now found myself on a new battlefield with my family cast as potential casualties.

Fortunately, while in Idaho, we only practiced the procedure. Though we had encountered some possible low-risk situations, things never escalated beyond that.

I only wish that was the end of the story but, as things turned out, it was far from it.

CHAPTER 26

YOU CAN GO HOME AGAIN

FLORIDA
JULY 2019

As much as my family and I enjoyed living in Idaho, I guess it was only a matter of time before we got homesick for the beach. After two happy and peaceful years, the negatives of being that far away from home started to outweigh the positives. I missed my mother and stepfather, and Shannon missed her grandparents, along with her birth father and his family—although she still had absolutely no desire to reconnect with Rusty and Sharon. Returning to Florida also allowed Shannon to resume her work as a part-time senior caregiver, a job she genuinely loved. Since we were living exclusively on my Veterans Administration disability compensation at the time, the extra income would also help us make ends meet.

We decided to move during the summer of 2019, which would give us enough time to get settled before our kids started at their new school. Upon our return, I learned Rich Vaughn had been named Investigator of the Year by Homeland Security, and Lindsay Campbell was promoted to a position at the Department of Justice in Washington. Cass Castillo, meanwhile, returned to private practice, and the other prosecutor on the case, Kelsey Bledsoe, was named chief statewide prosecutor for Florida. As for my old friend Joe Armstrong over in Wayward, I learned he had retired and was working as a private security consultant.

I let the FBI know we were returning, and they told me to inform local law enforcement of where we'd be living. The Bureau also provided a liaison at a local sheriff's office.

We found a house with a beautiful weeping willow in the front yard and the tributary of a lake abutting the back, located on a cul-de-sac that was secure in the sense that there was no pass-through. Any car that drove in had to be going to one of the houses situated there. And neither could anyone just walk randomly or accidentally up to my backyard. There was a safe, secluded beach on the grounds of a nearby military base that quickly became one of my favorite places. I reveled in watching my wife sitting in the sun, while my kids frolicked in the sand and water. Those moments were truly blissful, as close to normal as anything my family had experienced in longer than I cared to remember, but they belied a reality I couldn't dismiss: the fact that we had returned to an area where we were known targets.

I installed automatic robotic cameras around the exterior of our home and practiced regular security protocols. One precaution we took was that I wouldn't get into the car with my family until we got moving. Shannon would back the car up and start down the street, while I ascertained any potential threats in the area. Then she'd stop and I'd get into the passenger seat. We turned it into a game, and the kids always cheered when I climbed into the car.

Shannon always drove, so I could watch the route the whole way. We also redoubled our threat assessment protocols in terms of low risk, contact possible, and contact imminent, dreading the very real possibility that one of us would have to yell, "Fumble!" We were trying to achieve a delicate balance between not scaring our kids and developing situational awareness in them.

Given my background in intelligence gathering, I also got into the ritual of checking public venues for news of any organized activity that might be going on along the route we intended to use. This could have been something as simple as a parade or a road race, or as potentially dangerous as a protest demonstration or a march that could attract those I needed to avoid, as either participants or spectators. Then I'd check for traffic patterns, in order to develop a primary route and a secondary route. We might, for example, be on our way to see a movie in one location but have a backup multiplex in mind in case we encountered anything unexpected along the way. I utilized military terminology, specifically a sniper phrase used for terrain analysis of the battlespace, the acronym OCOKA, which stands for observation, cover and concealment, obstacles to overcome, key terrain, and avenues of approach.

Though the Klan had been decimated thanks to the arrests and the trial, Trump's 2016 election was allowing for its reconstitution, at least within the militia-style offshoots it had helped spawn and to which many of its former members had fled. Charlottesville was more than enough proof of that, and I didn't intend to take any chances. After all, I was the living embodiment of the Klan's demise, viewed nationwide as the man who had brought it down. As long as I was alive, an organization that had been thriving just a few years before would continue to be seen as weak and ineffectual, diminished to the point of irrelevance. In light of that reality, it wasn't hard to envision a former member or ghoul, even an organized group of them, taking a shot at me and my family to make the point that you still don't mess with the KKK.

Killing me would have been a great way to say: *We're still relevant.* But an organization that had terrorized the country since 1865 could no longer be taken seriously while I was still alive. My efforts and the successful prosecutions had left them looking over their shoulders in a way the mob families of New York had after the passage of RICO (Racketeer Influenced and Corrupt Organizations Act) left them paranoid and running for the hills. Nobody walks along the top of the dam when there's a crack showing.

After we moved back to Florida, Sharon and Rusty continued trying to reach out to my wife on social media, but she never responded to their overtures. They managed to trace us to our new home.

Fortunately, I was the only one there when they rang the bell one day in the summer of 2020, a year after we'd returned to Florida, then banged on the door. I held my gun in plain view of a window they were looking through and let them see, and hear, me calling the security liaison the FBI had provided to have the nearest officer respond. The couple fled but were pulled over by the responding officer minutes later. Shannon had maintained absolutely no contact with them since our move to Idaho, and this was the last time they tried to establish contact in person.

Shannon eventually did respond to her mother's overtures on social media. Sharon, though, refused to admit she'd done anything wrong. She was either delusional or in complete denial. Shannon insisted she was done letting herself be manipulated by her mother. The separation between them, after all we'd been through with Sharon and Rusty taking sides against me, could never be bridged.

Meanwhile, Shannon renewed ties with her birth father and his family. The problem was they lived in Gainesville, an extremely populous area where we could be spotted and recognized by someone who saw us before we had a chance to see them. We never ventured there without observing our security protocols and being prepared for the unexpected to arrive at any moment.

My mother and stepfather lived in northern Florida, and it was a blessing to be able to reconnect with them for the first time, really, in over four years. As soon as I hugged them, I knew we'd made the right decision by coming home. The fact that they now had a chance to be close to their grandchildren proved to be an immeasurable gift to them, as well as to my kids, who now had an extended family for the first time they could remember.

While my family and I managed to live more or less anonymously, there were some people in my wider circle of friends and family who had an inkling of who I was—rumors spread quickly, after all. I was approached on numerous occasions to pursue individuals the law either wouldn't or couldn't touch. But I strove to resist such overtures out of concern for further exposing myself to potential enemies. I had no desire to become a real-life version of *The Equalizer*; my family had already sacrificed enough because of me, and I had no intention of putting them through that particular hell again.

Occasionally, though, someone would come to me with a problem that forced me to stray from that path. No matter the level of threat I faced, at heart, the trauma of my childhood left me with a palpable hatred for bullies and an innate desire to stand up for those who weren't strong enough to stand up for themselves. I couldn't just flip a switch and stop being the man I'd always been. Having a happy and thriving family only served to increase my desire for others to have the same opportunity.

Meanwhile, the continuous watch I was performing online for potential enemies in our midst revealed that the Proud Boys had begun to hold what they openly called "prayer meetings," nomenclature previously reserved for the Klan, to describe planning violent activities or reprisals. In the Klan lexicon, such prayer meetings were often, if not usually, followed by prayer actions, like the planned killing of that truck driver in Wayward in 2009. That seemed to suggest that the Klan members who'd moved on to the likes of the Proud Boys, the Oath Keepers, and the Three Percenters had brought Klan influence and ideology with them. Prayer meetings of the sort held in Portland, Oregon, in August 2019 were the precursors of January 6, 2021, the canary in that particular coal mine.

The trend lines were there and steadily rising.

"[White nationalists] want to tap into beliefs that are still widespread and latent in the United States," Derek Black, who left the Klan in his twenties and became the subject of the Pulitzer Prize–winning book *Rising Out of Hatred*, told PBS's *Amanpour & Co.* in December 2020.

Those beliefs are rooted in racism and anti-Semitism, as well as a hatred for immigrants and anyone they feel is somehow threatening the hegemony of the white race, an absurd fallacy. The social grievances fueling such attestations have become the basis of a nascent political movement driven not by policy so much as a desire for an authoritarian leader they view as a savior.

Thanks to Donald Trump, the white nationalist movement the

Klan has been at the forefront of for generations moved from the shadows into the light, and his followers continued to flock to his dogma and his increasingly bombastic rhetoric from the White House. He openly courted the Americans who had rightfully been shunned and condemned to society's underbelly for generations. Sociologically, it was akin to ten small wildfires that are easy to fight while contained, but impossible to battle once they join up into a single, unstoppable scourge on the countryside. Living again in Florida, the epicenter of the whole movement, gave me a front-row seat for trend lines that confirmed my worst suspicions that America's arsonists were being supplied with not only matches but gasoline. I learned, for example, that the metadata I had supplied the FBI had unearthed a treasure trove of names, email addresses, and phone numbers of former Klansmen who were now known members of the groups that ultimately converged on the Capitol on January 6. The Invisible Empire the Klan had long pronounced itself to be was redefined and reworked into a model fitting the likes of Proud Boys leader Enrique Tarrio and Oath Keepers chief Elmer Stewart Rhodes.

Their actions and the radical views they espoused lured likeminded law-enforcement officials and former and current military members out of the shadows and into the light, no longer fearing reprisal, because they had a champion in the once and potentially future president. Trump was basically calling them to arms in the wake of his defeat in the 2020 election, sixteen months after our return to Florida. That's why January 6, 2021, wasn't a failure so much as a dress rehearsal. It also unearthed a disturbing, interconnected trend I had seen glimpses of first in the Wayward chapter of the Ku Klux Klan under William Hawley, and then again, even more pronounced, in the Bronson chapter under Jamie Ward and then Charles Newcomb: the pervasive infiltration of right-wing extremism into law enforcement.

CHAPTER 27

BE VERY AFRAID

NORTHERN FLORIDA
JANUARY 2022

A year later, in January 2022, I sat down across from an FBI agent I can't identify in a Florida restaurant I can't disclose.

"We're not having this conversation," he started, shuffling uncomfortably.

We were meeting because he knew who I was and was well versed in my exploits inside the KKK. He'd requested the meeting after I'd turned over information I had obtained in the course of one of those private investigations I undertook of my own accord, which in this case involved the sexual exploitation of women. Putting violent KKK members in jail went only so far to relieve the sense of obligation I felt to help others, while I continued to heal myself in the process. In the course of one of these "projects," I found evidence that several police officers from a nearby jurisdiction were active members of the Ku Klux Klan and other white nationalist groups.

"I need you to keep this quiet," he said, his voice barely raised above a whisper.

"This meeting?"

He nodded. "And the information you forwarded me. It would

hurt our ongoing investigation into the matter, if you were to go public with what you learned."

"Ongoing," I repeated.

"You're a man who knows how to keep things quiet."

"It's why I'm still alive," I told him.

"And I need you to keep what I'm about to tell you quiet," he continued. "We're investigating law-enforcement officials for alleged connections to white supremacist groups and far-right militias in more than a dozen states. And not just Southern states either. We have ongoing investigations in Michigan, California, Connecticut, Washington State, and Virginia. The more rocks we turn over, the more of them crawl out."

He wore his concern in the creases dug into his expression. "That's what I was afraid of," I said.

"You know better than anyone the damage these people are capable of doing. You know the Bureau's primary focus these days is on domestic terrorism."

"I do, yes."

"Well, the investigations focusing on militias and the like have turned up a slew of active links to law-enforcement officers across the board."

I told him a recent analysis by Reuters uncovered around twenty self-identified law-enforcement trainers and dozens of retired instructors in the database of the Oath Keepers.

"Those trainers are of a particular concern to us," he told me, "because it screams indoctrination of young recruits. But we've also uncovered hard evidence that groups like the Oath Keepers are planting active members in both law enforcement and the military, not just recruiting from within those bodies. I don't expect that surprises you, Joe."

It didn't. For the Klan to remain viable, it has to have its people in influential positions. White nationalist infiltration of police and the armed forces was a crucial component of the Klan's Invisible Empire. These militia groups boasted not only rising memberships in the wake of January 6 but also an even clearer adoption of established Klan ideology and dogma.

My FBI contact then illuminated an even more disturbing ongoing investigation.

"This doesn't leave the table, right?" he posed.

"Right."

I could tell he was nervous, uncertain, maybe even scared. "You're aware of the scandals in police departments located in pretty much every state, where officers have shared blatantly racist statements and posts on social media, right?"

"I know it's gotten bad, yes."

"Well, it's worse, a lot worse than that. It's not only the rank and file we're investigating, it's officers at the command level right to the very top. They're not just turning a blind eye to what's happening, they're outright encouraging it, Joe. They're actually hiring officers out of the police academies based on the kind of social views that were once seen as disqualifying. I've seen studies that put the number of avowed racists wearing badges at around ten percent. Those same studies estimate that percentage could be as much as a third in as little as ten years."

Further proof of the KKK's infiltration into law enforcement came courtesy of Associated Press investigative reporter Jason Dearen, who exhaustively looked into prison guards across the multitude of Florida penal institutions. As we've seen, in Florida, correctional officers are considered law-enforcement officials no different from police, and Dearen's findings were shocking. Apparently, he'd attended the 2017 trial of Charles Newcomb and David Moran and made great use of the evidence presented and the convictions, especially in the second of two articles that prominently featured me.

In December 2021, shortly after the second Associated Press article ran, I called Jason Dearen.

"Hello?"

"Jason, this is Joe Moore."

I knew he recognized my voice from my testimony at the trial and pictured him dropping the phone upon receiving my call. We spoke regularly into early 2022, with Jason providing more details about white nationalist infiltration into the Florida prison system. The warnings he'd been issuing about that were falling on deaf ears, evoking denials from Florida prison officials in the face of the evidence he presented to them. He shared some of the most outrageous claims he couldn't fully corroborate, and thus include in his reporting, about increasing numbers of guards joining the KKK and other similar organizations. Driver and Moran were only the tip of the iceberg, or more accurately the tip of the spear. He also highlighted a factor my FBI contact had failed to mention: the inability of well-intentioned law-enforcement officials to prosecute such offenders due to policies and procedures dictated by collective bargaining agreements. Even officials who truly wanted to do the right thing found themselves hamstrung not only by bureaucracy but also by the fear that such investigations would turn the rank-and-file officers against them. And that has turned white nationalist infiltration into the law-enforcement community into a self-fulfilling prophecy.

"So what are you doing about it?" I asked my FBI contact seated across the booth from me in January 2022.

"Good question," he said, leaning back. "It's not like we have the manpower to infiltrate every police department in the country. And even if we did, you can't arrest people for what they think, and what they say is an internal matter. Until it becomes criminal, there's nothing we can do."

"And by then it's too late," I said, thinking of that 33 percent figure he'd just quoted.

My FBI contact didn't respond. He didn't have to.

Those trend lines aren't getting any better as we approach the 2024 election. The warning lights I saw leading up to the election of Donald Trump in 2016 have only brightened. I was always far more concerned about a wholesale spread and adoption of the Klan ideology than I was about any individuals. You can arrest individuals and put them behind bars. You can't do the same with ideas, and the white nationalist movement that threatens the very future of this country has pretty much adopted the original Klan orthodoxy hook, line, and sinker.

Staying on the topic of law enforcement, I came across the headline "A Right-Wing Sheriffs Group That Challenges Federal Law Is Gaining Acceptance Around the Country" on the ABC News website. It was downright unsettling. This group, which is growing in numbers, claims local law enforcement is not bound by federal law and can disregard any laws passed that they don't agree with, enforcing only those they choose to.

"The sheriff's group has railed against gun control laws, COVID-19 mask mandates and public health restrictions," the August 2023 post stated.

It has also quietly spread its ideology across the country, seeking to become more mainstream in part by securing state approval for taxpayer-funded law enforcement training, the Howard Center for Investigative Journalism found. Over the last five years, the group has hosted trainings, rallies, speeches and meetings in at least 30 states for law enforcement officers, political figures, private organizations and members of the public, according to the Howard Center's seven-month probe, conducted in collaboration with the Arizona Center for Investigative Reporting. The group has held formal trainings on its "constitutional" curriculum for law enforcement officers in at least 13 of those states. In six states, the training was approved for officers' continuing education credits. The group also has supporters who sit on three state boards in charge of law enforcement training standards.

That sounds like tyranny, even anarchy, to me, and it's right out of the Klan playbook, especially because, once again, training was a key ingredient. That's another way of describing indoctrination, and just imagine a (near) future far-right president able to enlist and weaponize such a group in pursuit of their unconstitutional platforms. It would produce the effect of granting license to extremists to engage in questionable or even illegal activity, knowing they will be granted a pass for their actions. In the recipe for a civil war, cold or hot, the corruption of law enforcement in this manner is a prime ingredient and the first step toward the bifurcation of the country. The willful refusal of local municipalities to enforce federal law, county sheriffs making it up as they go along, represents a de facto secession from the rule of law and a blanket acceptance of a local interpretation.

Envisioning such a force on a national scale is more reason to be very afraid of the newly empowered far-right, white nationalist movement. In that respect, I have come to see January 6 as a dress rehearsal for what's coming next. In the aftermath of the 2020 election, the safeguards of our system bent but didn't break, while the perpetrators may well have learned how to break them next time. It's easy to make the case that the next civil war the Klan has been steadfastly working toward for more than a century is already underway, at least in the cold sense, where the weapons being wielded are ideas instead of guns.

Speaking of guns, how is it that over three quarters of Americans favor commonsense gun control, but few laws to that effect are ever passed? How is it that two thirds of the country favors abortion rights, but the fervent momentum for a near all-out ban continues to build? The answer lies in the fact that virtually all radically conservative movements currently spanning the globe rely on parliamentary systems that allow them to seize power under minority rule—the many dictating to the more. And while America has a party system to protect against such minority rule, the damage a third-party candidate, or candidates, could do on Election Day 2024 is as palpable as it is terrifying and incalculable. A relatively small percentage of the voting public in a mere smattering of crucial battleground states could easily tip the Electoral College to Donald Trump with little more than 40 percent of the vote and potentially somewhere in the mid- to high thirties.

Even a fringe candidate like Cornel West could mean the end of democracy as we know it. No less a source than Democratic strategist David Axelrod, who ran Barack Obama's 2012 reelection campaign, compared West to 2016 Green Party candidate Jill Stein, whom some blamed for splitting the vote for Hillary Clinton in key electoral states, potentially causing Clinton's electoral loss to former president Trump. Stein won more votes than Trump's margin of victory in Wisconsin and Michigan, states that would have tipped the outcome of the election if Clinton had won them and she is running again in 2024 on the Green Party ticket as well.

Be very afraid indeed. Reinstituting politically viable versions of poll taxes, intelligence tests, and Jim Crow laws would truly be all it would take to tip the scales of otherwise free and fair presidential elections for decades to come. And in some ways, this could even be scarier than taking up arms, because when you do that you expose yourself and there is recourse. But in a draconian authoritarian regime, there is no recourse. Remember, it's not so much who votes that counts, it's who counts the votes.

The far right is succeeding is turning this into an us-versus-them scenario, a classic zero-sum game in which for their side to win absolutely, the other side has to lose in the same manner. They're playing the long game here, while the rest of us are living between election cycles. And if a national divorce hasn't been cemented already, it certainly appears to be in the process. The far right has realigned itself. Groups that previously had no contact with one another have united in common cause, thanks to Trump in effect becoming their voice and giving them license to spout hate speech and take reactionary stances. They use racial hatred more as a tool than a foundation, luring those willing to take up arms out of hatred to stand as extremist symbols to rally more to their unholy cause.

And they have more than their share of journalists from media across the spectrum who are sympathetic to, if not downright supporters of, their cause, like Nate Thayer. In October 2022, I called Thayer, the journalist who revealed our identities, to ask him at the very least to take the names of my children out of the articles he had posted online. Thayer spoke in a weak, halting voice and expressed what sounded like genuine remorse over his behavior. He told me that honoring such a simple request was a long time coming. He admitted allowing himself to be used by Frank Ancona and the Seatons. To make amends, he removed those articles from the sites on which they'd been posted. Riddled with ailments, he died just a few months later, in January 2023, broken and broke, but I like to think at least a bit redeemed. It is very likely that among the last things he did in his professional career was take down the two articles that never should have been put up in the first place.

Had Thayer still been alive on August 26, 2023, I wonder how he would have greeted the news of a twenty-one-year-old white man just miles away from where I live gunning down three Black people he had never known or met. He killed them out of pure racial hatred the far-right fringe encourages in the hope that accelerationists like that shooter will continue to fan the flames of the fire they have set. The killings were undertaken while a peaceful March on Washington was taking place, commemorating the sixtieth anniversary of Dr. Martin Luther King's game-changing rally there, when he gave his legendary "I Have a Dream" speech.

By all appearances, the Jacksonville shooter, who displayed swastikas on the AR-15 rifle he used to murder those three people, was self-radicalized, a classic lone wolf in the tradition of Dylann Roof. But the truth is more complicated. The white nationalist and supremacist movement is extremely adept at sending up signal flares as thinly veiled instructions these individual accelerationists are prone to follow. Inside the Joint Terrorism Task Force during my tenures undercover, this was generally referred to as flash-bang. The "flash" describes the self-radicalization, potentially as a result of exposure to chat rooms or a popular figure who is emblematic of the ideology the subject has come to embrace. The "bang" is the response of the subject to signal flares fired off by that kind of popular figure, or more generalized movement, directing them to become operational. My work inside the JTTF revealed that the estimated time between the flash and the bang is as little as three months. The actual inciter could be as simple as language the subject sees as a green flag to kill for a cause to which they have surrendered their identity.

"When we consume stories about white power, of violence as single events, as a lone wolf attack," Kathleen Belew, associate professor of History at Northwestern University and author of *Bring the War Home: The White Power Movement and Paramilitary America*, told Rachel Maddow on MSNBC two days after the attack,

> *we are consuming them as if they are existing without connection to each other, without an ideological basis. So this is how we get stories about Jacksonville, as something separate from Christchurch, and Pittsburgh, and Buffalo, and Charleston. Many of these attacks have not only shared characteristics in the communities that are impacted, but they are all carried out by white power perpetrators, who are united through social ties. . . . And they are all working for the same purpose, which, by the way, is not limited only to mass attacks as a strategy, but also exists in precisely this landscape, where it is running into our national politics.*

The point being that today's social and political environment is ripe for those white nationalist signal flares to burst on the scene like fireworks. Having a leader who is perceived as strong rising up against one in power seen as weak is the ideal formula for the overthrow of any system already revealed as being vulnerable. The safeguards this country maintains to avoid such a debacle are nothing more than guardrails to be ignored or flattened by those willing to go further than the other side. This is reminiscent of the warning in the film *The Usual Suspects*: "They realized that to be in power you didn't need guns or money or even numbers. You just needed the will to do what the other guy wouldn't."

We need to fear that the 2024 election will signal the end of the checks and balances that have preserved our system through thick and thin since the time of the Founding Fathers. Government agencies, like the Department of Justice and the IRS, becoming thinly disguised tools to do the bidding of the administration means a permanent re-definition of the role of these agencies, just as the KKK has envisioned from the time of its founding. And since the far right would never dare to cede power back to the majority of the country, once in power they will be laser focused on gaming the system to assure they never relin-quish it in the fashion of other right-wing autocracies globally.

These organizations have already demonstrated that they are will-ing to engage in acts of violence in order to realize their agenda. Now we see them engaging in acts of manipulation, like donating money to the No Labels party in order to gin up interest in the right candidate to tip the scales away from Biden and toward an ideologue whose intention would be to never relinquish power again—and not so much the individual as the prevailing ideology. By their very nature, these people don't trust the system they're supposed to be engaged in. They're desperate to succeed, another reason why they should inspire fear in all of us. The kind of right-wing ideologues I spent a good portion of my life trying to bring down don't understand there are people in the world who want to get along with all people. They don't get that, because you're not allowed to think differently than they do. And if you think differently, you're the enemy. Period. They only ac-cept the results within the system that they agree with. It's both a foregone conclusion and a self-fulfilling prophecy.

The warning signs are already flashing in the rhetoric of Trump and others who inhabit the former fringe that has gone mainstream, three of which we need to pay special attention to: the dissolution of the Justice Department, the establishment of what amounts to a national militia or private police force, and the persecution of non-ideologues who don't toe the line. All three of these have become prime components of the policy platforms of Trump and others run-ning for president in 2024.

This country is being increasingly roiled by social fault lines. And the belligerents, those who would upend the system purportedly in order to save it, understand these social fault lines all too well, seeking to stoke conflict to widen them even more, like that young man in Jacksonville who gunned down three innocent people in cold blood for no other reason than that they were Black. On a wider scale, the groups we need to fear are accelerationist groups committed not only to lighting the fires but to seeing them spread.

Perhaps the most dire forecast for what's to come lies in recent elections held around the world that might well presage an overwhelming authoritarian, quasi-fascist wave spreading. In normally liberal-minded Holland, the so-called Freedom Party reactionary leader Geert Wilders won a dramatic victory. In Argentina, Javier Milei, an equally far-right candidate representing a party calling itself Liberty Advances, won an equally dramatic victory by trumpeting views virtually identical to those espoused by Donald Trump in his attempt to regain the presidency here. These aren't foghorns sounding, they are all-out screaming alarm bells warning us of the danger we face. A Trump victory would portend nothing less than the realization of the original doctrine the KKK established upon its founding in 1865, in which the Invisible Empire would become starkly visible, no longer confined to the shadows in which the movement has lurked for over 150 years.

No less an authority than Beryl Howell, a district court judge who has overseen a great number of the trials of those accused in the wake of the attack on the Capitol on January 6, 2021, recently said, "My D.C. judicial colleagues and I regularly see the impact of big lies at the sentencing of hundreds, hundreds of individuals who have been convicted for offense conduct on January 6, 2021, when they disrupted the certification of the 2020 presidential election at the U.S. Capitol. We are having a very surprising and downright troubling moment in this country when the very importance of facts is dismissed, or ignored. That's very risky business for all of us in our democracy. . . . The facts matter."

Or so we can hope, because the alternative is a precarious slide toward authoritarianism.

Against this backdrop, the wisdom proffered by none other than

George Washington, with regard to colonists who were fighting on the side of the British being taken prisoner, must prevail now as it did then. His officers wanted to execute them, but Washington wouldn't allow it. "We will treat these prisoners as you would treat yourselves," Washington said, "because eventually these people will be your neighbors."

January 6 lit a cauldron that has continued to simmer in its wake. But the fire on which that cauldron rests spurred hot spots that have spread across the country. When I find myself tossing and turning at night in fear for our future, in fear that the mentality I witnessed inside the KKK will infest the whole government, I think of the 2015 arrests and 2017 guilty verdicts I helped secure, which sent the Klan running for the hills. I find hope in the fact that I helped deal a devastating blow to that movement, even if my efforts didn't similarly devastate the ideology behind it. I find hope in the fact that the system prevailed.

And I find the most hope of all in my own family. My oldest, Jordy, born in the midst of my first infiltration of the KKK, is now a tenth grader. Even though we had to homeschool him for the two years we were in protective custody, he's reading at a level two grades higher. He's replaced his Elmo collection with dinosaur bones and meteorites, both of which we scour the area for to purchase to add to his new collection. My ten-year-old daughter, Tia, born in the midst of my second infiltration, is the athlete of the bunch, a natural at pretty much everything she tries. I sit on the beach thinking back to my tempting the big waves off Hawaii, while I watch her nimbly negotiating the Florida ones with a skill level far beyond her years.

My six-year-old son, Willie, meanwhile, is in kindergarten and has developed a fascination with heroes—not the cartoon or Marvel movie variety, mind you, but real-life ones. The other day, his teacher asked the class what each wanted to be when they grew up.

"I want to be a hero," Willie said when it was his turn.

He regularly goes on YouTube and plugs HERO into the search box, and then sits for hours at a time watching the product of reality instead of fantasy. Recently, he ran into my office to show me a video on his iPad of a dog pulling a drowning boy out of a swimming pool, and another of a police officer saving a choking infant as his hysterical mother looked on.

Willie might be our youngest, but he seems to boast the clearest grasp of all I did before he was born. And it's not just heroes on those videos who draw his worship. Recently, we were out shopping when we passed a police officer on foot patrol, and Willie veered over.

"Thank you for your service, sir," he said to the officer.

"Thank you, son," the officer said.

Then he knelt down and pulled a sticker in the shape of a police badge from his pocket. He peeled off the back and stuck it on Willie's chest, right over his heart. Then he saluted, and Willie saluted back, standing at attention.

He hasn't let us wash that shirt since.

EPILOGUE

Around the time I first reached out to Jason Dearen of the Associated Press, the outlet entered into an innovative, creative partnership with ABC News and George Stephanopoulos to produce documentaries based on AP stories for the Hulu network. Thanks to Jason, one of the first of these was about me, appropriately titled *Grand Knighthawk*. It documented an overview of my undercover experience, centered almost entirely on my infiltration of the Traditionalist American Knights of the Ku Klux Klan. I didn't believe the public attention posed any risk to my family's safety, because the bad guys already had all our personal information (in large part because of Nate Thayer), so there was no point in hiding anymore.

At the end of the filming, the producers arranged for me to meet Warren Williams. It turned out Warren did indeed like to fish, so what better way to get to know each other than to invite him over to my house so we could cast our lines into the river tributary that abutted my backyard?

He arrived at my home midafternoon on a Saturday, empty-handed, since he didn't have his own fishing rod. It was a late summer day, when the humidity is so thick that walking through it feels like parting a curtain.

"How you doing, Warren?" I greeted him as we shook hands.

"Nice to finally meet you. Thanks so much for coming over. I've got something for you."

I handed him the brand-new rod and reel I'd purchased that morning.

Warren's mouth dropped. "This is for me?"

I nodded. "You bet."

"But I didn't bring you anything," he said almost guiltily.

"Having you here is all I need."

I was choking back tears through my words, because eyeing this man, who was clearly quiet and gentle, a poet who had filled notebooks with words to express his feelings, put a human face on the heinous act the Klan had expected me to participate in out of racial hatred and a misguided desire for revenge. It just flat out blew my mind how people could have so much disdain for a fellow human being.

We headed down my sloped yard toward the water. I opened the gate, closed it behind us, and we took our place in the shade from the streaming sunshine cast by some sugar maple trees hanging over the shore. I could hear the chirp of crickets and the croak of frogs. Somewhere in the distance, a lawn mower engine revved, reminding me we were just steps away from my backyard.

Warren and I cast our lines and talked while we waited for the catfish, mudfish, or perch to bite. If we got really lucky, we'd snare a much-lauded bass, but I hadn't come across a lot of those this season.

"Can I ask you a personal question, Joe?"

"You can ask me anything you want."

"It has to do with me," Warren continued. "No matter who you are, no matter how old you are, you don't always make good decisions. Someone has to be there to protect you, stop others from taking advantage of you, when that happens."

"Like having someone you can go to for advice."

"Right, a person you can go to."

"So in your situation, you were not treated fairly. There are so many things wrong with that. And I sympathize with things that you might have gone through, and there's nothing more complicated than that."

"I appreciate that, I truly do," Warren said humbly, speaking in a hushed tone that typified his quiet demeanor and the way he carried himself. "And I appreciate you lending me this rod."

"It's a gift, my friend, yours to keep."

Just then his line vibrated, a fish having taken the bait.

"Looks like you caught one," I said as he reeled it in.

He was smiling from ear to ear. "I did, I sure did."

"Looks like a one-pounder," I said, smiling, too, as he hoisted the smallmouth bass from the river.

I watched Warren undo the hook lodged in the fish's mouth and gently place two hands beneath its squirming frame. Then he knelt down and gently released the bass back into the water, where it joined the flow of the current downstream, set free to live another day.

AUTHOR'S NOTE

This book opens with the famed quote attributed to Edmund Burke: "The only thing necessary for the triumph of evil is for good men to do nothing."

And a pernicious, corrosive evil is what I fought through two separate infiltrations of the Ku Klux Klan for the FBI. I could not stand by in the face of that evil and do nothing. As I had during my military service, I felt more loyalty to my nation than to myself and decided that risking my own life was worth it in order to expose the truth to preserve nothing less than this country's future. And make no mistake about it, that is what's at stake here. As a trained sniper, I learned and taught the skills necessary to gather intelligence and recall details from within a specific environment. When I was undercover, I relied on those details etched into my memory as much for my own survival as for the success of the mission, which unleashed a level of stress that probably would have killed the average person and nearly killed me.

I wrote this book because in my years undercover I was able to expose terrible truths about the KKK and the extreme right as a whole that not even the FBI was aware of. I think it's vital that you're made aware of those truths too. I began my service to my country more than twenty-five years ago, when I enlisted in the army. This book represents the culmination of that service, even though publishing it will certainly endanger my life and the lives of my family once more. My wife and I calling our children by names christened on their replacement birth certificates and living under new identities exemplifies the fact that we have already become refugees within our own country. I have to accept the pain I have inflicted upon my family in order to preserve and safeguard America. If the country has no future, my wife and children won't, either. I had to make quite literally a devil's bargain, because for ten years of my life I was dealing with the devil incarnate in the Klan.

I changed many of the names and likenesses of the characters in this book since, unlike the four KKK members I put behind bars, they did not face justice. The truth is their names don't matter nearly as much as the ideology they represent, one that threatens to deal a deathblow to the United States as we know it. Charlottesville happened because the KKK was so desperate that it sought to align itself with other like-minded organizations that followed the same beliefs that brought them—if not in body, then certainly in spirit—to Washington on January 6, 2021. That ideology spawned not just a day but also a movement that would live in infamy. Those names don't matter, either, when compared with the hatred and violence they spewed and cheered on.

I take great pride in dealing a hateful organization a devastating near deathblow. My first infiltration of the Klan was marked by enabling the first Black man ever to be elected president. My second infiltration climaxed when I saved the life of another Black man, not bound for greatness or glory but nonetheless deserving of a future of hope and happiness. In my mind, those two lives are equally important, as are all the nameless others still alive today because I stood against a pervasive evil composed of a regressive bloodline in which human rights are an afterthought.

And now it falls upon all of us to keep 2024 from becoming 1861. Ernest Hemingway once wrote, "The world is a fine place and worth the fighting for." So is America, and I fully intend to keep fighting for the country I love.

ACKNOWLEDGMENTS

I want to recognize those who both helped with the formation of this book and brought it to fruition, starting with Jason Dearen. His talented investigative instincts led to his crafting two stories for the Associated Press that began this book's journey.

That journey was shepherded by my agent, Kirby Kim, of Janklow and Nesbit, who reached out to the aforementioned Jason Dearen, because Kirby knew there was a much bigger story that needed to be told. He will be a friend for life, and I will forever appreciate his knowledge, expertise, and wisdom.

It was Kirby who brought me to Lisa Sharkey and her wonderful team at HarperCollins, which included a great editor in Maddie Pillari, a compassionate legal voice in Beth Silfin, and an outstanding copy editor in Jane Cavolina, among others who gave everything they had to this book.

My deepest appreciation to ABC, which, in conjunction with the Associated Press, partnered in their first-ever collaboration to produce the documentary film *Grand Knighthawk* for the Hulu network under the brilliant tutelage of George Stephanopoulos, along with the producers Emily De Sainte Maresville and Matt Cullinan. That documentary led to a two-page spread in *People*, which happened to be my mother's favorite magazine when I was growing up.

I can't thank the great author Brad Meltzer enough for being the first person outside the family to weigh in on this book and, especially, to Congressman Jamie Raskin for providing it the legitimacy and credibility I believe it fully deserves.

Of course, none of this would have been possible without the collaborative efforts of Jon Land, a fascinatingly creative talent I was lucky to have the opportunity to work with.

Finally, I want to thank my wife and kids for standing by me, supporting me, and suffering through this ordeal with me. The country is everything, but my family is always.

NOTES

PREFACE

xiii   between half and three quarters of all self-identifying Republicans: David Masciotra, "Right Wing Extremism Is Even More Common Than You Think," *Washington Monthly*, April 10, 2023.

xiv   "threats posed by domestic extremists": "DOJ OIG Releases Report on the Department of Justice's Strategy to Address the Domestic Violent Extremist Threat," press release, U.S. Department of Justice Office of the Inspector General, June 6, 2023.

xiv   "fingerprints are everywhere": Cassie Miller and Caleb Kieffer, "Hate and Extremism: In the Mainstream and on the Main Street," Southern Poverty Law Center, "The Year in Hate and Extremism 2022," June 6, 2023.

xiv   In June of 2023, a man named Taylor Taranto: Ryan Reilly and Fiona Glisson, "Jan. 6 Defendant Arrested Near Obama's Home Had Guns and 400 Rounds of Ammunition in His Van," NBC News, June 30, 2023.

xv   Congressman Paul Gosar of Arizona . . . and Congresswoman Marjorie Taylor Greene: Shawna Chen, "Gosar Claims Video Appearance at Event Hosted by White Nationalist Due to Staff Error," Axios, April 1, 2022.

xv   Gosar also has two alleged white nationalist sympathizers on his staff: Ryan Randazzo, "Rep. Paul Gosar Blasted by Jewish Groups After 2 Staffers Linked to White Supremacist," *Arizona Republic*, May 15, 2023.

xv   Senator Tommy Tuberville said: Meg Kinnard, "Sen. Tuberville Criticized for Remarks on White Nationalists," Associated Press, May 11, 2023.

xv   A librarian of the Kingsland Branch Library: Asher Price, "Texas Librarian Alleges She Was Fired for Not Removing Books," Axios, March 18, 2022.

xvi   the number of military veterans who participated in the January 6 insurrection: Tom Dreisbach and Meg Anderson, "Nearly 1 in 5 Defendants in Capitol Riot Cases Served in the Military," NPR, January 21, 2021.

xvi   *Business Insider* reported: Tom Porter, "31 Police Officers Are Under Investigation over Their Suspected Involvement in the Capitol Riot, as Departments Face Pressure to Weed Out White Nationalists," *Business Insider*, January 25, 2021.

xvi   Law enforcement officials: *White Supremacist Infiltration of Law Enforcement*, Federal Bureau of Investigation Intelligence Assessment, October 17, 2006, https://www.justsecurity.org/wp-content/uploads/2021/06 /Jan-6-Clearinghouse-FBI-Intelligence-Assessment-White-Supremacist -Infiltration-of-Law-Enforcement-Oct-17-2006-UNREDACTED.pdf.

CHAPTER 1: A CALL TO THE FBI

18   "Although white supremacist groups": Federal Bureau of Investigation, *White Supremacist Infiltration of Law Enforcement*.

CHAPTER 5: FIREWORKS

50   Forrest is infamously remembered for perpetrating a massacre: "Fort Pillow Massacre," History.com, updated June 21, 2019.

51   Ku Klux Klan Act in 1871: "Ku Klux Klan Act Passed by Congress," History.com, updated April 16, 2020.

55   "the most reprehensibly racist film in American history": Ed Rampell, "'The Birth of a Nation': The Most Racist Movie Ever Made," *Washington Post*, March 3, 2015.

55   he proclaimed himself Imperial Wizard of the Invisible Empire of the Knights of the Ku Klux Klan: DeNeen L. Brown, "The Preacher Who Used Christianity to Revive the Ku Klux Klan," *Washington Post*, April 10, 2018.

55   The revived Klan was given a further boost: "Rosewood Massacre," History .com, May 4, 2018.

56   the Klan's national membership: Olivia B. Waxman, "How the KKK's Influence Spread in Northern States," *Time*, October 24, 2017.

56   Mary Elizabeth Tyler and Edward Young Clark: Joshua D. Rothman, "When Bigotry Paraded Through the Streets," *The Atlantic*, December 4, 2016.

57   the Christian Front: Terry Gross, "Rachel Maddow Uncovers a WWII-Era Plot Against America in 'Ultra,'" NPR, *Fresh Air*, December 15, 2022.

58   Kennedy took matters into his own hands: FBI History: Famous Cases & Criminals, "Mississippi Burning," FBI.gov, undated.

58   "The Greensboro massacre": Shaun Assael and Peter Keating, "The Massacre That Spawned the Alt-Right," *Politico*, November 3, 2019.

CHAPTER 6: CAMPAIGN VISIT

63   "Kissimmee, on October twenty-ninth": "Obama Campaign Event in Kissimmee, Florida," C-SPAN, October 29, 2008.

CHAPTER 8: GONE FISHING

77   the WKKK would organize boycotts of anti-Klan businesses: Emily Cataneo, "A Brief History of the Women's KKK," JSTOR Daily, October 14, 2020.

CHAPTER 9: MAKE THE GUY PAY

82   significant rise in hate crimes: Matthew Bigg, "Election of Obama Provokes Rise in U.S. Hate Crimes," Reuters, November 24, 2008.

83   "individual police officers have sent overtly racist emails": Kevin Rector and Richard Winton, "Law Enforcement Confronts an Old Threat: Far-Right Extremism in the Ranks. 'Swift Action Must Be Taken,'" *Los Angeles Times*, February 17, 2021.

CHAPTER 11: THE CALL

113   the November 2008 murder of Cynthia Lynch: Carlin Miller, "KKK Leader Pleads Guilty to Murdering Recruit Who Wanted Out, Gets Life in Prison," CBS News, May 7, 2010.

CHAPTER 12: KNIGHT FLYER

115   twenty-three right-wing nationalists or white supremacists ran for office: Robert Steinback, "Electoral Extremism: 23 Candidates on the Radical Right," Southern Poverty Law Center Intelligence Report, February 23, 2011.

CHAPTER 13: FERGUSON

123   Insult was added to injury: Julie Bosman and Joseph Goldstein, "Timeline for a Body: 4 Hours in the Middle of a Ferguson Street," *New York Times*, August 23, 2014.

132   the FBI and others had classified the Klan as a terrorist organization: Susan Campbell Bartoletti, *They Called Themselves the K.K.K.: The Birth of an American Terrorist Group* (New York: Houghton Mifflin, 2014).

132   "It's interesting that people who are making": Chris Hayes, "KKK: Ferguson Protests Awakened Sleeping Giant," *All In*, MSNBC.com, November 12, 2014.

CHAPTER 14: POWDER KEG

134   "Missouri is definitely on fire": Danny Wicentowski, "Missouri KKK Leader: Ferguson Protests Are Boosting Recruitment," *Riverfront Times*, November 12, 2014.

135   "The 56 largest cities saw 17 percent more homicides": Dara Lind, "The 'Ferguson Effect,' a Theory That's Warping the American Crime Debate, Explained," *Vox*, May 18, 2016.

136 published a book called *The Lost Cause*: Michel Paradis, "The Lost Cause's Long Legacy," *The Atlantic*, June 26, 2020.

138 He was convicted of first-degree murder: Staff and wire report, "Deland Man Gets Life Without Parole for Killing 2 Bikers in NY," *Daytona Beach News-Journal*, October 22, 2015.

139 "Based on investigations between 2016 and 2020": Josh Margolin, "White Supremacists 'Seek Affiliation' with Law Enforcement to Further Their Goals, Internal FBI Report Warns," ABC News, March 8, 2021.

CHAPTER 15: HOT TIN ROOF

143 Abarr claimed it would be all-inclusive: Kirsten Cates, "Many Suspicious of More Inclusive Montana KKK Chapter," *Great Falls Tribune*, November 2, 2014.

CHAPTER 16: THE THREE AMIGOS

155 lead conspirator Edgar Ray Killen: FBI History: Famous Cases & Criminals, "Mississippi Burning."

155 Steven Joshua Dinkle: "Former Alabama KKK Leader Sentenced to Prison for Cross Burning and Obstruction of Justice," press release, Department of Justice, May 15, 2014.

CHAPTER 20: TAKEDOWN

195 interview with the murderous Khmer Rouge leader Pol Pot: Seth Mydans, "Nate Thayer, Bold Reporter Who Interviewed Pol Pot, Dies at 62," *New York Times*, January 10, 2023.

195 he had developed alcohol and substance abuse problems: Mydans, "Nate Thayer, Bold Reporter Who Interviewed Pol Pot, Dies at 62."

195 many stemming from shrapnel damage: Anthony Kuhn, "Nate Thayer, the Rebel Reporter Who Interviewed Pol Pot in the Cambodian Jungle, Has Died," NPR, January 6, 2023.

196 over thirty-five thousand dollars had been raised: Mydans, "Nate Thayer, Bold Reporter Who Interviewed Pol Pot, Dies at 62."

CHAPTER 25: MY OWN PRIVATE IDAHO

239 the number of Klan chapters fell by almost a third: Mark Potok, "Extremism in the Mainstream," Southern Poverty Law Center, "The Year in Hate and Extremism," February 15, 2017.

240 "A surge in right-wing populism": Potok, "Extremism in the Mainstream."

243 "Are the pro-democratic forces": Debbie Elliott, "Charlottesville Was a Wake-Up Call for Many About the White Supremacy Movement," NPR, *Morning Edition*, August 11, 2022.

CHAPTER 26: YOU CAN GO HOME AGAIN

249 the Proud Boys had begun to hold what they openly called "prayer meetings": KOIN News Staff, "Antifa to Proud Boys: 'Go Home, Nazis,'" We Are Iowa, August 17, 2019.

249 "tap into beliefs that are still widespread": "What Made Fmr. White Nationalist Derek Black Change His Mind," PBS, *Amanpour & Co.*, December 17, 2020.

CHAPTER 27: BE VERY AFRAID

252 a recent analysis by Reuters: Hassan Kanu, "Prevalence of White Supremacists in Law Enforcement Demands Drastic Change," Reuters, May 12, 2022.

253 prison guards across the multitude of Florida penal institutions: Jason Dearen, "White Supremacist Prison Guards Work with Impunity in Fla.," Associated Press, November 19, 2021.

255 "The sheriff's group has railed against": T. J. L'Heureux et al., "A Right-Wing Sheriffs Group That Challenges Federal Law Is Gaining Acceptance Around the Country," ABC15 Arizona, August 21, 2023.

257 compared West to 2016 Green Party candidate Jill Stein: Nate Robertson, "Axelrod Warns Cornel West Bid Could Tip Election to Trump," *The Hill*, July 8, 2021.

259 "When we consume stories about white power": MSNBC, *The Rachel Maddow Show*, August 28, 2023.

261 "My D.C. judicial colleagues and I": Josh Gerstein, "Judge Key to Jan. 6 Cases Warns US Faces 'Authoritarian' Threat," *Politico*, November 28, 2023.

ABOUT THE AUTHOR

Born in Jacksonville, Florida, JOE MOORE enlisted as a private in the army, completing basic training in 1995 before being selected for sniper school in 1997. Because of his military service, Joe was first recruited by the FBI and the Joint Terrorism Task Force in 2007 to infiltrate the Ku Klux Klan. His first stint as a confidential human source lasted three years and was followed by a second infiltration into a second KKK klavern beginning in 2013, which lasted two years and resulted in numerous successful prosecutions of noted Klan officials in 2017. He lives today in an undisclosed location with his wife and three children.